Contents

Appendixes

Introduction

At 12:11 A.M. on January 1, 1995, I welcomed my first-born into the world after 22 hours of labor and a C-section. On January 3, I experienced my first panic attack. Just home from the hospital, I had easily fallen asleep, only to be awakened out of a dead slumber a few hours later, gasping for breath and heart racing.

I had no idea what was happening. I remember jumping out of bed, stumbling down the stairs, and throwing the door open. The cold January air seemed to snap me back to reality and help me regain control of my breathing. I spent the next few hours terrified of going back to sleep, afraid of the dark, and wondering if I was experiencing some weird reaction to the anesthesia or if I was losing my mind. Over the next six weeks, as the panic attacks recurred, I began to believe the latter.

There's an irony here. With a family history of depression, I was not unaware of the risk of post-partum complications. I had read up on postpartum depression and was ready to deal with any baby blues that might linger longer than usual. But postpartum panic? During all my years of clinical training, postpartum anxiety was something I had never heard of.

After I got better, I realized that there had been warning signs during my pregnancy. I had always enjoyed flying; during my nine months of pregnancy, I dreaded boarding any airplane, and the slightest turbulence would have me gripping the arm of the unlucky stranger who happened to sit next to me. When an elevator door got stuck for a few minutes when I was about five months along, I felt so claustrophobic and panicked I wanted to scream. There were enough little scares during my pregnancy that I came to feel as if I were receiving random electric shocks; just as I was relaxing into expectant motherhood, another worry would jolt me back into a state of alarm.

Before the Tipping Point

Before my postpartum days, if you had ever asked me if I was an anxious person, I would have laughed. So, I'm sure, would any of my family or friends. It drove my mother crazy that I seemed to "thrive under pressure," often waiting until the last minute to get my homework done. My messy room and disorganized approach to life were a testament to the fact that I didn't have a compulsive bone in my body. I had a lot of friends and did well in school.

At the same time, there were early clues that anxiety was a way I responded to stress. I was a nail biter. I always had a lot of "nervous energy" and often fidgeted. During a particular rough patch in my childhood, I went through a period where I stuttered. And I always had a terror of speaking in public, so much so that I became paralyzed with fright when I was supposed to stand up and say a few words to my classmates. Speech prepared, I stood up, walked to the podium, froze—and pretended the microphone was broken.

My mom had a more direct relationship with anxiety. She was a worrier. Throughout my growing-up years, she seemed to have a lot of fears and concerns about her health, and often developed physical symptoms when under stress. I often wondered if having suddenly lost her father at age 10 was the cause of it. I didn't know it until years after my son was born, but she had also experienced panic attacks after the birth of my younger sister.

A Dark Road but a Bright Future

Fast-forward through a lot of pain, guilt, fear, and hard work, and I'm a happy, healthy career woman and mother of four. I am happily married and am lucky enough to have a lifestyle I love. Some of the positive steps I have been able to make in my life's journey have been *in spite of* my anxiety. And yet, although I would once have never believed this, I think some of my present fulfillment is also because of it. The personal growth my anxiety forced me into has not only taught me to deal with uncertainty and discomfort, it has also helped me be a more empathic parent. I have gained more self-respect, quit procrastinating (most of the time), and given up some nasty mental habits—such as perfectionism and self-criticism.

Am I cured? Who knows? I still get occasional blips of anxiety when I'm under stress, but it's been a long time since I've had a full-blown panic attack. We anxiety sufferers learn the hard way not to take too much for granted; symptoms can always rear their ugly head. I can tell you that I don't fear the fear anymore. If it comes, it won't wrestle me to the ground like it once did.

—Joni Johnston

However, this book is about *you*, not us. Joni shares her personal story to show you that she comes at this topic from an up-close-and-personal viewpoint as well as a professional one. We are more concerned with helping you make your daily life better than whether you fit neatly into any diagnostic category. As such, although the focus of their application is on anxiety, many of the self-help skills in this book are *life* skills that will benefit anyone. And, of course, we also explore anxiety-disorder-specific self-help (that is, how to cope with panic symptoms and how to recover from phobias). Joni also uses her dual perspective to address the interplay between self-help and professional assistance.

How This Book Is Organized

Part 1, Exploring Anxiety, takes a look at what is a normal amount of anxiety and what is not. In these chapters, you have a chance to evaluate how much worry and anxiety impacts you on a day-to-day basis and learn how mental-health professionals make their diagnoses. We then shift the focus to why some people are more vulnerable to anxiety, what the path to recovery looks like, and how to stay on track when the road gets bumpy.

In **Part 2, Fighting Your Way Through the Fright,** we build a foundation for tackling your fears by strengthening your ability to manage everyday emotions and stop anxiety-related habits. We also explore how anxiety and fears can result in a tendency toward procrastination, and we explore assertiveness and how you can develop more empowering habits.

Part 3, Taming Those Alarming Ideas, arms you with the mental weapons to slay negative thoughts and defeat irrational beliefs that have long held many of us captive. Not only do you learn to challenge negative thoughts that fuel generalized anxiety, we also get down to the core of your beliefs, correcting myths around your need to be perfect or your constant need to earn approval. We then explore how these ingrained beliefs can congeal into self-defeating personality traits and how you can build more flexibility and self-acceptance into your life.

In **Part 4, Boosting the Mind-Body Connection,** we capitalize on the inseparable link between mental health and physical health. This part explores the relationship between anxiety, exercise, diet, and sleep. You learn how certain foods can rev you up and others promote a calming effect. You also learn how to prevent anxiety and worry from robbing you of a good night's sleep, and how exercise can serve as a buffer from daily hassles and situational stress.

Part 5, Survive and Thrive Strategies for Diagnosed Distress, takes on three of the "big boys"—the clinically diagnosed anxiety disorders. Building on the foundation developed in the preceding three parts, we look at state-of-the-art self-help strategies for panic disorder, social anxiety, and phobias. We also explore when professional help can boost your personal efforts and what the evidence says is the best anxiety-related treatment for your buck.

Part 6, Keeping Anxiety from the Next Generation, offers empowerment for any anxiety sufferer who is, or plans to be, a mom or a dad. This part starts by exploring one of the best-kept postpartum secrets—postpartum anxiety—and how you can keep anxiety from ruining your joy during pregnancy and after delivery. We also explore parenting traps that can increase tension and worry in children and how much power parents have in fostering resilience in their offspring. And finally, we explode the myth of the "carefree" childhood, develop ways to help children tackle normal fears, and learn how to be advocates for children should they need professional help.

Extras

In addition to the main narrative of *Idiot's Guide: Overcoming Anxiety* are nuggets of useful information designed to cut to the chase about a particular anxiety-related topic. Look for these sidebars:

ANXIETY ATTACK

Quick tips on how to tackle tough situations.

MYTH BUSTER

True facts that debunk popular myths and misconceptions about anxiety.

ON THE CUTTING EDGE

Short summaries of the latest anxiety-related research.

STRESS RELIEF

Positive strategies for improving everyday life.

Acknowledgments

"People often say that motivation doesn't last. Well, neither does bathing—that's why we recommend it daily." This quote by Zig Zigler pretty much sums up the process of writing this book—and coping with anxiety. With every new study I absorbed and each story I put down, I was reminded of how life is like writing; it happens a word at a time, we have to show up for it daily, and we have to pay attention to the process. The sentences we "write" on our psyches today, dictated by our actions and our attitudes, eventually become the "stories" of our lives.

How fortunate for me, therefore, to have had the opportunity to revisit my own personal values and daily choices at the same time I worked diligently to create a self-help road map for the brave readers who were ready to take control of their anxiety. Special thanks to the people who encouraged me on this journey, including the following:

My literary agent, Evan Fogelman, who continues to exceed all expectations.

All the mental-health professionals who have been brave enough to publicly share their personal battles with anxiety. You know who you are.

Every anxiety sufferer who has used his or her personal pain to help others. I was continually inspired by the notes of encouragement and self-help tips I found among anxiety sufferers in online communities, chat rooms, and websites.

To the four Z's in my life—Zach, Zhanna, Zane, and Zaylin—who provide all the motivation I need to stay on my path of personal growth. May the lessons I learn make you stronger, wiser, and happier.

To Alex. If consciousness *does* survive after death, I hope I get to spend eternity with you.

Special Thanks to the Reviewers

The first edition of *Idiot's Guides: Overcoming Anxiety* (2006) was reviewed by an expert who double-checked the accuracy of what you'll learn here, to help us ensure that this book gives you everything you need to know about overcoming your anxiety. Special thanks are extended to Sandra K. Trisdale, PhD, who is the author of over 30 articles on mental health issues. A former therapist, she is now involved in mental health research in San Diego, California.

Dr. O. Joseph Bienvenu, MD, PhD, Associate Professor of Psychiatry and Behavioral Sciences at Johns Hopkins University School of Medicine and director of the Johns Hopkins Anxiety Disorders Clinic and the Johns Hopkins Residents' Outpatient Clinic, went through the text with a fine-tooth comb for the new edition, updated information that had changed since the first publication, and added his insights throughout. Dr. Ann R. Fischer, PhD, Associate Professor of Counseling Psychology at Southern Illinois University, reviewed the edited manuscript and provided invaluable input and insights to make the book as helpful and accurate as possible.

Exploring Anxiety

"I'm nervous about that test coming up next week. That phone call sent me into a panic."

For better or worse, we use anxiety-related words on a regular basis. On the plus side, all of us know what it feels like to have excessive worries, knots in our stomach, or a strong desire to avoid a scary or tense situation. On the downside, it can be hard to know how much anxiety is too much or pinpoint when our fears take control of our lives.

That's what this part is about: illustrating the difference between normal anxiety and an anxiety disorder, becoming familiar with the different faces anxiety wears, shedding light on anxiety's causes, and predicting what the road to anxiety recovery looks like—and why we should travel down it.

Just the Jitters?

"Well, Miss Gordon, how are you today?" he [my psychiatrist] asked. I was shocked to hear myself burst into a monologue of almost feverish intensity.

"What's new, Dr. Allen, is that I can't walk the streets of the city I love alone. Unless I'm stoned on pills or with someone. I can't do it. I can't function without Valium. I'm growing too dependent on something other than myself to function. I'm growing too dependent on pills. Why? Tell me why!"

He interrupted. "But I've told you many times, Miss Gordon, they are not addictive. They can't hurt you." And he crossed his legs and sat back in his chair to hear my response.

In This Chapter

* The symptoms of anxiety
* Discover when normal anxiety crosses the line
* Conduct your own anxiety self-assessment
* Learn who is vulnerable to anxiety disorders
* Physical problems that cause anxiety

Barbara Gordon was a talented, award-winning American filmmaker—with an anxiety disorder. She was prescribed Valium and visited a psychiatrist once a week for more than 10 years with no noticeable improvement. Barbara Gordon documented her life with an anxiety disorder in the best-selling book *I'm Dancing as Fast as I Can,* describing in detail her struggle with her anxiety disorder, the Valium addiction she developed when she sought help, and her ultimate recovery. There are at least two takeaway messages from this book:

- People from all walks of life develop debilitating anxiety.

- We are ultimately responsible for taking the necessary steps for our own recovery.

In this chapter, we talk about what anxiety is and what it's not, when it helps and when it hurts, what's normal and what isn't, and what other illnesses can masquerade as an anxiety disorder.

What Is Anxiety?

If someone asked you to define anxiety in 25 words or less, could you do it? Probably, because the odds are you've experienced it. Perhaps you'd say "worrying too much" or "feeling uptight." Perhaps you'd describe flip-flopping in your stomach or tightness in your chest. Anxiety involves all these and more; in fact, it can show up in many ways: *physically, emotionally, cognitively,* and/or *behaviorally.*

 MYTH BUSTER

"Anxiety is a sign of weakness." Wrong! Big, strong, macho guys get anxiety disorders, too. Famous men known or strongly suspected to have suffered from an anxiety disorder include Abraham Lincoln, actor James Garner, football star Earl Campbell, and even Winston Churchill.

Physical Symptoms: From Butterflies to Insomnia

Ever had to give a speech without preparation? How about swerved at the last moment to avoid hitting someone with your car? Then you probably know firsthand the physical signs of anxiety:

- Nausea or indigestion ("butterflies" in the stomach)

- Sweating, especially sweaty palms, forehead, or underarms

- Shortness of breath

- Racing pulse or a feeling like your heart is pounding

- Trouble swallowing or feelings of choking

- Dizziness or headache

- Chills or hot flashes

- Muscle tension

- Skin changes ("goose bumps")

- Trembling or shaking

- Difficulty sleeping

 ANXIETY ATTACK

Starting to feel nervous in a situation? *Breathe.* Concentrate for a few minutes or even a few seconds on taking slow, deep, regular breaths. When some of us begin to get anxious, we start breathing quickly and shallowly, which sets up a whole chain reaction in our bodies that can cause *more* anxiety.

Emotional Symptoms: Fear

Fear is the main feeling associated with anxiety. And when it starts, it can snowball (especially for those of us with panic disorder). First we're anxious in a certain situation; then we become anxious about being anxious—and afraid that *next* time we're confronted with that situation, we'll get anxious again.

Other emotions associated with anxiety include feelings of nervousness, irritability, and the sense that something bad is about to happen. Molehills seem like mountains, and it is harder to control our tempers. Or perhaps we feel as if we're outside ourselves watching what's happening rather than being involved. In fact, sometimes our feelings can be numbed or blunted; it may be hard to recognize any emotion.

Cognitive Symptoms: Thoughts

Cognition is just another word for "thinking." Being anxious can affect the kind of thoughts we have, and it can certainly affect our concentration!

For difficult tasks, we need a certain level of arousal or alertness in order to focus properly. Both too little and too much arousal can interfere with difficult tasks. For example, it is hard to solve complicated math problems in our heads if woken up suddenly from deep sleep. On the other hand, if we are extremely anxious while taking questions from an audience, it can be very difficult to "think on our feet" and remember what we actually (usually) know. Two psychologists, Robert Yerkes and John Dodson, described this relationship in the early 1900s, as illustrated in the following figure.

In addition, what we think can affect how we feel, and unhelpful ways of thinking are common in anxiety disorders. Some common unhelpful ways of thinking that contribute to anxiety include the following:

- Thinking about fearful situations over and over without resolving anything

- Focusing too much on tiny details, not seeing the big picture

- Overestimating the real danger of everyday activities or situations

- Doubting our ability to cope

- Worrying that any physical symptom is either the beginning of an anxiety attack or a sign of a life-threatening illness

- Overestimating the likelihood of a negative outcome

- Thinking excessively about the possibility of failure or of drawing negative attention

 STRESS RELIEF

> When speaking or performing in public, some people get so anxious about making a mistake that their anxiety gets out of control. Some therapists who specialize in anxiety disorders actually suggest that performers intentionally make a small error at the beginning of their performance so that they can let go of the internal pressure to be perfect, and relax.

Behavioral Symptoms: Either Take Charge or Run Away!

The last aspect of anxiety involves our response to our fear. Because anxiety feels threatening, it's no surprise that, in response to it, we either fight or "fly" away. Common behavioral responses include the following:

- Avoiding situations that have made us anxious in the past

- Freezing up

- Avoiding situations that we are afraid might make us anxious

- Refusing to try new things

- Procrastinating—putting things off for later

- Using drugs or alcohol to try to cope

Donny Osmond: A Familiar Face with Anxiety

Here's another real-life example of a celebrity who has met anxiety up close and personally. Singer/performer Donny Osmond learned to cover up his anxiety for years until it got so out of control he could no longer hide it.

Osmond reported the emotional signs of anxiety, which centered on his escalating fear of performing onstage: "There are times I remember before I walked on stage, where if I had the choice of walking on stage or dying, I would have chosen death."

He has described some of his anxiety-related thoughts, including the pressure to be perfect and the fear of scrutiny: "I knew at least somebody in that audience was looking at me all the time."

He eventually ended up having a full-blown panic attack, with all the physical and behavioral symptoms that accompany them. "I remember shaking in bed, and I just, I couldn't get out of bed. Something was wrong and my wife took me to the hospital."

Through psychotherapy, Osmond eventually learned to cope with his social anxiety disorder.

 ON THE CUTTING EDGE

Some people apparently need more anxiety. Recent research has shown that some people don't feel much anxiety even in dangerous or life-threatening situations. These people tend to take extreme risks and are more likely to die in thrill-seeking activities. Apparently, a certain amount of anxiety keeps us on our toes when we need to pay extra attention and proceed with caution.

Cautious, Nervous, or Dealing with a Disorder?

If you look at all the different anxiety symptoms, you might think we all suffer from anxiety—and you'd be right! There's nothing wrong with a little anxiety. In fact, we need some in order to survive.

For a physical comparison, think about the sensation of pain. No one likes to hurt, but people who are born without an ability to feel it are at chronic risk of serious injuries and tend to die earlier; there has been at least one case of a toddler who could not feel pain who walked into a pretty bonfire on purpose and stayed there. And if pain didn't accompany a heart attack, we wouldn't seek the medical attention we need to survive. So pain isn't much fun, but we often need it. In a way, the same is true for anxiety.

For example, suppose you need to cross a busy street, but cars are rushing by in both directions. A little jolt of anxiety will motivate you to be extra vigilant and cautious and wait until you can cross safely. If you weren't worried at all, you might just walk out into traffic and get hit by a car.

In addition, people who don't become anxious in normally anxiety-causing situations may have difficulty learning from mistakes. They may be even more likely than the rest of us to make the same mistakes over and over.

Although not everyone with a chronic anxiety deficit is a criminal, it is true that some criminals have a low ability to become anxious. That may explain, in part, people who make the same mistakes time and time again, even if they are punished for making them. It may also help explain how the presence of anxiety can be an important signal tweaking our conscience, telling us that we are acting, behaving, or thinking in a way that conflicts with a deeply held value or belief.

As discussed previously, normal anxiety can be good for you; it can give your conscience a necessary tug or inspire you to prepare just a little bit harder. There is a continuum of anxiety, and we want to be somewhere in the middle range. So how much anxiety is too much? There are a few ways of telling.

Context and Continuum

First, most people with diagnosable anxiety disorders experience feelings of anxiety, fear, or terror in situations that don't justify it. Either it's a situation (context) in which most of us wouldn't feel particularly anxious (such as driving a car), or the level of anxiety is much greater than the circumstances warrant. For example, most of us might feel a little bit uneasy entering a grocery store we've had a bad experience in, but the person who associates panic attacks with a particular store may avoid it no matter the personal or relationship costs.

Of course, the continuum of normal anxiety depends upon the situation, how most people experience it, and your unique personal makeup. So if your palms are sweaty when you stand in line for that new thrill ride at the amusement park, join the crowd! Got a few butterflies in your stomach going in for that important job interview? Perfectly normal. But if you're so terrified of the thrill ride that you refuse to even enter the amusement park, that's not how most people would react. It would be pretty extreme. And if your anxiety gets so out of control that you blow off the interview, or get there and freeze up, unable to answer questions, then it's a problem.

Here's a true story: a colleague of Joni's interviewed at several graduate schools before selecting one. During the interview process, one university conducted group interviews so the staff could see how well potential students handled themselves. In front of the group, this intelligent, articulate woman began to respond to a question, stopped, blushed, and completely froze up. She was unable to answer or even function at all. Although all the candidates had high test scores, high grade point averages, and excellent credentials, this woman's anxiety ended up getting her rejected as a candidate.

 ANXIETY ATTACK

Getting back on the horse that threw you can be good advice. When people are frightened by a certain situation, they may start avoiding that situation and others like it. The best thing to do is face the situation again as soon as you can by any means possible—with a friend's support, in gradual steps, and so on.

States and Traits

Anxiety can be divided into either state anxiety or trait anxiety. *State anxiety* refers to your level of anxiety in a particular situation. Maybe you stay cool during job interviews, but you're terrified of spiders. You're not anxious all the time, just in certain situations.

Trait anxiety refers to our tendency to respond to a wide variety of situations with either too much or not enough anxiety. Those who take big risks tend to have low levels of trait anxiety—even when a higher level might be helpful or appropriate. But people with high levels of trait anxiety tend to be much more anxious in general, even in situations that most of us don't think of as particularly stressful.

Although certain types of state anxiety can be very unpleasant and can impact your life significantly, high levels of trait anxiety tend to be the most crippling.

 MYTH BUSTER

Some people believe that religious faith will overcome anxiety. You might feel that if you're just a devout enough Christian, Jew, Buddhist, Wiccan, Muslim—whatever—you can overcome anxiety. But anxiety disorders are just as real as other medical illnesses. Rather than try to overcome a broken leg (or severe anxiety) through faith alone, why not just bless the doctor who helps you heal?

How Bad Is It?

One way to look at how much your anxiety affects you is by how much it keeps you from dealing with everyday life. Let's look at three different people with anxiety about the same issue. Betty, Bob, and Brittany are all anxious about heights. But they deal with their fears differently.

Betty works on the twenty-sixth floor of a building. Every time she rides up or down the elevator, she closes her eyes and concentrates on her breathing to keep from getting overly nervous. She has a corner office with a great view, but she keeps the blinds pulled because the view scares her. When she and her husband went to Paris and he went up the Eiffel Tower, she decided to stay on the ground and take photos. When she flies on business, she requests a seat as close to the middle of the row as possible. If she sits by the window, she closes the shade and reads a book for distraction.

Bob works in a city on one side of a major river. It's a dead-end job, and he could do better if he was willing to get a job in the city on the other side of the river, but he just can't bring himself to drive across that suspension bridge every day. Once when a job assignment involved giving a presentation on the other side, Bob called in sick. His bosses weren't happy, and the guy who covered for him got the next promotion. Bob met a great woman at a party once. They went out a few times, but she lived across the river. When she found out Bob wasn't willing to drive across the bridge to see her, she called him a "wuss" and dumped him. Bob is sometimes afraid she was right—maybe he is a wuss. His self-esteem is pretty shot, and he hasn't dated anyone in a while.

Brittany is terrified of heights—any heights. When her family went to the Grand Canyon when she was a child, she curled up in a ball on the floor of the family car. Everyone in her family teased her about her fears. She won't get in an elevator, and escalators scare her even more. She has to pay a neighbor's son to come change her light bulbs because she can't stand on a stepladder. Brittany's husband left her years ago; one of the reasons was that he was tired of his life being so affected by his wife's fears. Brittany's grown daughter lives in Hawaii and is getting increasingly angry with her because she won't fly out to see her new grandchild. But Brittany has never been on a plane—the mere thought makes her shake all over. She walks out of the movie theater if a scene unexpectedly shows a view from a great height or if someone is shown climbing a mountain, driving over a high bridge, or parachuting. She has trouble getting to sleep and often has nightmares about falling. She knows her fears have taken over her life, but she doesn't know what to do about it.

Three people, one fear, and three different outcomes. Betty is anxious about heights, yes, but it doesn't have a huge impact on her life. She has developed coping strategies that work for her. The anxiety does not keep her from doing what she wants or needs to do. Brittany clearly has a full-blown anxiety disorder. Her anxiety is impacting her life negatively in a variety of ways. Bob's anxiety is also affecting his life negatively, but it's more subtle. He qualifies as having an anxiety disorder, too, but it's not as severe as Brittany's.

Does any of this mean that Betty is smarter, stronger, or somehow better than Brittany or Bob? Absolutely not! Though Betty may enjoy life more without her anxiety about heights, Betty is doing fairly well. Bob and Brittany need some help in dealing with their anxiety; with treatment, they could both end up doing the things that today seem impossible.

 ANXIETY ATTACK

Anxiety makes it hard to look on the bright side. To prepare in advance for anxiety-provoking situations, psychologist Daniel Wegner suggests writing down a list of happy memories, tough times you've conquered, or things you're looking forward to. It might be helpful to keep such a list in your pocket to review when you get stressed.

Assess Yourself: How Much Is Too Much?

Although different anxiety disorders have their own clusters of symptoms (which we discuss in upcoming chapters), some general signs suggest that your anxiety is severe enough that it's time to take some action. To determine whether your anxiety has crossed the line, ask yourself the following questions—and be honest!

- Does your anxiety cause you to avoid specific places, events, objects, or situations?

- Are these places, events, objects, or situations that other people don't seem to be afraid of or consider relatively harmless?

- Does your anxiety interfere with your ability to work?

- Does your anxiety cause problems in your relationships with other people—or prevent you from having relationships at all?

- Does your anxiety keep you from taking care of your responsibilities around the home?

- Does your anxiety cause you discomfort or distress on a regular basis?

- Do things seem to be getting worse over time?

- Have friends, family members, or employers expressed concern over your anxiety or its effect on your life?

- Do you sometimes feel that your thoughts are out of control?

- Do you frequently feel irritable?

- Do other people tell you that you always look stressed out?

- Do you feel like your mind often just goes blank?

- Do you often have trouble falling or staying asleep?

- Do you worry about the same things over and over?

In general, the more questions to which you answered "yes," the more likely it is that you have an anxiety disorder.

However, this is just an informal screening. We culled symptoms from several different anxiety disorders, so even the most anxious person is unlikely to answer "yes" to each and every question. A person suffering from generalized anxiety disorder, for example, may not identify with the person who avoids social situations out of embarrassment—and may be completely unable to relate to someone who avoids crowds because of fear of panicking and having difficulty getting out. Yet all of these individuals have anxiety disorders.

Of course, the bottom line, as we said at the beginning of this chapter, is your own experience. If your anxiety is causing you significant pain or is limiting your life, then it's a problem for you. Whether or not you meet the clinical criteria for an anxiety disorder, what matters is that your life gets better—and easier. And it can!

Primary Anxiety or Something Else?

So you've looked at the self-assessment questions in this chapter, and you may be sure you have an anxiety disorder. However, it is important to note that a number of other conditions can cause anxiety (secondary anxiety) and be mistaken for run-of-the-mill (primary) anxiety disorders. It's important to rule out these other conditions first.

General Category	Examples
Cardiovascular (heart)	Paroxysmal supraventricular tachycardia
Respiratory (lung)	Asthma, emphysema, scleroderma
Central nervous system	Psychomotor epilepsy/seizure disorder
Metabolic/hormonal	Hyperthyroidism, Cushing's disease
Nutritional	Anemia, folate deficiency
Intoxication	Caffeine, amphetamines
Withdrawal	Alcohol, sedatives
Psychiatric	Depression, ADHD

For instance, several different types of heart conditions can cause symptoms of anxiety; sometimes a heart attack and a panic attack can be hard to tell apart. Another heart condition, paroxysmal supraventricular tachycardia (PSVT), is characterized by sudden attacks of palpitations, chest pain, shortness of breath, anxiety, and dizziness—similar to panic attacks.

Certain diseases of the lungs can also cause anxiety symptoms. It's terrifying to not have enough oxygen; our bodies need it!

How healthy are your eating habits? If you have a poor diet or difficulty absorbing some critical vitamins or minerals, you could end up with symptoms of anxiety; in particular, low levels of thiamine, pyroxidine, and folate have all been associated with anxiety, as has iron-deficiency anemia. So take your vitamins if your doctor says you need them!

Many illicit drugs can cause anxiety, the most notorious of them being stimulants like speed, cocaine, or meth. But another anxiety-inducing intoxicant is perfectly legal: caffeine. Although many of us can drink coffee with relatively few side effects, some of us are very sensitive to caffeine, and a little coffee or tea, even an over-the-counter pain reliever with caffeine, can cause substantial anxiety. The worst part is that these sensitive people may not connect the anxiety with the soda or the chocolate bar they had earlier.

 STRESS RELIEF

Want to reduce your anxiety? Cut out (or at least cut down on) the coffee. Excessive caffeine can make you anxious and jittery. If you suffer from anxiety or panic attacks, even small amounts of caffeine can exacerbate it. How much is too much? It depends. If you have trouble falling asleep, if you find it hard to concentrate during the day, or if you drink more than 5 cups of coffee a day, you may be getting too much caffeine.

Other psychiatric disorders can sometimes look like anxiety disorders. Individuals with attention-deficit hyperactivity disorder, or ADHD, can display leg/foot movements, hand tapping, and other physical signs that may be mistaken for anxiety. Poor concentration—common in anxiety—is also common in depression. In addition, some people with anxiety disorders may have other disorders (depression or substance use disorders) that make diagnosis more complicated. Is the substance use an attempt to self-medicate anxiety? Did depression come before the anxiety, or is a person depressed because of persistent anxiety?

If anxiety is making you miserable, get a thorough medical checkup to be sure an underlying physical illness isn't causing it. Start with your primary health-care provider, and go from there.

What's the Difference?

What if you're free of any other medical problem, and you've already been diagnosed with an anxiety disorder? But your cousin has an anxiety disorder, and her symptoms are completely different from yours! Why?

Each anxiety disorder shares something in common with the others, but each one is different. These disorders may have partly different origins and often have different treatments, as we discuss in the following chapters.

The key things to remember with any anxiety disorder are *you are not alone* and *there is hope*. Other people suffer from the same disorder you do; other people have gotten better. *You can feel much better!*

Having anxiety is nothing to be ashamed of; in fact, the main reason we focused on celebrity experiences of anxiety in this chapter is to show you (and perhaps your doubting or judgmental friends or family) that anxiety is not something anyone *wants* to have; that no one is immune; and that richer, more famous, better-looking, and smarter people than we have been down the same road.

In the next chapter, we take a look at the different anxiety disorders—and you can find the path you need to take to emotional freedom.

The Least You Need to Know

- There are four components of anxiety: physical, emotional, cognitive, and behavioral.
- The best way to determine whether your anxiety is truly a problem is by how much it affects your work, school, social, or personal life.
- Many medical conditions can cause anxiety; a physical checkup is always a good idea before deciding that you have an anxiety disorder.
- Each anxiety disorder has its own set of symptoms; your disorder may not look much like someone else's.

The Anxiety Disorders

I'm going crazy. I can't breathe. I've got to get out of here. I know the doctors have missed something; maybe I have AIDS! I'd rather die than get up in front of that group .... I can't turn off these thoughts racing around and around in my head.

This is the world of anxiety. Unless you've suffered from it, it can be quite difficult to understand how someone's life can be so affected by what may appear quite trivial. Unfortunately, a lot of people have firsthand experience; anxiety disorders plague 40 million people in the United States alone.

However, whereas all anxiety disorders share certain features, there are differences across conditions. In this chapter, we take a look at each clinical anxiety disorder, find out what an anxiety disorder diagnosis really means, and learn how to translate a terrifying experience into something your friends and family members can understand.

In This Chapter

- What a diagnosis really means
- Anxiety disorders and related conditions
- What these disorders do—and don't—have in common
- Getting support from friends and family

What's the Diagnosis?

Sam goes to his doctor complaining of chest pains, shortness of breath, trouble sleeping, and irritability. His symptoms began after a divorce and escalated after he got a welcome yet stressful promotion at work. His brother, Max, goes to his doctor with an arm injury he received in a flag-football game. Max's doctor does an x-ray and easily diagnoses a broken arm. Ten other physicians could perform the same test and would reach the same conclusion. Unfortunately, this isn't the case for Sam.

Sam's mental state is a changeable collection of thoughts, physical symptoms, and feelings. Though anxiety disorders clearly have a physical basis, the doctor can't x-ray his mind, and other kinds of brain imaging are not helpful for diagnosis. Sam's diagnosis is likely to be made by default; the doctor may do several tests to rule out easy-to-measure physical problems and essentially conclude that Sam's problem involves his brain. How sensitively and knowledgably the doctor communicates this will depend upon his or her beliefs about the cause/nature of mental illness.

 ON THE CUTTING EDGE

A 2004 study found that 25 percent of 9,000 randomly interviewed Americans met the criteria for a mental illness within the past year; fewer than half of those in need had gotten treatment.

The Pros and Cons of Labels

When considering anxiety disorder diagnoses, it's important to keep in mind what they're good for and what they aren't.

For instance, a diagnostic label can provide a useful shortcut for describing (and making sense of) a collection of thoughts, feelings, and behaviors that tend to go together. It can be reassuring to know that there's a name for this terrifying, imprisoning experience, that other people have had—and gotten better from—similar illnesses, and that there are doctors out there who've treated similar problems. That is, we are not alone.

On the other hand, although a diagnosis can tell us *what we have,* we should never let it tell us *who we are.* When you get an anxiety disorder diagnosis, take all the benefits you can from the structure, clarity, and reassurance it can provide—and take heart in the route to recovery it reveals. But don't let it be a confining and limiting label or think of it as a precise analysis encompassing everything about your unique human experience.

ON THE CUTTING EDGE

Anxiety often accompanies depression, and an addiction may accompany a mood or anxiety disorder. Unfortunately, even though 50 percent of people with one mental disorder also meet the criteria for a second, research suggests that mental-health treatment is often geared toward a single problem or disorder.

Co-occurrence

An obstacle to the "right" diagnosis is the fact that disorders often coexist with each other; 58 percent of patients diagnosed with one anxiety disorder also meet the criteria for a second. A person diagnosed with panic disorder may also suffer from agoraphobia; he or she may also show signs of depression and social anxiety.

Zeroing in on—and treating—one disorder may bring partial relief but not address the whole problem. For example, an antidepressant may significantly reduce panic symptoms but inadequately address the crippling avoidance that limits careers and puts love lives on hold. In terms of treatment, then, a diagnosis is a great starting point, but ideally the finish line should be clear of any limits our anxiety disorder is currently imposing on our lives.

Difficulty with Objectivity

Another challenge with diagnosing a mental condition is the fact that the source of our symptoms (the brain) is also the source of information about those symptoms. Max's mind should be able to clearly recall and describe the circumstances surrounding his injury, but Sam may not be able to be so objective. Asking a distressed mind to calmly describe itself can be like asking a ball of wool to unravel itself.

STRESS RELIEF

Tracking symptoms (noting time, length, triggers, and so on) on a daily basis can not only help our doctors make better diagnoses, it can help us get some distance from our anxiety symptoms. In addition, loved ones can sometimes provide essential information to doctors, so we often encourage patients to bring loved ones along to appointments, especially early in the diagnostic process.

Cultural Differences

Finally, cultural differences can get in the way of a clear and objective diagnosis. Although people of all races, cultures, and social classes experience anxiety disorders, there are cultural differences in how individual symptoms are regarded and expressed.

Cultural differences in emotional expression and social behavior can be misinterpreted as "impairments" if clinicians are not sensitive to the cultural context and meaning of exhibited symptoms. For example, in some cultures, it is normal and natural to channel stress symptoms into physical complaints. In the United States, however, this tendency is sometimes frowned upon by physicians. In turn, these physicians may not have the sensitivity or knowledge to effectively communicate that the problem is anxiety related.

On the other hand, serious emotional distress can be overlooked if the person's description or behavior doesn't match what the physician expects. In some Native American languages, there is no equivalent translation for *anxiety;* savvy clinicians have to rely more on descriptions of stressful events. Similarly, several studies have shown that Asian Americans tend to report feeling more social anxiety in comparison to numerous other groups; however, in these studies, Asian Americans were much less likely to avoid socially uncomfortable situations or show behaviors that many clinicians would look for in diagnosing social anxiety disorder. Absent the anticipated outward signs, the internal turmoil might be missed.

STRESS RELIEF

Choosing a mental health professional who is culturally similar to you—or who has worked extensively with members of your culture—can reduce misdiagnosis or mistreatment.

The Anxiety Disorders

Now that we have some perspective on what an anxiety disorder diagnosis means, let's take a look at the anxiety disorders listed in the fifth edition of the *Diagnostic and Statistical Manual.* You'll see that the anxiety disorders have a lot in common; for instance, they all involve chronic or difficult-to-control fear; numerous physical symptoms; and a strong desire to avoid/escape uncomfortable situations. However, they're also unique; the sudden spontaneous terror of a panic attack may be completely unfamiliar to someone with generalized anxiety disorder.

Generalized Anxiety Disorder: Chronic Worry

At some point, most of us have worried about a child who's out later than usual, stressed over a dwindling bank account, or imagined that a minor illness was a symptom of a more serious one. During times of stress, it's pretty normal to find ourselves stewing over things we can't control.

For the 4 million Americans suffering from *generalized anxiety disorder* (*GAD*), worry is a daily companion. Even if sufferers realize their anxiety is more intense than the situation warrants, they just can't seem to shake it. Not surprisingly, a constant, low-level state of fear takes its toll, leading to physical symptoms such as headaches, muscle tension, stomach problems, and a disrupted sleep pattern. Over time, these can wear a person down, making life a tiring, uphill series of events.

 ANXIETY ATTACK

> GAD is diagnosed if symptoms are present for more days than not during a period of at least six months. The symptoms also must cause substantial distress or interfere with daily life.

In the 1990s and 2000s, Drs. Robert Spitzer, Janet B. Williams, Kurt Kroenke, and colleagues developed the Patient Health Questionnaire (PHQ), in an effort to help primary physicians identify and treat common mental illnesses in their patients. Materials are freely available online (phqscreeners.com/overview.aspx), with the following language: "No permission required to reproduce, translate, display or distribute."

The following questionnaire, the GAD-7, is useful to screen for GAD and monitor symptoms over time. If relevant for you, feel free to make as many copies as you'd like for monitoring purposes.

Over the **last two weeks,** how often have you been bothered by any of the following problems?

	Not at All (0)	Several Days (1)	More Than Half the Days (2)	Nearly Every Day (3)
1. Feeling nervous anxiety or on edge	❏	❏	❏	❏
2. Not being able to stop or control worrying	❏	❏	❏	❏
3. Worrying too much about different things	❏	❏	❏	❏
4. Trouble relaxing	❏	❏	❏	❏
5. Being so restless that it is hard to sit still	❏	❏	❏	❏
6. Becoming easily annoyed or irritable	❏	❏	❏	❏
7. Feeling afraid as if something awful might happen	❏	❏	❏	❏
GAD-7 Score:	❏	= _____	+ _____	+ _____

In order to rate the severity of generalized anxiety symptoms, count each symptom rated "1" ("several days") once, each rated "2" ("more than half the days") twice, and "3" ("nearly every day") three times (i.e., symptoms rated "2" or "3" should be multiplied by 2 or 3). A total score of 5 to 9 indicates mild generalized anxiety symptoms; 10 to 14, moderate symptoms; and 15 or more, severe symptoms. Put another way, a score of 10 to 14 draws attention to a possible clinically significant condition, while a score of 15 or more indicates that treatment is probably warranted.

Note that, besides restlessness, tiredness, and muscle tension/aches (including headaches), many people with generalized anxiety experience other physical symptoms, such as sweatiness, nausea, frequently needing to use the bathroom, and even trembling.

Also, people with generalized anxiety tend to see potential problems as more likely and more catastrophic than others do, and they are sometimes jumpy or easy to startle.

Up to a quarter of people with GAD develop an additional anxiety disorder. GAD sufferers may, for example, choose to stay at home—a place of safety—as in agoraphobia. Or they may avoid social contact, as in social anxiety disorder.

Experience has shown that professional treatment can have a positive impact on GAD. In addition, sufferers can take some action to control some of their symptoms, as you will see later in this book.

Social Anxiety Disorder: Beyond Butterflies

James was always a little shy in elementary school. He described himself as "excruciatingly self-conscious" during his teen years. However, after joining the military, with its built-in social network, he thought his shyness was a thing of the past. Until he left the army and his marriage failed.

His civilian job required interaction with new people on a regular basis, and James found it increasingly difficult to put on his game face. When he was asked to give a presentation, he stressed about it for days and finally called in sick. He began avoiding the lunchroom and felt increasingly self-conscious in meetings. By the time he finally got help, he had passed up at least two promotions and had become so lonely and isolated he was experiencing fleeting thoughts of suicide.

ON THE CUTTING EDGE

A 2006 study found that people suffering with social anxiety disorder have increased activity in a part of the brain when confronted with threatening faces or frightening social situations. Though methods of imaging brain activity are currently quite expensive and of limited usefulness for individual patients, they may eventually be feasible to help objectify how severe a person's social phobia is, as well as the effectiveness of treatments.

As you can see, there's a quantitative difference between social anxiety disorder—also called social phobia—and the nervousness many of us feel when asked to speak at a conference or give a wedding toast. A phobia of public speaking is the most common form of social anxiety disorder, and this phobia can cause substantial suffering and missed opportunities. However, many people with social anxiety disorder can become afraid of everyday social interactions such as shopping or going to a party with co-workers. Over time, this anxiety perpetuates itself, resulting in …

- Extreme self-consciousness in social settings.

- A strong urge to avoid social interaction.

- An excessive fear of looking or sounding foolish in front of people.

Although we can all feel shy at times, particularly among strangers or when we are asked to perform a task in front of others, social phobia is normally diagnosed when these shy feelings become almost overwhelming, accompanied by physical symptoms of extreme nervousness, and when these symptoms begin to impact a person's ability to function socially.

 MYTH BUSTER

"Social phobia is just shyness." This is an oversimplification. Moderately shy individuals don't stress about an upcoming social event for weeks, sweat, tremble, and feel terrified during it, or take drastic measures to avoid it. Though our temperaments can influence the likelihood of developing social phobia, being shy doesn't mean we can never enjoy social activities.

Panic Disorder: The Tsunami of Anxiety

It's virtually impossible to do justice in describing the terror and fear involved in a panic attack; if you've had one, you know what it's like; if you haven't, it can be hard to imagine. A panic attack is a sudden episode of overwhelming fear and anxiety, with accompanying physical sensations and/or thoughts.

 ANXIETY ATTACK

The frightening sensations of a panic attack typically peak within 10 minutes; our bodies can't sustain that level of anxiety and fear for much longer.

Not everyone who has experienced severe anxiety, including panic attacks, has panic disorder. That is, panic disorder is defined as having more than one spontaneous or out-of-the-blue panic attack, along with negative effects of this spontaneous anxiety on a person's life.

The Patient Health Questionnaire includes a panic disorder section that can be helpful in establishing the diagnosis:

Questions about anxiety.

		No	Yes
a.	In the last 4 weeks, have you had an anxiety attack—suddenly feeling fear or panic?	❑	❑
b.	Has this ever happened before?	❑	❑
c.	Do some of these attacks come suddenly out of the blue—that is, in situations where you don't expect to be nervous or uncomfortable?	❑	❑
d.	Do these attacks bother you a lot or are you worried about having another attack?	❑	❑

Think about your last bad anxiety attack.

		No	Yes
a.	Were you short of breath?	❑	❑
b.	Did your heart race, pound, or skip?	❑	❑
c.	Did you have chest pain or pressure?	❑	❑
d.	Did you sweat?	❑	❑
e.	Did you feel as if you were choking?	❑	❑
f.	Did you have hot flashes or chills?	❑	❑
g.	Did you have nausea or an upset stomach, or the feeling that you were going to have diarrhea?	❑	❑
h.	Did you feel dizzy, unsteady, or faint?	❑	❑
i.	Did you have tingling or numbness in parts of your body?	❑	❑
j.	Did you tremble or shake?	❑	❑
k.	Were you afraid you were dying?	❑	❑

If a person responds "yes" to all 4 of the "questions about anxiety" and "yes" to at least 3 accompanying symptoms during their last bad anxiety attack, that person is likely to have panic disorder.

Note that some people with panic disorder have other symptoms. For example, it's common to feel a sense of impending doom (something terrible is about to happen) with a panic attack. Also, panic attacks can be accompanied by a feeling of losing control or "going crazy." Finally, some people have odd perceptual experiences during panic attacks, including the sense that the environment around them is not real or that they are outside their bodies.

Given this bombardment of bodily sensations, no wonder a panic attack can make someone feel as if the world is coming apart. And it can happen anywhere. Sometimes panic sufferers experience attacks truly out of the blue. Other times they will have attacks in certain situations (for example, in crowded restaurants).

Not all panic attacks develop into panic disorder. Some people have one panic attack and never experience another one. Some have a few that get better or worse as life stressors change. When a person has suffered at least two unexpected panic attacks—and at least a month of fear and worry over having another one—a clinical diagnosis is likely. Even then, a sufferer may develop coping routines to avoid extreme stress, such as leaning on family or friends. Regularly calling and getting together with friends, for example, can be helpful in managing everyday stress. Staying connected like this is good in the long run, too; research shows that people are less likely to have panic symptoms when they feel cared for by friends and family.

 MYTH BUSTER

"Years of suffering requires years of therapy." Actually, guidelines among therapists now call for improvements to be noticeable within 6 weeks. And studies show that 70 to 90 percent of patients with panic disorder can be helped with treatment.

For some people, particularly when such support isn't available, the only option apparent to them is to withdraw from society—which is called agoraphobia.

Agoraphobia: Fear of the Marketplace

Literally meaning "fear of the marketplace," agoraphobia is an anxiety disorder whose sufferers sometimes feel that the only safe place is home. In a sentence, agoraphobia is a fear of being in a situation or a place from which there is no easy escape. The clinical definition of agoraphobia is marked fear or anxiety in two or more of the following types of situations:

- Public transportation like buses and planes

- Open spaces like marketplaces and bridges

- Enclosed places like shops and theaters

- Being in lines or crowds

- Being outside of the home alone

A person with agoraphobia fears/avoids these situations because they are difficult to escape, or help might not be available if the person becomes incapacitated or develops embarrassing symptoms. Patients with agoraphobia often find that being in such situations is tolerable if they are with a trusted companion; however, it is not always easy on family members, etc., to be available.

Panic disorder and agoraphobia are strongly related. Though people with these kinds of situational fears have not always experienced panic attacks, it is clear that panic attacks can trigger or acutely worsen agoraphobia. A person feels insecure, worried about another attack, and even though there may be no evidence that further attacks will happen or happen anywhere other than a specific place, a person may begin to feel that the home is their only safe haven.

A tendency to develop agoraphobia can run in families and apparently has a genetic basis. Nevertheless, effective treatments have been found to significantly reduce the symptoms. These include cognitive behavioral therapy, medications, and lifestyle changes, which we discuss later.

ANXIETY ATTACK

The quicker a person gets treatment for an anxiety disorder, the better the odds of improvement. However, all persons with anxiety disorders can get better.

Specific Phobia: Targeted Fear

Melissa, age 40, loves visiting family on the east coast. Each year she makes the trip from her home in Santa Monica, driving the more than 2,500 miles, making stops on the way to refuel and rest. Though she knows the trip would take a fraction of the time by air, she can't bring herself to even visit an airport. Melissa has a phobia of flying. Unlike a person with agoraphobia, she doesn't fear being stuck high in the air and unable to escape; she fears crashing.

Unlike general anxiety, a specific phobia is triggered by a specific inciting factor—dogs, heights, or confined spaces. More than six million Americans suffer from such phobias, and although in many cases a phobia isn't a serious condition (in that it doesn't always interfere with everyday life), some phobias can limit or control a person's behavior.

Remember Indiana Jones, fearless hero and adventurous archeologist? Indy had one chink in his armor—his phobia of snakes. Phobias have nothing to do with bravery or rational logic—the strongest, most intelligent people can suffer from phobias.

Related Conditions

Until recently, obsessive compulsive disorder (OCD) and post-traumatic stress disorder (PTSD) were considered anxiety disorders, and many experts argue that there are good reasons for that. However, there are also advantages to considering these conditions and their *other* close cousins separately. In this book, we note that OCD and PTSD share some features in common with the anxiety disorders just introduced, and we note that some of the principles outlined throughout the book are also relevant to OCD and PTSD. In addition, we felt it was important to discuss depression as well, as anxiety disorders and depression tend to co-occur within persons and within families.

Obsessive Compulsive Disorder: The Broken Record

Here's Mark's story:

> During the third grade, I started having unusual symptoms. I kept having vivid, unwanted thoughts and images—horrible things such as killing a family member. I worried that I had actually done something terrible, and felt trapped, unable to escape the thoughts. I couldn't stand to be around knives, and I insisted that my parents put them away in drawers. My parents eventually brought me for treatment and, with the help of medication and a great therapist, I began getting control over my thoughts, feelings, and behaviors. I was amazed to discover how many other people were suffering from OCD ... . OCD was the most terrible experience of my life, but in some ways it hasn't been all bad—I am now more confident, and I can really understand how other people feel.

You know how it feels to worry that you didn't lock the door or turn off the stove before leaving home. You've probably had the sudden impulse to do something irrational or out of character. Although many people can choose to ignore or override such doubts, about 2 percent of the U.S. population finds these compelling thoughts or urges impossible to ignore, ultimately setting in motion a repetitive, energy-draining cycle of behavior aimed at controlling and reducing the emotional discomfort. This repetitive cycle is often obsessional thoughts followed by repetitive actions that are geared toward managing or alleviating them.

An *obsession* is an unwanted thought, image, or urge that intrudes into consciousness. A person may experience upsetting thoughts, repugnant sexual images, concerns about germs or contamination, or unwanted urges to harm himself or loved ones. A *compulsion* is an overwhelming urge to do something, often in response to obsessive thoughts. For example, some people wash their hands excessively in an attempt to reduce anxiety about germs. Others feel compelled to count objects in a certain way to reduce anxiety. The compulsion—or behavior—is a response to the anxious feeling.

For example, an OCD sufferer may feel compelled to repeat actions, checking things even though rationally they know there is no need. For some, the disorder can take forms that others cannot easily observe. A person may compulsively monitor their own breathing or avoid certain numbers or colors.

Unfortunately, although persons with OCD may receive a feeling of temporary relief from performing compulsions, sufferers report that such relief is short lived. With passing time, or in the right circumstances, the feelings of insecurity heighten again.

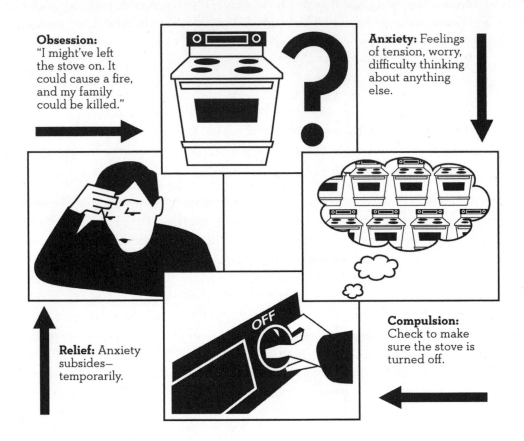

Post-Traumatic Stress Disorder: The Endless Movie

Mike can't sleep. He tells his doctor he feels dazed and numb, as if he's in another world. Loud noises make him jump, and he has this constant undercurrent of fear. He starts to cry as he explains how his relationship to his wife and children is becoming strained by his behavior.

Three weeks ago, Mike witnessed his friend accidentally shoot himself in a hunting accident. Two days later, his symptoms became pronounced. At present, Mike is suffering with acute stress disorder, an emotional condition that can emerge after a person has either witnessed or experienced death, serious injury, or sexual violence. If his symptoms continue for more than a month, his diagnosis will become post-traumatic stress disorder. Its symptoms include the following:

- Reliving the event through unwanted memories, nightmares, flashbacks (the sensation that the event is occurring now), or intense distress or physical reactions to reminders of the event

- Avoidance of thinking about or reminders of the event

- Changes in thoughts and mood (e.g., thoughts that the world is more dangerous than is the case, less interest in activities that used to be enjoyable)

- Hyperarousal (e.g., difficulty sleeping, a tendency to startle easily, trouble concentrating, and a general sense of restlessness and being on edge)

Whereas any of us would be extremely upset following a life-threatening trauma such as a serious car accident, rape, or a life-threatening illness, for many of us the symptoms would lessen considerably over time. Our risk for this disorder goes up or down depending upon the severity of the trauma and our own personal tendencies, and some experts believe that symptoms persist, at least in part, because of avoidance. That is, if a person is able to "talk out" and process what happened, and if they "get back on the horse of life" (continue their normal everyday activities and don't run away with drugs and alcohol), the symptoms will decrease with time.

 ON THE CUTTING EDGE

Until recently, mental health professionals didn't realize that patients who survive critical illnesses and intensive-care unit treatment are at relatively high risk for post-traumatic stress disorder. Critically ill patients often have horrific memories of being out of control and confused, with frightening experiences of being tortured, etc.

Depression: Churchill's Black Dog

In Chapter 1, we mentioned that Winston Churchill suffered from anxiety, but he also famously suffered from clinical depression, which he referred to as his "black dog." Those of us with anxiety disorders are at increased risk for major depressive episodes as well, especially without treatment. Often, but not always, anxiety disorders emerge earlier than depressive episodes.

The Patient Health Questionnaire includes a depression section that can be helpful in establishing the diagnosis and monitoring symptoms over time. This section is often referred to as the PHQ-9. If relevant for you, feel free to make as many copies as you'd like for monitoring purposes.

Over the **last two weeks,** how often have you been bothered by any of the following problems?

	Not at All (0)	Several Days (1)	More Than Half the Days (2)	Nearly Every Day (3)
1. Little interest or pleasure in doing things	❑	❑	❑	❑
2. Feeling down, depressed, or hopeless	❑	❑	❑	❑
3. Trouble falling or staying asleep, or sleeping too much	❑	❑	❑	❑
4. Feeling tired or having little energy	❑	❑	❑	❑
5. Poor appetite or overeating	❑	❑	❑	❑
6. Feeling bad about yourself—or that you are a failure or have let yourself or your family down	❑	❑	❑	❑
7. Trouble concentrating on things, such as reading the newspaper or watching television	❑	❑	❑	❑
8. Moving or speaking so slowly that other people could have noticed? Or the opposite—being so fidgety or restless that you have been moving around a lot more than usual	❑	❑	❑	❑
9. Thoughts that you would be better off dead or of hurting yourself in some way	❑	❑	❑	❑
PHQ-9 Score:	❑	= _____	+ _____	+ _____

To rate the severity of depressive symptoms, count each symptom rated "1" ("several days") once, each rated "2" ("more than half the days") twice, and "3" ("nearly every day") three times (i.e., symptoms rated "2" or "3" should be multiplied by 2 or 3). A total score of 5 to 9 indicates mild depressive symptoms; 10 to 14, moderate symptoms; and 15 or more, severe symptoms. Put another way, a score of 10 to 14 draws attention to a possible clinically significant condition, while a score of 15 or more indicates that treatment is probably warranted.

Anxiety's Effects on Others

Because anxiety disorders affect the way we feel, think, and act, our friends and family may be affected by them, too. Maybe we've canceled plans with a friend because of our fears, or our anxiety has made us on-edge and irritable. Now that we know what the problem is, how can we explain our anxiety disorder to others in a way that makes sense and allows us to get the support we need?

Friends and family can be supportive only if they know about a problem. At the same time, no magic words can guarantee a positive response; no matter how you say it, some people will be judgmental or skeptical. Most of the people we care about will be supportive of our attempts to get better; they may be less so if they think we're using our diagnosis as an excuse to justify a short fuse or continue avoiding things we're afraid of.

The trick is to prepare in advance, being clear with yourself about why you are telling the person, what you want from him or her, and how you will respond to whatever reaction they might have. For example, before talking to a friend or family member about your anxiety disorder, ask yourself the following:

Why do I want or need to tell this person? If you're telling your boss, for example, you should probably stick to how it impacts work, what help or assistance you need, and what you are doing to get better.

What do I want from him or her? For instance, do you want emotional support or do you want this person to participate in your treatment?

How has this person responded to other challenges in the past? How does the person handle his or her own emotional bumps and bruises?

Write down what you want this person to know about your anxiety disorder. In addition to telling your own story, it can be useful to find some basic reading material you can recommend they use as a reference. Don't sabotage yourself by sharing with your loved one when you're in the middle of an argument, when either of you is pressed for time, or when either of you is in a bad mood.

> **ANXIETY ATTACK**
>
> Before sharing the fact that you have an anxiety disorder with anyone at work, be sure you know why you are doing it, what the possible consequences are, and what legal rights you have.

Now that we've met the anxiety disorders and related conditions, remember what we discussed about diagnosis. These lists of symptoms represent psychiatry and psychology's best attempt to summarize conditions that affect real people. Your experience will be unique, and your path to emotional freedom will be your own; in later chapters, we discuss what the best self-help and professional assistance have to offer.

But before we get to problematic symptoms, let's take a look at the "why" behind the "what." An anxiety disorder diagnosis often raises as many questions as it answers. Why me? Why do only some people develop anxiety disorders? Is it nature (biology) or nurture? In the next chapter, we discuss the causes of anxiety disorders: the genetics, the biology, the environment, and the internal triggers that either cause them or keep them going.

The Least You Need to Know

- All anxiety disorders share an undercurrent of fear, various physical symptoms, and attempts to avoid.
- An accurate diagnosis of any mental condition is challenging because it is based on self-report, symptoms often change, and cultural influences may cloud the picture.
- Obsessive compulsive disorder, post-traumatic stress disorder, and depression can be considered anxiety-related conditions.
- Family support can be critical in overcoming an anxiety disorder. Before talking with loved ones, it is helpful to know why you want to share with them and how you'd like them to help you.

Why Me?

Monica's parents describe her as a happy, sensitive, and eager-to-please child. Sure, in fifth grade, she went through a brief period of what she calls "nervous stuttering" and nail biting, but these subsided as she adjusted to a new school and her parents' separation. High school was fine, even though Monica always felt anxious at parties and was terrified in her speech class. However, she had many good friends. And although she suffered for hours before a speech, she always managed to get through it. In fact, she was valedictorian of her high school class and received an academic scholarship to an Ivy League college hundreds of miles from home.

The first semester away was rough. For the first time, Monica felt dumb; academic competition among her peers was fierce, and Monica found herself doubting her ability to succeed. She also worried that she would lose her academic scholarship and let her parents down. Then in November of her freshman year, she learned her father had prostate cancer. On December 1, walking to class on a sunny but cold fall day, Monica had her first panic attack.

All of us experience stress and pressure. Many of us have lost someone close to us or faced the possibility. Yet not all of us develop an anxiety disorder. In this chapter, we look at why anxiety disorders develop and what clues their origins provide to help us regain control over our lives.

Who Gets Anxiety Disorders?

Although anyone can get an anxiety disorder, they are twice as common in women as they are in men. Anxiety disorders also show up more often in certain age groups; they can appear at any age, but most people experience their first symptoms in childhood, adolescence, or young adulthood.

Anxiety disorders also run in families. If someone in your family has an anxiety disorder, you are several times more likely to develop one yourself; in general, the closer the genetic link between you and your anxious family member, the more your risk increases. But even if your identical twin has an anxiety disorder, it doesn't mean you will.

Certain life experiences also put us at risk for an anxiety disorder. A childhood history of abuse can increase our odds of adult anxiety, as can childhood parental loss or separation. In addition, children with highly reactive temperaments may be innately more sensitive to their environments and, as a result, more reactive to environmental stressors and the physical cues they generate.

So where do these disorders come from? Are they psychological or physical? The most commonly accepted model of mental illness is the *diathesis-stress model*. This theory proposes that some people are born with a predisposition for a given illness such as generalized anxiety disorder or panic disorder that may or may not develop, depending on what life throws at them. For instance, a natural worrywart may get along just fine until she is diagnosed with breast cancer. A shy teenager may develop full-blown social anxiety only in response to a humiliating school event or a bully's constant teasing.

The answer, then, is that anxiety disorders often develop for biological and psychological reasons. When they do develop, what we put in our bodies and how we use our minds can make them better or worse.

 ON THE CUTTING EDGE

Recent research suggests that anxiety and depressive disorders run together in families and share a genetic basis.

Psychology and Anxiety

Many years ago, psychiatrists and psychologists believed that anxiety was usually explainable in terms of unconscious conflicts, and psychodynamic theories still often focus on anxiety symptoms in this way. For example, the rituals associated with obsessive-compulsive disorder (OCD) are viewed as a way to ward off unacceptable impulses or internal conflicts. Phobias are sometimes interpreted as a use of *displacement*, a psychic defense mechanism whereby a person redirects thoughts, feelings, and impulses from a source that causes anxiety to a safer, more acceptable one. From a psychoanalytic point of view, a boy who develops a fear of horses may really have an unrecognized fear of his father.

Even today, from the psychodynamic perspective, anxiety is sometimes interpreted as reflecting basic, unresolved conflicts in intimate relationships or hidden anger. Treatment often centers on uncovering these hidden conflicts, impulses, and feelings. Unfortunately, there's not much evidence that this treatment works as well as other treatments, at least for some anxiety and related disorders, particularly OCD and phobias (see Chapter 19).

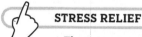

STRESS RELIEF

There is some evidence that women may ruminate more about distressing life events than men, suggesting that learning to monitor and acknowledge thoughts and worries may be especially useful tools.

Behavior

The behavioral model focuses on how we learn to be afraid. According to behaviorists, we learn in three different ways: *classical conditioning, operant conditioning,* and *modeling.* All of these have implications when it comes to anxiety.

Classical conditioning is when you learn by automatically associating two different things or stimuli. In particular, the emphasis is on how we learn to pair a normal reflex action with a "neutral" stimulus nearby. If you feed your dog canned food, you can witness classical conditioning firsthand. Watch her drool when she hears the electric can opener running—even if you're opening a can of pineapple! She associates the sound of a can opener (a neutral stimulus) with being fed and, as a result, is drooling in the absence of dog food.

How can this relate to anxiety? In a famous experiment, social scientist John Watson (1878–1958) intentionally induced a phobia in an 11-month-old boy by pairing a loud noise with a little white rat. (Please note that ethical standards have changed; no university would allow such an experiment now.) Every time little Albert reached for the rat, Watson clanged away. Not only did Albert begin to associate the white rat and the noise, becoming anxious around the rat, he also began to generalize. He became anxious around other white, furry objects, including a rabbit, a fur coat, and a Santa Claus beard.

But this doesn't have to happen in a laboratory. For example, let's say that when you were young you ate a chocolate-mint Girl Scout cookie, and shortly afterward you were violently ill with a virus affecting your gut. You might feel sick and avoid eating (or even thinking about) that kind of cookie, or Girl Scout cookies in general, for years afterward–even though the original cookie had nothing to do with your nausea and vomiting! This is classical conditioning at work, and it's not hard to imagine how this could be useful in some circumstances; that is, it is not good to eat food that makes us sick. However, we don't always know what makes us sick. Sometimes we have strong aversions without a reasonable basis, and we don't even realize where these aversions come from.

Next, any parent understands *operant conditioning;* it simply means we learn to do things we're rewarded for, and we stop doing things that lead to painful or negative consequences. Although this risk/reward strategy works well most of the time, it can backfire when our avoidance interferes with doing what we love or when short-term rewards lead to long-term problems.

For instance, most of us tend to stay away from things we fear. According to operant conditioning, this avoidance behavior tends to be reinforced because when we avoid (or escape) unpleasant situations, we feel better. An unfortunate side effect, though, is that this strategy reduces opportunities for us to overcome our fears. An attempt to avoid unpleasant feelings can have life-altering—even life-threatening—consequences. For the right person, a bad encounter with an inexperienced nurse and a needle could lead to avoidance of much-needed medical care for years. Fears of driving after a car accident could adversely impact our careers and our relationships.

Note that avoidance is not the only behavior reinforced in anxiety disorders; compulsions are also highly reinforcing! Unfortunately, though compulsions temporarily decrease anxiety, they don't cure it—anxiety almost always comes back if the cycle below is not interrupted.

Finally, *modeling* is another way we may pick up fears. If Mom is terrified of snakes, we may decide all snakes are dangerous without ever coming near one. If everyone in the family is anxious about the same thing, we're even more likely to jump on the bandwagon.

So is all anxiety learned? It appears that some anxiety disorders are more so than others. For instance, one study found that more than three quarters of people with a needle phobia had had a bad experience with an injection or blood draw. That may reflect learning at work, at least to some extent. On the other hand, a study of children who were terrified of water showed that more than half of them exhibited the fear at their very first aquatic encounter! Obviously, not all anxiety can be associated directly with learning.

 MYTH BUSTER

"Stress causes mental illness." In reality, stress may trigger an episode or cause worsening symptoms (e.g., of anxiety or depression), but this is just one part of a complex picture. There are probably many things that can contribute to mental illness—the causes are not yet fully understood.

When Twisted Thinking Leads to Anxiety

Cognitive theories of anxiety focus on the way our thoughts influence us. Here's an example: picture yourself about to give a big speech at school or work. Imagine that you're thinking to yourself, "Okay, I can handle this. I'm well prepared. Everyone here wants me to do well. Even if I make a few mistakes, it won't matter."

Now imagine that you're in the same situation, but instead you're thinking, "I can't do this. I'm going to throw up. I'm going to pass out. The speech I prepared is pure garbage. Everyone is just waiting for me to screw up. One mistake and I'll get an F [or get fired]."

It's the same speech! But there's no question about which situation would make you, me, or anyone else more anxious. It's not just reality that matters—it's what we *think* about what happens or what might happen that influences how we feel about the situation.

Cognitive distortions occur when our thoughts become unreasonable, irrational, or even ridiculous. Psychologists have a whole list of ways we distort our thinking when we become anxious. Some of these may ring true with you (note that these can overlap).

Catastrophizing happens when we turn a molehill into a mountain. "Oh my Lord, it's the end of the world—I have to give a talk and I have a run in my pantyhose!" The reality? Most people won't notice—or care.

Dichotomous reasoning means seeing everything as black or white. You're either a success or a failure (and one mistake can make it seem like you're a failure). In reality, none of us are perfect, and none of us are completely flawed.

Disqualifying the positive happens when you ignore the good feedback you get. Ten people say you look great today, but you find reasons to discount what they say.

Emotional reasoning happens when you decide that what you feel must really reflect reality. For example, you feel incompetent, so you must really be incompetent. Remember that our feelings can mislead us.

Fortune telling happens when you act as if your worst fears will certainly come true. You're not worried the worst *might* happen; you're *sure* it will.

Labeling occurs when we give a global label to ourselves (e.g., "I'm a failure") rather than seeing something as a single event (e.g., "Well, I blew that one, but I'll do better next time").

Mind reading is when we assume others are reacting negatively to us, even when we have no evidence.

Minimization is when you don't give yourself credit for your good qualities or accomplishments. You might be able to tell someone all your faults but nothing good about yourself.

Overgeneralization means taking one event and basing reality on that. For example, he says he loves you at the end of 99 phone calls, but if he forgets to just once, it must mean he doesn't really love you.

Personalization means taking everything personally and ignoring other factors. "She didn't smile; she must hate me!" (In reality, her cat just died, or she doesn't feel well today.)

Selective abstraction happens when you focus on one part rather than the whole; you get five A's on your report card and one B minus—and all you can think about is the B minus.

"Should" and "have to" statements can mess up your mind if you go overboard with them. Some 12-step programs refer to overdoing this as "should-ing all over yourself."

 STRESS RELIEF

One way anxiety can influence thinking is described in a metaphor of a lake. We don't actually perceive things as they really are—we perceive them as they are reflected by our emotions, as in the surface of a lake. If we are emotionally unsettled, angry, afraid, depressed, or anxious, the reflection is distorted, and we cannot see things clearly.

Biology

What about biology? We discuss this later in the book in more depth, but we'll take a brief look here. You may remember from high school biology that your nervous system transmits information throughout your whole body.

Your nervous system is divided into two parts: your central nervous system (the brain and spinal cord) and your *peripheral nervous system*, which transmits information back and forth to your central nervous system.

Next let's get more specific. The peripheral nervous system is also divided into two parts: the *somatic nervous system*, which controls our voluntary actions, and the *autonomic nervous system*, which controls our internal organs.

The autonomic nervous system divides down yet again into two parts: the *parasympathetic system*, which helps us relax, and the *sympathetic system*. The sympathetic system activates our survival responses to perceived threats.

In extreme instances, this survival response is known as *fight or flight*. Your body is preparing you to either run away or do battle. This was probably great for our caveman ancestors. You see that mammoth approaching, and it's time to run like heck or get ready to try to put it on the dinner table.

But this survival response is often no help with modern stressors. When we're at the dentist's office, it's not appropriate to jump out of the chair and run or to challenge the dentist to a duel. It's time to open our mouths and let the dentist do her job of taking care of our teeth.

 STRESS RELIEF

Learning through rewards and punishments still works, no matter how old we get. But we can reward ourselves, too. Got a stressful event coming up? Depending on how stressful the event (and how much money you've got), a reward might range from a chocolate milkshake to a new dress to that getaway vacation you've been dreaming about.

The Fear Pathway

So what happens in the brain during fight or flight? The startling noise of a mammoth—and every other piece of worrying sensory information—takes two pathways. One pathway is to the frontal cortex, the reasoning part of the brain, where every perception is analyzed and interpreted with powerful processing tools.

But this processing takes precious time, so there is another, shorter route. On this route, the perception is rapidly matched by the amygdala against possible threats. The *amygdala* is an almond-shaped structure in the limbic system whose job is to trigger responses to danger. If there is a close enough match, the amygdala will hit the emergency button, raising the heartbeat, changing breathing, and revving up the engines for action. However, because the amygdala's focus is on survival, it tends to err on the side of caution; accuracy takes a backseat to speed, and innocuous situations can be misperceived as dangerous. Right or wrong, the amygdala takes a stand long before the rational mind has processed the incoming data.

Of course, sometimes the amygdala serves us well in getting us out of real danger quickly. But many times this life-saving system activates our panic mechanisms needlessly. Even when the rational mind catches up and concludes there is no threat, it takes a while to calm down the systems that have been alerted.

All the physical symptoms of fear—the shortness of breath, the nausea, the need to use the bathroom, the speeding pulse, the restlessness—are caused by the amygdala's response to a perceived threat. In the case of an anxiety disorder, this pathway becomes well trodden, a default pattern of response that becomes all too familiar—and difficult to maneuver around.

 MYTH BUSTER

"It's all in your mind." Wrong! Anxiety, like all emotions, produces physical reactions in our bodies, too. Sometimes, particularly when the anxiety is extreme, the physical reactions can cause other changes, such as a reduced immune system from chronic stress.

Life Experience and Anxiety

We know that biology affects psychology: if your body is pumping adrenaline into your bloodstream, you're unlikely to stay in a calm, peaceful frame of mind. But psychology can also affect biology.

Think about the last vivid dream you had. Was it scary, thrilling, funny, or just plain weird? Dreams are perhaps the most dramatic and challenging type of thought we have—and despite the frankly bizarre imagery, we usually completely believe dreams while we're having them. This is because the analytical, fact-checking higher cortex of the brain is largely shut down while we dream. So when we wake up, we are often charged with all the emotions of the dream; the body is responding as if the dream is real. If the dream is frightening, the sympathetic nervous system accordingly opens up all the channels needed to deal with the apparent reality. In other words, your body is responding to *nothing but your mind*.

In a sense, our brain chemistry changes with every thought. Each time a brain cell makes a connection with another brain cell, a chemical called a *neurotransmitter* is released to jump the gap. And different neurotransmitters are produced for different types of thought. So our state of mind can clearly affect the biology of our brains.

What's the Cause—Genes or Environment?

The simple answer is that it's probably a mix of both. There's no doubt that the genetic makeup we inherit from our parents sets a precedent for how we behave—we are all set at different emotional levels, and these levels are largely determined by our genes. However, this does not mean we are genetically doomed. Even if we are more inclined to respond with fear or anxiety to a given situation, learning how to manage emotions and irrational thinking is a powerful way to manage what nature and nurture have given us.

Take a look at the following table to compare the anxiety risk factors we face from both our biological makeup and what daily life can throw at us.

Diagnosis	Biological Risks	Environmental Risks
Social phobia	Moderately heritable: anxious/introverted temperament	Learning, often in adolescence
GAD	Moderately heritable: anxious temperament	Work/life stresses
Panic disorder	Moderately heritable: anxious temperament	Work/life stresses
Agoraphobia	Moderately heritable: anxious/introverted temperament	Learning
Specific phobias	Moderately heritable	Learning, often in childhood

It's clear that biology and the environment can both influence our susceptibility to anxiety disorders.

What Triggers Your Anxiety?

Film actress Scarlett Johansson recently divulged her anxiety trigger: work. She suffered severe panic attacks on the set of one of her movies. "I usually feel nervous before every film, but this time it was a lot worse. I was so nervous that, by the time we were ready for the first scene, I was nearly dead from anxiety."

 STRESS RELIEF

Daily hassles are minor irritants—misplacing or losing things, an unreliable car, continuous interruptions by a co-worker—that can create wear and tear on an anxious psyche. Dealing directly with these and building a strong support system can significantly cut down on chronic stress.

Understanding the causes of your own anxiety provides a basis for coping with and managing it. Studies have shown that there are some common causes for anxiety and anxiety disorders, but each person will have his or her own experience and triggers. What are yours? Rate your anxiety level for each of these known triggers.

Anxiety Trigger Checklist

Triggers	Strongly Anxious	Anxious	Not Anxious
Work worries	❏	❏	❏
Relationship dilemmas	❏	❏	❏
Money problems	❏	❏	❏
Recent loss of a loved one	❏	❏	❏
Health concerns	❏	❏	❏
School difficulties	❏	❏	❏
Life trauma such as a road accident	❏	❏	❏

In addition to these common stress inducers, you may also need to think about whether any of the following are already affecting your physical state:

- Are you taking medication that can cause excitement, nervousness, or irritability?

- Is your caffeine intake too high?

- Are you taking illicit drugs such as cocaine or cannabis?

Anxious feelings can spread easily. When we feel anxious, our perspective can be altered, and it can be hard to pinpoint the source of stress. So it's important to analyze your physical state and anxiety level with respect to triggers when you are at your calmest.

You can also discover your own anxiety triggers by completing a stress diary, explained later in the book. Make a note of the situations in which you feel most anxious. Notice when your anxiety levels decrease. This is invaluable information in learning to manage your own type of anxiety.

Now that we've talked about the types of anxiety disorders, and the causes and triggers of your own anxious feelings, what can we do about them? Is it possible to change, or should we accept what we have and live with the consequences? And if we are to change, how do we keep up the motivation when the going gets tough? In the next chapter on what to expect on the road to recovery, we talk about these issues and more.

The Least You Need to Know

- You are not alone; anxiety is a very common phenomenon.
- Anxiety has biological and environmental roots.
- Biology can affect your thinking, and thinking can affect your biology.
- Understanding your own anxiety triggers helps to form the basis of recovery.

What to Expect on the Path to Recovery

As a young girl, Eleanor Roosevelt developed a terror of water after the steamship she was traveling on was involved in a mid-sea collision with another vessel. She and her father barely managed to get in the same lifeboat. Afterward, she refused to go on another boat trip and, as a result of her fear, never learned to swim.

After her husband contracted polio, he could no longer play as actively with their children. Eleanor found herself taking over many parenting tasks—and, once again, came face to face with her water phobia. This time, though, she wasn't willing to give in to it. Out of her love for her children, Eleanor also found the motivation, and the strength, to break free of her phobia. She took swimming lessons and gradually became comfortable in the water. In fact, overcoming her fear of water gave her so much courage that she decided to conquer another personal challenge: she learned to drive.

Eleanor's motivation didn't make her fears go away. Instead, Eleanor found her way *through* her fear. In fact, her lifelong motto became, "You must look fear in the face. You must do the thing you think you cannot do."

In This Chapter

- A peek into your journey to reduced anxiety
- How to anchor your values
- The secrets of staying power
- Develop a winning attitude in the contest against anxiety

Tackling anxiety, whether it's a temporary state of mind or a chronic problem, is a journey. It's common for us to feel afraid, to have ups and downs, and, at times, to have to do things that are the opposite of what our instincts tell us. To keep ourselves on the path to freedom, let's explore what to expect and how we can overcome our initial fears, rally our motivation, gain momentum, and bounce back when things don't go as we planned.

Values

Anxiety and worry drain our energy and sap our motivation. So how do we muster the strength to take it on when it's already taking its toll? How do people ever make changes? These are important questions.

Identifying and focusing on our values can be one source of strength and motivation. A value is a belief, a mission, or a philosophy that is important to us (e.g., hard work, independence, or concern for others). These serve as the inspiration for our goals; if honesty is a value, for instance, I probably won't aspire to be a con artist. A concern for others might lead me to do volunteer work or choose a helping profession.

We're happiest when the way we live our lives is consistent with our core values. Unfortunately, anxiety, worry, and fear can keep us from doing so by either tempting us to *avoid* activities that would fulfill our values or by leading us to *do* things that are contradictory to how we would like to be. If Eleanor Roosevelt had let it, her fear of water could have prevented her from being the courageous, involved parent she wanted to be. A person with extreme social anxiety might find herself lying at the last minute to get out of a work talk, violating her personal values of honesty and keeping commitments.

 MYTH BUSTER

"Change is just a question of willpower." Not always. Determination is key, but we also need the skills and the resources.

Core values can help us stay committed to conquering our anxiety by keeping the "big picture" in mind. This gives us something to move *toward* in the struggle to master our fear. It can also help us tolerate temporary discomfort by keeping in mind the payoff at the end of the road, much like an expectant mom is willing to go through labor pains to get that bundle of joy.

So what are your personal values? What core beliefs form the bedrock of who you are? What's your basic philosophy or personal mission statement?

Consider some of the following values, and determine which of these are most important to you.

Adventure	Honesty
Calm, quietude, peace	Honor
Commitment	Independence
Communication	Inner peace
Community	Innovation
Concern for others	Integrity
Creativity	Justice
Discovery	Knowledge
Faith	Leadership
Family	Love, romance
Friendship	Loyalty
Fun	Meaning
Goodness	Money
Gratitude	Openness
Hard work	Pleasure
Harmony	Positive attitude

Which of these would be your top five? How do you act them out in your everyday words and actions? Write them down and put your list in a place where you can readily see it. Let it serve as a quick measure by which you evaluate your everyday decisions and choices.

 STRESS RELIEF

What do you want to be remembered for? How would you want your closest friends and family to describe you at your funeral? Writing your obituary can be a dramatic way to help clarify your personal values and make contact with what you care about.

Anxiety's Costs

Now that you've got a clearer picture of what values are closest to your heart, take a close look at how anxiety clouds the picture. Because anxiety is an attention grabber, it can take our focus away from the very things we treasure most.

For instance, if we worry excessively about harm befalling someone we care about, we may not give our child growing room to explore the world on his or her own. Our fear of flying might prevent us from attending a cherished friend's wedding or a loved one's funeral. Unmanaged stress might cause us to snap at people we care about, alienate co-workers, or abuse drugs or alcohol.

As painful as it is, getting a snapshot of how anxiety limits our lives is critical, especially when there's so much immediate relief in *giving in to* what our anxiety or fear is telling us. Yes, maybe we can avoid a panic attack if we don't get back behind the wheel of our car, but think of what this costs us. Think of our dependence on others to take us places, our child's confusion over why Mom or Dad can't carpool, and the secret shame and guilt we feel about it.

How does your anxiety affect you? What personal costs have you had to pay? What about the lifestyle changes and relationship issues caused or made worse by your anxiety?

Here's an exercise designed to help you see, on a daily basis, how costly giving in to your anxiety really is. For the next seven days, make daily recordings of situations or events that trigger your anxiety, concerns, or worries. Write down how you experience that anxiety; this should include your physical symptoms, feelings, thoughts, and concerns. Then record what your coping strategy was, what emotions your coping strategy produced, and what the lost-opportunity costs were. Here's an example of what your log might look like.

> **Situation:** Asked to give a talk at work.
>
> **Anxiety:** Afraid of being embarrassed, scared my anxiety would cause me to lose my train of thought.
>
> **Coping strategy:** Tried to talk myself into it but called in sick at the last minute.
>
> **Emotional impact:** Felt like a failure, felt guilty and ashamed, frustrated.
>
> **Opportunity cost:** Boss was irritated, lost chance to impress the sales group.

A warning: this exercise takes courage. Many people who initially commit to this exercise wind up avoiding it or "forgetting" to do it. Don't let yourself be one of them. If it helps, remind yourself that taking stock doesn't commit you to making any behavior changes; it's just a look-see. It's also a reminder that avoiding anxiety comes at a price, one that ultimately might be higher than going through it.

Developing the Right Attitude

Getting clear about anxiety's costs can be a powerful motivator. Another ally is to develop the right attitude—toward ourselves and toward our anxiety symptoms. We're not talking about looking on the bright side; we're talking about the deliberate cultivation of some healing beliefs that can help us put our anxiety symptoms in perspective and show respect to ourselves.

Let's take a look at five attitudes that can get your mind, your heart, and your willpower working together.

I Am Not Ashamed of Myself or My Symptoms

If people knew how I really felt, they'd think I was crazy. I must really be a loser if I can't even control my own feelings. I can't tell my husband; he couldn't handle it.

There are valid reasons why many of us keep our anxiety a secret, such as the very real stigma society still puts on mental-health challenges, or the common confusion between everyday worry and a clinical disorder. Whether you decide to tell others about your anxiety is less important than having the *emotional option* to tell them. If, out of our fear of rejection or sense of shame, we *have* to keep our anxiety a secret, we are making decisions based on what will protect us from the rejection or scrutiny of others, not what will help us heal.

Anxiety Is My Teacher; What Can I Learn?

Ever tried a Chinese finger trap? It's a tube of woven straw about 5 inches long and $\frac{1}{2}$ inch wide. You slide both index fingers into the straw tube, one finger at each end. If you then attempt to pull your fingers out, the tube catches and tightens. The only way to regain some freedom and space of movement is to push the fingers in first and then slide them out one at a time. One of us once gave them out as favors at her 5-year-old's birthday party and can still picture a frantic mother running down her driveway, fingers stuck in each end, shouting, "I can't get out!"

Anxiety can be like that. If, at the first uncomfortable physical sensation, we tighten up and try to fight our feelings, more often than not they will get worse. We are now adding anxiety about our symptoms to our initial fear. See how this can snowball?

On the other hand, rather than pushing against our anxiety, what if we add something to it? Perhaps we step back and add a scientific observation, almost like we're describing someone else's experiences: "Hmm, for me, anxiety seems to start with a flip-flop in my stomach, almost as if I'm riding a roller coaster." Perhaps we rate it: "That's about a three on the anxiety scale." "Wow, that was a big wave; I'd give it an eight." Or perhaps we adopt an attitude of curiosity: "I wonder what these feelings are trying to tell me."

By going with our anxiety, rather than fighting it, we are much more likely to flow through our discomfort rather than make it worse or get trapped by it. And whereas it can be a mean teacher, anxiety does sometimes have important lessons for us; it has helped us take better care of ourselves, set better limits with others, and get a clearer sense of what is important to us.

 **MYTH BUSTER**

"I should never feel anxious." Anxiety is a normal human emotion—we all feel it at times! In fact, trying to avoid anxiety can make you feel more anxious.

Symptoms Are an Opportunity to Practice—Not a Test

If you've decided to tackle your anxiety, we can assure you that you *are* going to take steps forward and get knocked back. Perhaps we find ourselves "relapsing" into worry after a parent dies or can't control our terror in anticipation of a visit to a new dentist. Maybe we promise ourselves we'll stay at the party until 8:30 and then flee at 7 or leave the grocery store during a panic attack even though we promised ourselves we'd ride it out.

Okay, so you didn't meet your initial goal. Let that experience be feedback to you as you take corrective action. What can you adjust? Maybe you need to get some help with your grieving or join a self-help group. Perhaps you need to visit the dentist's office before your appointment, to make it a more comfortable place. Maybe it would be easier to stay at the party if you planned some ice-breakers and conversation starters.

Talk to yourself about setbacks in the same way you would talk to a child who is having a tough time learning a new skill. You'd encourage her. You'd put temporary setbacks in perspective. You'd problem-solve with her when she faced glitches and bumps in the road. And you'd *never* call her a failure.

ON THE CUTTING EDGE

People who suffer from anxiety disorders may be more likely to experience relapses following attempts to quit drinking, suggesting that anxiety treatment may be a necessary component—and great benefit—to individuals who self-medicate with alcohol.

Anxiety Is Uncomfortable, but It's Not Dangerous

Anxiety is uncomfortable. It's unpleasant. It can feel overwhelming. As a result, when anxiety hits, our instincts tell us to *do* something. Move. Get out of there. Make it stop!

How ironic it is; going against the flow may ultimately result in smoother sailing. Allowing ourselves to get used to wading through moments of emotional discomfort can do wonders in building up our confidence to deal with the really tough times. Internal messages such as "I'm feeling anxious, and that's okay" can go a long way toward defusing our fear's power.

STRESS RELIEF

When we feel we've hit a roadblock in reaching a personal goal, seeing our journey from a third-person perspective—as if looking at one's past self in a movie—can help us appreciate the progress we've already made and give us the strength we need to keep going.

I Can't Stand It. I've Got to Get Out of Here. What If It Gets Worse?

Every time we allow these thoughts to stay in our heads, we create a picture of ourselves as vulnerable and weak.

In addition, uncertainty is especially distasteful for those of us who crave control. Trying to anticipate, avoid, or escape pain can put you in a tense state of vigilance, constantly monitoring your environment for signs of threat. To overcome anxiety, you need to be willing to lower your defenses and tolerate some uncertainty. By accepting the risk of a negative outcome, you are lessening your need for certainty, and your anxiety will reduce.

With these five attitudes as your base, take a look at some additional ways you can keep yourself steady on your journey.

Remaining Motivated

We've already mentioned several ways we can keep on the path as we work to control our anxiety. We've talked about defining and living according to our personal values, keeping track of what our anxiety costs us, and developing a healing perspective.

Let's take a look at some other top tips for remaining motivated:

Reward yourself. Praise yourself for every little step you take in the right direction. In addition, if you've taken a big leap, by staying in a tough situation or breathing through some scary symptoms, reward yourself with something you enjoy.

Build a skills base. If you're nervous in social situations, work on your communication skills. For chronic tension or worry, learn meditation or take a course in biofeedback. For performance anxiety, try visualization or self-hypnosis. These life skills can help anyone, anxious or not, lead a better life.

Don't go it alone. Find people you can share your struggles with, whether it's an online support group or a close circle of family and friends.

On the surface, making the decision to deal with anxiety seems like a no-brainer. Who doesn't want to feel better? In reality, though, taking steps toward emotional freedom requires some upfront commitment; we've got to be clear about our goals, develop helpful attitudes, and suffer through some emotional bumps and bruises. Just as labor pains and sleepless nights are part of parenting, we may have to go through some rough spots before we get where we want to be.

This chapter has examined the mixed feelings so many of us have when we start on the path to recovery from anxiety. On the one hand, we're sick and tired of anxiety taking up so much of our valuable time and energy; on the other hand, what if nothing we do makes any difference? *What if we feel worse?*

In the next chapter, we look at how we can build our emotional reservoir by strengthening our emotional intelligence. We explore the value of emotional self-awareness as well as basic strategies for managing our emotions. We tackle the whole issue of emotions—what they are, what they do, and how anxiety impacts them.

STRESS RELIEF

Need another motivator? Reducing anxiety can improve relationships, and recent research confirms that people involved in committed relationships are generally happier than others.

The Least You Need to Know

- The journey from anxiety to peace is never straightforward or discomfort-free, but it is worth it.
- Being clear about our personal values, and honest about anxiety's costs, can be powerful motivation to plow ahead.
- Developing healthy attitudes about the recovery process can buffer us from setbacks and bumps in the road.
- Anxiety often creates a paradox; if we fight it, it gets stronger. On the other hand, if we flow through it, it lessens.

PART

2

Fighting Your Way Through the Fright

Fear is perhaps the most primitive emotion we have. Because of its survival focus, it quickly takes over our thoughts and drives our behavior.

This part looks at how you can build up your emotional intelligence to better manage your everyday emotions and use difficult emotions, such as anger, to your benefit. From there, we talk about the role of anxiety in avoidance behavior and how you can give up self-defeating behaviors such as passivity and procrastination that ultimately make your anxiety worse.

Getting in Tune with Your Emotions

How are you? It's a common enough question, one we hear every day. But honestly, how do you *feel*? Feelings are, after all, a part of much of what we think about and do, so it's an important question.

Ideally, our emotions are our teachers, telling us what's important about our needs, our wants, and how the world around us is treating us. They can serve as a warning system when we need something. Even when they seem counterproductive—like the fear accompanying a panic attack or the chronic worry that underlies generalized anxiety—they can teach us things about ourselves.

But what if we've lost touch with them? What if we ignore them? And what happens when our emotions start shouting? Becoming in tune with how you feel and responding appropriately to your emotions takes a little skill and practice.

In this chapter, we discuss the role of our feelings in managing anxiety, how emotions affect us, and what it means to be emotionally intelligent.

In This Chapter

* The role of emotions in anxiety problems
* Discover the feelings underneath your worries
* Evaluate your emotional intelligence
* Better manage your emotions

Feelings

Artists often trumpet their feelings as being responsible for their art. William Wordsworth described poetry as the spontaneous overflow of powerful feelings. Picasso once said the artist is the receptacle for the emotions that come from the world around. For the rest of us, our feelings make us human, allow us to fall in love, tempt us to get even, and motivate us to climb the corporate ladder.

Feelings have often taken a backseat in the field of psychology. In fact, it was long believed that our thoughts were the major force behind our actions. But as a good car salesperson knows, our feelings have a much more persuasive influence on the choices we make. How many of us chose a mate based on a careful analysis of that person's strengths or weaknesses. It's more likely we fell in love *in spite of* our logic. Sometimes our thoughts come in to justify getting what our feelings want!

Emotions are produced by the brain in response to the balance between our needs and wants and what the outside world is offering us. Falling in love is a combination of internal needs for intimacy and closeness coupled (hopefully!) with the right timing and chemistry with another person. The correspondence of needs/wants with the outside world produces feelings.

Temperament

Although we all share the same basic feelings—love, sadness, happiness, guilt, and so on—we differ in the particular feelings we experience at any given time and how strongly we feel them. Some of us are more high strung, often prone to strong negative feelings (like anxiety), whereas others seem more emotionally cool. Some of us easily express our emotions, whereas others prefer a poker face.

Individual differences in emotional sensitivity and expressiveness are an interesting result of both nature and nurture. It probably comes as no surprise that we inherit much of our emotional tuning from our parents. Some of this inheritance shows up in the temperament we're born with.

For example, from birth, children differ in how sensitive they are to different stimuli in their environment, and how intense their response. Joni's oldest son has always been extremely aggravated by shirt tags, tight hugs, bright lights, and loud noises. On the other hand, one of her younger kids could probably wear a shirt made out of Brillo pads and enjoy a TV show while a marching band played in their family room.

Intensity of reaction refers to the energy level of a person's typical response. For example, a child who has a low threshold of responsiveness but a high intensity of reaction may respond to a bad-tasting medicine with a very loud "Yuck!" and lots of facial grimacing and spitting. On the other hand, another child with the same threshold of responsiveness but a low intensity of reaction may only wrinkle his nose in distaste. (We discuss temperament further in Chapter 10.)

Parenting and Response Styles

Whereas some characteristics are no doubt genetic, research is casting light on the patterns of emotional behavior we learn while growing up. It seems that not only do we get our emotional setting (high strung or laid back) from our parents, we also learn our patterns of dealing with our feelings from watching our parents:

> Honey, you don't really feel that way. How can you say you were mad that I missed your birthday party; don't you know how hard I work? Snap out of that bad mood, young man, and quit being so selfish.

Were you able to blow off steam in your house without upsetting anyone? How comfortable were your parents in expressing their emotions—both positive and negative? Children from homes in which family members are expected to express feelings, whether in shouting matches or calm conversation, are more likely as adults to do likewise, whereas children from homes where emotional expression is taboo are more likely to be emotionally reserved (or inhibited) as adults.

One fascinating study compared parents of anxiety-disordered children to parents of children with no mental health problems to see how these families coped with emotional challenges. Specifically, the researchers recorded parents' habits in dealing with or discussing their children's feelings to see whether there were any differences in parenting style. The results? Parents of children with anxiety disorders were less inclined to talk to their children about feelings. In some cases, parents of anxious children tended to discourage emotional discussions by ignoring the child's attempts to do so or by changing the subject.

Learning to understand and express emotions is an important developmental experience through which children develop emotional competence. Children look to their parents for guidance on how to deal with their own feelings. Some treatments for young anxiety sufferers now include a family component, in which parents are helped to better manage their own stress and anxiety and model more effective emotion management by openly discussing emotions with their children.

ON THE CUTTING EDGE

Human emotions are universal, but the culture in which we are raised gives us rules about when and where our feelings can be expressed. A child raised in a typical Italian family, for example, may be more emotionally expressive than one brought up in Finland.

Acknowledge Feelings

Let's pretend your 17-year-old sister calls you because she's upset. She's just broken up with her boyfriend, and she's got a ton of college applications due out in a few weeks. She still hasn't gotten her SAT scores back and is imagining the worst. You love your sister, but, to be honest, you're not in the best frame of mind yourself. You've been working 14 hours a day, and you've just heard rumors about a work layoff, which, because you've just bought a car you can barely afford, worries you even more than it normally would. Plus your sister has repeatedly broken up with her boyfriend, who, in your opinion, is a class-A jerk.

So you respond with something like, "Oh, Sis, quit being so dramatic. You've aced every test you've ever taken, you'll probably get accepted to Harvard, and as for your ex-boyfriend—the jerk—I'm glad you broke up and I'm sick of hearing about it."

Whether what you're saying is true or not, the odds are that this response is going to get you the opposite of what you want. You're trying to get your sister to be less emotional and more rational; by discounting her feelings, however, the odds are she's going to become *more* emotional (and possibly less rational).

Feelings, ours and anyone else's, are like that. Like them or not, we are best advised to accept them, listen to them, and understand why they are there. We don't—and shouldn't—give in to them or use them as an excuse to justify our behavior. But they are important signals and, if we ignore them, they're likely to get louder until we stop and listen.

STRESS RELIEF

One way of letting go of fear is to allow yourself to feel afraid—even briefly. In other words, instead of trying to think it through, just feel it through. By letting the feeling do its job, it can then stop alarming you, allowing your higher-reasoning powers to process the information and make a secure judgment.

Managing Emotions

No matter how much we try, there are some feelings we can't control. The primary emotions—fear, anger, happiness, sadness—are hardwired into every one of us; they're the feelings that kept our ancestors alive. And yet many of us think we should be able to avoid or control negative feelings, and that we've failed if we can't.

Did you know that by not listening to your feelings, you may be telling yourself that you are not important enough to listen to? Ignoring how you feel can shake your self-esteem. Pretty soon you may be carrying around lots of unexpressed and unaddressed feelings, which may lead to other problems.

 MYTH BUSTER

"Ignoring feelings makes them go away." Not necessarily. In fact, sometimes our feelings seem to shout louder to get our attention—by raising our heart rate, releasing stress chemicals, and slowing down rational thought, making it hard to concentrate—in other words, by inducing feelings of anxiety.

Vicious Cycles

Anyone who has had a panic attack can feel panicked at the thought of having another one. This fear of panic is a secondary feeling; it's based largely on the things we're telling ourselves about the first panic attack. Thinking *I couldn't stand to feel that bad again* can quickly turn discomfort into terror. Thinking *Dan's not home and I've got that bad feeling; maybe it's a sign that something terrible has happened* can turn concern into crippling anxiety.

These secondary feelings can cause substantial psychic problems. Often the original feelings aren't as severe and hard to manage as the secondary feelings make it seem. It takes practice to distinguish our original feelings from the thoughts and feelings we have about those original feelings. Yet this process frees us to focus on building the capacity to accept our primary feelings—which we can't directly control anyway—and eliminate the secondary feelings that we're feeding with our frightened thoughts (see Chapters 8 and 9).

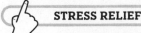

Music is a great mood modifier. Start off with a tune that closely matches your mood and gradually work your way to something more relaxing. Your brain will readily accept the mood-matched music, and by gradually introducing something more soothing, you'll transition into a calmer state.

Emotional Intelligence

Learning how to handle everyday emotions builds up our strength for handling an anxiety disorder. In addition, learning to handle everyday emotions might be the single best predictor of how successful we will be in life. You may have heard the term *emotional intelligence* bantered around at a company meeting or in a magazine article on relationships. Those who can effectively manage emotions—both their own and those of the people around them—are thought to have a high emotional intelligence quotient, or EQ.

Make a quick assessment of your emotional intelligence. For each item that follows, circle the answer that best describes you. Although informal, this can give you an overview of your strengths and weaknesses. The first half will help you evaluate your ability to manage your own feelings; the second half is geared toward your awareness of, and sensitivity to, the emotions of others.

1. I stay relaxed and composed under pressure.
    1 = Very true   4 = Mostly not true
    2 = Mostly true   5 = Not true at all
    3 = Sometimes true

2. I can identify negative feelings without becoming distressed.
    1 = Very true   4 = Mostly not true
    2 = Mostly true   5 = Not true at all
    3 = Sometimes true

3. I calm myself quickly when I get angry or upset.
    1 = Very true   4 = Mostly not true
    2 = Mostly true   5 = Not true at all
    3 = Sometimes true

4. I can pull myself together quickly after an unexpected setback.
   1 = Very true   4 = Mostly not true
   2 = Mostly true   5 = Not true at all
   3 = Sometimes true

5. I am aware of how my behavior impacts others.
   1 = Very true   4 = Mostly not true
   2 = Mostly true   5 = Not true at all
   3 = Sometimes true

6. When I'm in a bad mood, I know what or who is upsetting me.
   1 = Very true   4 = Mostly not true
   2 = Mostly true   5 = Not true at all
   3 = Sometimes true

7. Even when I do my best, I feel guilty about the things that did not get done.
   5 = Very true   2 = Mostly not true
   4 = Mostly true   1 = Not true at all
   3 = Sometimes true

8. When I am upset, I can pinpoint exactly what aspect of the problem bugs me.
   1 = Very true   4 = Mostly not true
   2 = Mostly true   5 = Not true at all
   3 = Sometimes true

9. I am able to get over guilt about little mistakes that I made in the past.
   1 = Very true   4 = Mostly not true
   2 = Mostly true   5 = Not true at all
   3 = Sometimes true

10. I am able to stop thinking about my problems when I want to.
    1 = Very true   4 = Mostly not true
    2 = Mostly true   5 = Not true at all
    3 = Sometimes true

11. I will do whatever I can to keep myself from crying.
    5 = Very true   2 = Mostly not true
    4 = Mostly true   1 = Not true at all
    3 = Sometimes true

12. People who know me tell me that I overreact to minor problems.
    5 = Very true   2 = Mostly not true
    4 = Mostly true   1 = Not true at all
    3 = Sometimes true

13. No matter how much I accomplish, I have a nagging feeling that I should be doing more.
    5 = Very true   2 = Mostly not true
    4 = Mostly true   1 = Not true at all
    3 = Sometimes true

Now add all the numbers under the 13 questions; your total score should fall somewhere between 13 and 65. To get your average score for managing your own feelings, add the total of your score and divide by 13. If your total falls between 2 and 3.5, you are fairly average in managing your feelings. Below 2 means you are above average. Higher than 3.5 means you may benefit from tools to help manage your emotions.

Now answer the following questions about your reactions to other people's feelings:

1. I am not satisfied with my work unless someone else praises it.
   5 = Very true   2 = Mostly not true
   4 = Mostly true   1 = Not true at all
   3 = Sometimes true

2. People who are emotional make me uncomfortable.
   5 = Very true   2 = Mostly not true
   4 = Mostly true   1 = Not true at all
   3 = Sometimes true

3. I need someone's push in order to get going.
   5 = Very true   2 = Mostly not true
   4 = Mostly true   1 = Not true at all
   3 = Sometimes true

4. It seems to me that people's reactions come out of the blue.
   5 = Very true   2 = Mostly not true
   4 = Mostly true   1 = Not true at all
   3 = Sometimes true

5. I panic when I have to face someone who is angry.
   5 = Very true   2 = Mostly not true
   4 = Mostly true   1 = Not true at all
   3 = Sometimes true

6. Some people make me feel bad about myself no matter what I do.
   5 = Very true   2 = Mostly not true
   4 = Mostly true   1 = Not true at all
   3 = Sometimes true

7. I pay attention and listen to others without jumping to conclusions.
   1 = Very true   4 = Mostly not true
   2 = Mostly true   5 = Not true at all
   3 = Sometimes true

8. I can receive feedback or criticism without becoming defensive.
   1 = Very true   4 = Mostly not true
   2 = Mostly true   5 = Not true at all
   3 = Sometimes true

9. I am sensitive to other people's emotions and moods.
   1 = Very true   4 = Mostly not true
   2 = Mostly true   5 = Not true at all
   3 = Sometimes true

Use the same scoring suggestions as the first half of the quiz.

So how comfortable are you with the emotions of the people around you? How does your own self-awareness compare with your sensitivity to others? Are you better at listening and understanding other people's feelings than your own, or are you able to interpret and cope with what's going on inside you but find other people's feelings confusing or overwhelming? Ideally, of course, you will be able to manage your responses to your own and others' emotions.

Pitfalls on the Way to Better Emotion Management

Developing emotional intelligence can be tricky. As with any skill, there are old habits to break and pitfalls to avoid. There are also a few myths about what it means to be more emotionally intelligent; for example, some people think developing a higher EQ means "I should always be able to control my moods" or "I should be more emotional" (neither is correct). As you become more aware of, and respectful toward, your feelings, the following are some things to be wary of.

STRESS RELIEF

Increase self-awareness by checking your emotional status several times a day. Rate yourself on a 1 to 10 scale of negative emotions (i.e., anxiety, sadness, and anger); jot down your score, what was happening at the time, and how you responded to your feelings. Taking notice of feelings in this way can diffuse stress because you are listening to your inner self rather than trying to ignore it.

Feelings Are Faster—and Stronger—Than Thoughts

Our thoughts are always playing catch-up to our feelings. Consider this: the limbic system, the center of our emotions, operates at speeds of a thousandth of a second. In contrast, the rational mind, the neocortex, operates at about one tenth of a second. The helpful part of our emotional edge is that our feelings can help us react quickly in life-and-death situations, before we've even had time to think about the danger. The downside is that we can become sidetracked by our emotions.

Strategy: Pay attention. Feelings may not be intense immediately; they often build up gradually, so we have time to become aware of them as they build. When feelings first arise, ask yourself, "What is this feeling? What is it telling me?" Processing your feelings in this way can prevent them from snowballing out of control.

ON THE CUTTING EDGE

Recent research suggests that self-control is like a muscle, and when we use it, we may need some time to regain strength. Following a period of self-control when facing tempting food, alcohol, or tobacco, people were found to have less physical stamina, problem-solving ability, and impulse control. But take heart: the more we use our self-control, the stronger it becomes.

Feelings and Thoughts Can Get Tangled Up

Strong negative emotions can cloud our thinking; when we feel angry, we think angry thoughts (and may become even angrier). Perhaps we conjure up angry memories from the past. We may even behave angrily—by shouting, slamming a door, or giving the target of our anger the cold shoulder. Conversely, if we're emotionally inhibited, we may find ourselves thinking critical or judgmental thoughts or acting vengefully, without noticing that we are angry.

Strategy: Don't make any important decisions (or pronouncements) when you have strong feelings. Instead, buy yourself some time and get some perspective on your feelings. Talk about the situation with a friend or write down your thoughts, feelings, and options in a diary or journal, as in the following table. (Feel free to make as many copies as you'd like.)

The Decision (or Pronouncement):		
My thoughts:	My feelings:	My options:

In other words, listen to your feelings, but only respond to them *once you understand them*. Only then can you make the best judgment about what to do.

Self-Medication for Bad Feelings Can Backfire

Lots of pleasurable (and sometimes anxiety-reducing) activities can temporarily tamp down negative feelings: drugs, alcohol, food, shopping, sex, gambling, etc. The pleasurable effects, however, are predictably short lived, not only because we haven't attended to the original feelings, but now we might have added other feelings (guilt, shame, embarrassment) on top of them. We may have even made our real circumstances worse. A short-term "fix" can have a long-term price tag.

Strategy: If you find yourself reaching for an outside solution to uncomfortable feelings, build in delays. Put buying that dress on hold, or go for a walk before you eat that second piece of cake. Unless they're ingrained habits, most impulses will subside within 15 minutes if you remove yourself from the temptation and give yourself a breather.

 ON THE CUTTING EDGE

When people are anxious or stressed, they're less capable of giving themselves the mental boost they need. If you can't see the bright side on your own, find someone who can! Talk to an upbeat friend or go to a place associated with fun, such as a park or a party.

Judging Your Feelings Doesn't Help

Although it's worthwhile to evaluate your emotions and decide how to respond to them, you shouldn't just dismiss negative feelings as being "bad." Your feelings may have something to tell you that you can address.

Worry

Worry might be considered transforming your fears into thoughts. Instead of *feeling* anxiety, people channel it into anxious *thinking.* In fact, some experts believe worry is another way to avoid anxious feelings. More often than not, we wind up with the worst of both worlds; there's still that undercurrent of tension, and our thoughts become less productive and rational.

Because our thoughts play such a critical role in anxiety, we spend two whole chapters (Chapters 7 and 8) learning how to recognize and remedy self-defeating or fear-inducing thoughts. For now, start to explore some of the possible fears underneath those worries, and investigate in what situations you have felt similarly. For instance, any parent is terrified at the thought of losing a child; however, a parent who lost his mom to cancer at age 14 may have a much harder time stopping the "what ifs" when his child gets the flu.

MYTH BUSTER

"All uncomfortable emotions are bad." Not true! Emotional discomfort can signal real danger or threats. Research found that carefree individuals were more likely to ignore signs of cancer than those who showed moderate levels of anxiety.

Fine-Tuning Your Alarm System

We human beings are "wired" with impressive alarm systems, including anxiety. Ideally, we notice our anxiety, investigate why we are anxious, and decide whether we need to take action or wait and see.

Sounds pretty simple, but it's not. Some of us have an extremely sensitive alarm system. Some of us have learned, either through life experiences or early socialization, to either ignore our feelings or to avoid or fight whatever triggers them. And, of course, if we have an anxiety disorder, our alarm system may not be functioning correctly. Anxiety can develop in response to an overly active alarm system, and anxiety can send our everyday emotions into overdrive.

This is particularly true when it comes to anger. The Greek philosopher Aristotle rightly said, "Anyone can become angry—that is easy. But to be angry with the right person, to the right degree, at the right time, for the right purpose, and in the right way: this is not easy." In the next chapter we explore the relationship between anger and anxiety, how you can use anger as a motivator, and how you can prevent it from sabotaging yourself and your relationships.

The Least You Need to Know

- Negative emotions may be signals that your goals, needs, and wants are not being met.
- Babies come into the world wired with different levels of emotional sensitivity and reactivity. These traits can be heightened or suppressed by their environment.
- Emotional intelligence is the ability to effectively use your feelings and to be aware of, and positively influence, the feelings of others.
- Primary emotions are those that our ancestors relied on for survival—such as fear and anger. Secondary emotions, on the other hand, are a result of our interpretation of the primary emotion-triggering event.
- Anyone can boost his or her emotion-management skills. It starts with self-awareness or paying attention to early emotional signals.

Understanding and Managing Anger

We humans have many ways of being angry. We can be afraid of our anger, repressing it and trying to appear as if we feel differently than we do. We can deny our anger—to others and ourselves—and let it come out indirectly, by "forgetting" to do things others ask of us or by making snide remarks. We can explode like lightning and thunder, releasing all of our anger in a sudden, uncontrolled outburst. We can use our anger to feel in control by threatening or bullying others. We can also use our anger as a mask to hide the fear, shame, and uncertainty we really feel.

In the preceding chapter, we talked about the purpose and value of our emotions. In this chapter, we focus on one particular—and often problematic—emotion: anger.

Why choose this particular emotion for a whole chapter? Well, anger is a natural part of the human condition, but few of us are effective in using it. Many of us spend too much time either trying to squash it or trying to clean up the aftermath after letting it loose.

In This Chapter

- Discover the link between anxiety and anger
- Explore the effects of anger on you and your relationships
- Find out how to manage anger and aggression
- Learn some techniques for dispersing anger and frustration

Anxiety makes it harder to cope with anger. On one hand, feeling afraid and on edge can make us irritable and more likely to lash out when we get annoyed. On the other hand, some of us may be so frightened by our anger that we panic at the thought of getting mad at the people we care about. Let's take a look at the many faces of anger and how we can use these feelings to make our relationships—and our lives—better.

 MYTH BUSTER

"Anger isn't a problem for me—I don't shout or get aggressive with people." Keep in mind that anger can appear in open confrontation, but it can also appear in quiet ways such as resentment, lack of communication, or sarcasm.

Anxiety and Anger

Bill is worried about his job. There have been layoffs recently, and there are rumors about more. He can't sleep; he wakes up at all hours thinking through every comment his boss made the preceding day to see whether there's some sign that he's about to get laid off. He's becoming increasingly competitive with his colleagues and is snappy and defensive when anyone makes even constructive suggestions to him. As a result, his co-workers avoid him whenever possible, and his boss is giving him fewer assignments because she thinks Bill is under too much pressure. When his boss hands yet another plum assignment to a colleague, Bill loses his temper, calls his boss unpleasant names, and storms out of the office, slamming the door.

Michelle, on the other hand, has a different scenario. After the birth of her second child, she suffered a serious bout of post-partum panic disorder. With her high level of anxiety, she found it harder and harder to be patient with her 2-year-old, who was naturally responding to a new sibling with temper tantrums and increased clinginess. Even her newborn's cries set her teeth on edge. The shame she felt over her anxiety made it that much more difficult to accept that she was *angry* that life was so tough right now. Instead of using these feelings as a signal to get the help and support she needed, she felt increasingly depressed.

Am I more or less irritable when I feel anxious? Your answer to this question is a valuable clue in understanding the link between your anxiety and your anger. For most of us, anxiety leaves us feeling sensitive and irritable—less severe forms of anger. Recent research, for example, found that individuals with generalized anxiety disorder (GAD) are twice as likely to experience anger-related relationship problems in comparison to non-sufferers, with 7 out of 10 sufferers confirming that their anxiety created relationship problems, from having arguments to problems with sexual intimacy.

Typically a person who suffers from anxiety can feel anger because they …

- Feel a lack or loss of control.

- Think it is not appropriate to discuss negative feelings with someone, allowing these feelings to build up.

- Feel frustrated about being anxious.

- Worry about rejection.

A feeling of losing control is usually at the heart of anger. Some people may, for example, be angry about anxiety itself, feeling that they are powerless to change their condition.

What Is Anger?

Anger starts with frustration, the feeling we experience when we don't get what we want or feel we deserve. Our goal, whether it's to be happy, to feel good about ourselves, or to get to work on time, has been threatened or blocked. Then we start looking for someone or something to blame.

If our frustration is strong, and the goal important enough, we feel anger. We experience an urge to take back some control. Sometimes our anger pays off; most wrongs that have been righted in the world have started with a deep sense of outrage that spawned an unwillingness to tolerate unacceptable or abusive circumstances. To make this clear, think of a time when your anger helped you protect yourself or get to a better place, perhaps by leaving a bullying boss or finally letting go of an energy-draining friend.

 MYTH BUSTER

"The best way to get rid of anger is to let it out." This is not necessarily true. Research has shown that expressing hostility gets easier with practice, a fact that calls into question the wisdom of getting rid of aggression by beating up a punching bag. It's better to find out what triggers your anger and then develop strategies to keep those triggers from toppling you over the edge.

Anger can also be seductive. We may call it getting our own back, settling the score, or an eye for an eye. Being aggressive toward someone who has hurt our feelings or treated us unfairly makes us feel better. But it also makes us more likely to hurt that person or others even more later on. It can give a person who feels out of control a sense of being back in the driver's seat. When we're angry, our pulse rises, our breath quickens, more blood flows to our muscles, our pain-relieving chemicals are released, and our pupils dilate. Sound familiar? The list of physical responses is very similar to what happens when a person is passionately making love!

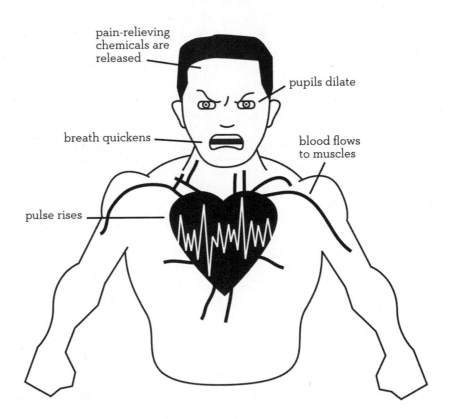

No matter how seductive, though, letting loose or feeding anger can make matters worse. Anger can easily lead to aggression and the intentional act of harming someone. Experience has shown that it is very difficult to control our responses when we are aroused by anger. It can be a very dangerous state of mind.

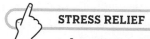

Recognizing Anger

For many of us, anger is a chameleon (a lizard that can change colors to blend into its background). Your experience and expression of it will depend on your beliefs, your views of yourself, and the source of your frustration. It may be easier to control anger at your boss than to suppress your frustration with a sibling.

So if anger can take on different forms, how can we detect it in ourselves? What clues do we look for? The following table outlines some signs and symptoms that may reflect anger.

Physical Cues	Behavioral Cues	Mental Cues
Clenching your jaws or grinding your teeth	Raising your voice, screaming, or crying	Exaggerating: "You always," "I never," "You idiot!"
Shoulder and neck tightness	Losing your sense of humor or using sarcasm	Blaming: "It's not me—it's this system," "If only you were more reasonable"
Stomachaches or headaches	Hurting: malicious gossip, stealing, trouble-making, not forgiving, being judgmental	Characterizing: "Men are lazy," "Women are stupid," "Doctors are idiots"
Sweating, shaking, or trembling	Rebelling: antisocial behavior; defiance; refusal to talk or cooperate; being disruptive or distrustful; sulking	Being suspicious: "If you really loved me you would …," "You cheated!"
Increased heart rate	Withdrawal: quiet remoteness, silence, lack of communication	Fantasies of revenge or getting even

If it's too threatening to be open with our anger, we can always express it in other ways. This indirect expression is often called *passive-aggression,* a pattern of sabotaging the object of our anger by doing the opposite of what he or she wants. We may drag our heels after making a verbal commitment, make frequent critical remarks, and verbally agree ("sure, whatever") but inwardly remain defiant—with excuses like being "sick" for being late. Although not as outwardly hostile, this way of expressing anger is just as real and can be just as damaging.

At the extreme, there are perpetual "victims," those who have developed the habit of accepting their powerlessness and resigning themselves to their emotional discomfort and pain. The flip side is the need to avoid responsibility and blame; after all, through no fault of their own, they have been mistreated. Those stuck in the victim role are hard to cheer up or help; they won't cooperate. They are more likely to sulk or try to cause someone to feel guilty instead of openly expressing anger—and they reject helpful suggestions offered to them.

ON THE CUTTING EDGE

Good friends aren't good at everything! Studies at the University of Virginia have shown that hidden anger is more easily noticed by mere acquaintances than close friends, perhaps because friends don't want a relationship to be threatened by anger, or because friends don't want to be viewed in an unflattering light by a pal.

Misdirected Anger

When we feel angry, we may avoid expressing anger toward one person and instead express it toward someone "safer." For example, a person may have a bad day at the office and come home and argue with their spouse or partner. People have long believed that repressed anger, hidden in the mind, will leak out—displaced—causing rifts with innocent scapegoats. Unfortunately, the scapegoat is often a close confidant, the person with whom we feel safest. So how do we avoid hurting the ones we love?

ANXIETY ATTACK

Anger often masks our deepest fears. In an anger-inducing situation, ask yourself what deep fears it might be stirring in you.

The Personal Cost of Anger

What about the personal cost of anger? Anger can disrupt our mental health; in fact, some believe that chronic depression can be caused by anger turned inward.

From a physical standpoint, chronic or frequent anger puts pressure on the cardiovascular system, leading some experts to claim that chronic anger kills. And the effects are even more serious for people who already have heart or blood pressure problems. In addition, research has shown that when we are angry, our blood prepares to clot in anticipation of a wound. This can prove fatal to people who have narrowed or blocked arteries.

It seems that our anger response was designed for emergencies, not for our everyday routines. Our bodies are simply not designed to be constantly angry.

STRESS RELIEF

It's not easy to see things clearly when we are emotionally charged. If it's not possible to walk away and take a "time out," take yourself away in your mind, using visual imagery to approach the problem with a wider perspective.

Remaining Balanced

Does anger ever help us? Of course! The feelings of control and righteousness that come from anger can motivate us to challenge and change difficult interpersonal and social injustices. If handled correctly, our anger can motivate others to help us. Anger can help us overcome feelings of vulnerability and release tensions and frustrations. It can provide the energy and resolve necessary to defend ourselves when we've been wronged or threatened.

On the other hand, acting immediately on all of our angry feelings, without choosing from a range of thoughtful responses, will leave us with few friends and possible heart problems. The goal is to allow anger to do its job *and* let the rational mind do its job. A negotiation between anger and rational thinking will give you the best balance available.

Anger is an emotion designed to alert us to something that *may* require attention. Don't make the mistake of assuming your anger *must* be acted upon. Instead, as with anxiety, we should acknowledge anger and consider why it's there.

STRESS RELIEF

Giving people a "heads-up" when challenging emotions are wreaking havoc on your self-control can help minimize relationship damage. For instance, an "I'm sorry, I'm having a really bad day today, please excuse me if I seem rude" can prevent others from taking your remarks personally.

Another way of looking at anger is to liken it to a crying baby. We should acknowledge the noise and think carefully about the best way of proceeding, gently holding the baby and calming it down, while we check to see what the real problem is and tell ourselves, "It could be nothing, or there may be a real problem. Let's see."

ON THE CUTTING EDGE

Anger—in moderation—does have an upside. In studies, people who responded to challenging circumstances with fear suffered more stress as time passed than those who reacted with anger.

What to Do with Anger

Effective anger management involves responding appropriately when we become angry, as well as structuring our everyday lives to decrease the likelihood that we will become angry. It may be helpful to manage your anger by …

- Dealing with irritating daily hassles so that they don't build up over time.
- Avoiding aggressive movies or TV shows, hostile or resentful company, or negative self-talk.
- Developing calming habits like meditation or yoga.
- Calmly disrupting destructive thoughts and fantasies.
- Keeping a daily gratitude journal (for example, writing down five things you're grateful for each day).
- Rewarding yourself for staying in control of your anger, and keeping track of any negative consequences for outbursts.
- Distracting your thoughts with humor.
- Learning to monitor your thoughts to keep them from feeding your anger.

But what about the times when anger rises suddenly? What about unfair situations that need to be addressed, limits that need to be set, or verbal abuse that needs to be stopped? In the next chapter, we look at the art of assertiveness and how we can express our anger in a way that will maximize the odds that we will get what we want.

For now, the trick is to give yourself enough time to keep your emotions from leading you to harm. The first step, of course, is becoming aware of your anger; the sooner you notice it, the less likely it will get out of control. And the best way to do this is to start connecting what happens, your thoughts about it, how you feel about it, and what you do.

ANXIETY ATTACK

Imagine that anger opens an options menu, like on a computer screen. We could select the best option, rather than automatically using the defaults that our feelings suggest.

Anger Diary

An anger diary or journal is one of the best ways to keep track of your relationship with anger. To get the most out of such a diary, make daily entries that document the following information for each anger-provoking event:

- What happened?

- What provoked the situation?

- What thoughts were going through my mind?

- On a scale of 0–10, how angry did I feel?

- What did I do?

- What were the consequences of my behavior for me and others?

- Was I already keyed up or stressed about something else? If so, what?

- What physical symptoms did I have?

- What was my first impulse (what did I want to do immediately)?

- How did I feel immediately after the episode?

- How do I feel about it now?

After recording this information for 14 days, look back through it and see what recurring themes or "triggers" make you mad. For many of us, the themes will look something like this:

- Other people doing or not doing what I expect them to do (spouse not listening, customer taking up too much of my time)

- Situational events that get in my way (repeated interruptions at work, traffic jams, car problems)

- People taking advantage of me (boss requesting too much from me, family member asking to borrow money again)

- Being angry and disappointed in myself (acting in ways that I'm ashamed of, failing to get an assignment or promotion)

Also look for anger-triggering thoughts that recur. We can recognize these particular thoughts because they will generally involve one or more of the following themes:

- The perception that I have been victimized or harmed.

- The belief that the person who provoked me meant me harm.

- The belief that another person was wrong and that he or she should have behaved differently.

- The belief that life is "not fair"—for example, another person is getting more than his or her share in life while I am getting less than I deserve.

Use your anger diary to identify instances when you felt harm was done to you, why you thought the act was done deliberately, and why you thought that it was wrong.

Tracking your thoughts will also help you begin to see the underlying assumptions that guide those automatic thoughts. We discuss assumptions—and how to deal with them—in Chapter 9. For now, here are some examples of underlying assumptions that lead to angry thoughts and negative feelings:

- People don't care about me.

- People demand/expect too much of me.

- People try to take advantage of me.

- People think only of themselves.

- People don't treat me the way I should be treated.

- People don't give me the help I need.

- People try to control or manipulate me.

And here are some situations in which these assumptions are likely to occur:

- When stating a difference of opinion
- While receiving and expressing negative feelings
- While dealing with someone who is being uncooperative
- While talking about something that irritates or annoys you
- While disclosing sensitive information
- When saying "no" or standing up for yourself
- While responding to undeserved criticism
- When asking for cooperation

Most people find a few thoughts that frequently trigger their anger. Look for situations that trigger your anger, and see whether you can identify the particular set of thoughts that really send you over the edge.

The purpose of your diary is to help you identify patterns of behavior and specific recurring situations that really "push your buttons." The more accurately you can observe your feelings and behaviors and the more detailed your anger diary, the more likely you will be able to identify anger triggers and how you react to them. Of course, the bigger goal is to use this insight so that you can plan more productive strategies for responding to these feelings.

Pause Before Acting

As you've discovered, anger-triggering thoughts occur automatically and almost instantaneously. It takes some conscious work to identify these thoughts and to substitute something more accurate or useful.

For example, imagine you ask your spouse how his day went and he snaps at you. It's hard to step back and take notice of your physical reaction when your first impulse is to snap back. However, taking a deep breath and noticing your stress symptoms gives you some perspective on the situation; it allows you to look at the situation more objectively, instead of going with your first impulse to attack. You may consider all the possible explanations for his outburst: perhaps he had a bad day; maybe he's still upset after the argument you had this morning; and so on. It doesn't mean you excuse his behavior or justify his actions; considering all the possibilities just gives you the freedom to seek more information—and take care of yourself in the process—before reacting.

In this chapter, we have examined the emotion of anger: what it is, how it affects us, and what we can do about it. For better or worse, anger is a powerful motivator; at its best it can help eliminate a sense of vulnerability and motivate us to take much-needed action. In the next chapter, we take a look at two "actions" that are often paired—procrastination and assertiveness—and how we can become active to make our lives better.

The Least You Need to Know

- Anger is a powerful motivator that you can use to your benefit or to your detriment.
- Anxiety can make it harder to control your anger, and being afraid of your anger can make you anxious.
- How you experience—and express—your anger is influenced by your inborn temperament and by what you've learned.
- Effective anger management requires you to investigate your triggers and how you respond to them.
- Daily monitoring of your frustration level can be a powerful tool in anger management.

Assertiveness

Some of us anxious folks are so ultraresponsible that you wouldn't think we'd have any trouble getting things done. Often, though, we're too good at getting *other people's* things done. I'm not about to suggest that you ditch everyone in your life and start over. But I am suggesting that you learn to act assertively when faced with other people's agendas so that you can move forward with your own life.

In this chapter, we take a look at conflict avoidance and procrastination and the role they can play in aggravating anxiety. We also focus on how you can be more proactive and assertive, reducing the risk that last-minute emergencies (either self- or other-created) will disrupt your peace and sabotage your priorities.

In This Chapter

- Find how fear of conflict feeds procrastination
- Discover the link between procrastination and anxiety
- Learn how to stand up for yourself
- See how shrinking your to-do list can shrink your stress

Doing Good—and Doing Yourself In

How often have you found yourself in one of these situations?

- You've just agreed to baby-sit your niece's children—again—even though you have a stressful work project due this Friday.

- Your neighbor drops in uninvited several times a week and spends hours telling you her personal problems. As a result, you're behind on your writing deadline.

- Your husband is going through a rough patch at work and constantly takes his frustrations out on you by being rude, picking fights, or silently fuming. Even though you know it has to be done, you find yourself "dragging your feet" when he asks you to finish paying the bills.

What themes emerge when you look at these scenarios? Procrastination? Lack of assertiveness? Resentment? By not saying "no" to your niece, your work project is now delayed. If you were able to set limits with your neighbor, you'd send her on her way—maybe with a recommendation of a good therapist—and get your writing done. If you were able to confront your husband effectively about his mistreatment, you might be more motivated to get those bills paid.

Conflict Avoidance and Anxiety

All three scenarios show how people can avoid conflict with others at the expense of getting their own needs met. However, the more we do that, the more anxious (and angry) we are likely to feel. The more anxious we feel, the more likely we are to put off challenging or stressful things, and the more chaos we invite into our lives to justify putting things off.

Of course, things do happen that are beyond your control. You can learn, however, to be discriminating about what is and is not your responsibility. Passivity and procrastination do not cause anxiety disorders. In fact, you can think of them as misguided attempts to manage your anxiety by avoiding unpleasant confrontations or tasks. However, in the long run, procrastination—whether in setting limits because you don't want to deal with conflict or in tackling a must-do—adds to your stress level. If procrastination or conflict avoidance becomes a habit, you can aggravate any anxiety you already have.

Crossing off every item on your to-do list won't cure an anxiety disorder—but it will sure lighten your stress load. And sometimes, remedying bad habits that can lead to worry and stress can ultimately help you manage your anxiety.

Saying "No"

If you've ever "put up" with a situation until you "blew up," you know what it's like to change quickly from passive to aggressive. Many of us who declare our limits by losing our cool learn the wrong lesson. Either we feel so guilty about losing it that we try even harder not to say anything the next time, or we feel so much better that we give ourselves permission to do it again.

It is possible, though, to say "no" before you reach the breaking point. In fact, saying "no" with calm and confidence is a sign of healthy assertiveness. It's not an insult or a rejection. It's just a piece of information.

"Is it raining outside?" "No."

"Will you baby-sit for me today?" "No."

Can you imagine being able to say "no" without tagging on a litany of excuses? It's hard. And yet, in the English language, the word *no* makes up a complete sentence. So why does "no" seem mean, selfish, or incomplete, when it's really the right answer?

One reason is simply that many of us were taught *not* to say "no." When a teacher or parent asked you to do something, "no" wasn't really an option. How would your third-grade teacher have responded if you'd politely declined her request for you to write an answer on the chalkboard? The normal socialization process encouraged us to be "nice" and accept birthday party invitations from kids we didn't like.

In other words, we learned that it's not okay to say "no" just because we don't want to do something. As an adult, all this early learning can make it difficult to tell the difference between "have-to's" and "want-to's." It can also lead us to the main reason that we have trouble with saying "no": fear.

There are the "little" fears, of course. There are fears of being judged selfish, lazy, or incompetent. There's the fear of hurting someone's feelings. There's the fear that the other person won't be able to cope if we say "no."

But all of these fears and more can be mini-versions of a larger fear of abandonment. "If I say no to my friend's request, she won't like me anymore." "If I tell my husband I need more help with the kids, he'll be mad at me." "If I talk to my boss about the work overload I'm experiencing and ask him to prioritize, he'll think I can't handle the pressure."

More often than not, there is no real substance to this fear. Your friend may prefer that you say "yes," but it probably isn't going to jeopardize your relationship. People may sometimes try to control you with their disapproval; if you can learn to see this for what it is, however, it loses its power. And consider the likely consequences of *not* talking to your boss about too much work: missed deadlines, sloppy work, and focusing on the wrong assignment.

MYTH BUSTER

"Being assertive is being selfish." Wrong! Being assertive is being honest. Assertiveness is about acknowledging *all* opinions as important. It conveys the message "I matter, and you do, too."

An Assertive Attitude

The ability to say "no" gracefully is a skill that can be easily learned, but true assertiveness comes as much before we open our mouths as when we do. It's first and foremost an attitude, a stance toward oneself and the outside world that says "I matter, and you do, too."

Dealing with a Pet Peeve

For example, let's pretend that one of your pet peeves is being late. You believe it's disrespect-ful to be late because it communicates to the other person that you don't value his or her time. In your mind, timeliness is linked to trust; you want to be able to count on it when a person says, "I'll meet you there at 7." Occasional glitches aside, if someone is frequently late, you think it suggests a lack of discipline or caring.

Here's the problem: you've just fallen head over heels for Mr. Wonderful-but-Laid-Back. Because you're so crazy about him, you try your best to overlook the fact that he's half an hour late for every date you make. He always calls if he promised to, but it might not be *when* he said he would. You're starting to realize that this quirk or habit of his is becoming a *big deal* to you.

An assertive attitude starts from the perspective that you both have legitimate viewpoints, that your new beau might not have the same beliefs about time, and you have the right to express your feelings and ask for what you want.

What an Assertive Attitude Includes

An assertive attitude would include the following:

- Confidence that you can handle conflict. ("Resolving this issue will prevent me from feeling resentful.")

- A positive, optimistic outlook. ("I think we can figure out a way to improve this situation.")

- Clarity about what you need or want. ("It's important to me to be on time.")

- Calm communication without attacking the other person or giving in. ("I hear you telling me to 'lighten up.' I realize being on time may not be as important to you.")

- Negotiation, if it turns out the two of you want different things. ("I can see how you might be running a few minutes late. I'll tell you what; if you're not here by 6:45, I'll meet you at the movie theater.")

- Sticking to clear boundaries. ("If you're not ready to leave by 7:30, I'll go ahead and see you when you get there.")

In all of these examples, nonverbal communication is at least as important as what you say. Tone of voice and body language make a difference in how your words are received. An open, relaxed stance and a calm, low voice convey confidence and respect.

 ANXIETY ATTACK

Some research suggests that women, in particular, are likely to feel anxious when they have to say "no" because it threatens their need to stay connected by pleasing others. However, saying "yes" when we want to say "no" is dishonest and ultimately disconnects us from other people and ourselves.

The Many Benefits of Assertiveness

When we don't trust ourselves to directly ask for what we want, it's tempting to do it in sneakier ways. Giving our mom the "silent treatment." Sulking when our spouse forgets our anniversary. Instead of talking to our boss about our excessive workload, we let it pile up on our desk and hope she'll notice that we have too much to do. These are all ways of trying to communicate indirectly and regain a sense of control. The problem is that our communication can be easily misinterpreted or overlooked—or, worse, be used as justification for someone to continue treating us unfairly.

Assertiveness, by contrast, is not about controlling people or situations. Truly assertive people give others the same rights they give themselves. They are willing to communicate what they want and leave other people free to say yes or no. If the needs of other people don't mesh with their own, assertive people don't panic or fume. They are willing to negotiate toward a solution that best meets everybody's needs. This creates a relationship and environment that invites creative solutions and allow everyone to get their needs met.

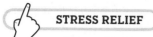 **STRESS RELIEF**

Research suggests that, in business, 20 percent of success depends on technical skill, and 80 percent depends on an adaptive, positive personality.

Acquiring Assertiveness Skills

When we realize that assertiveness is as good for the people we care about as it is for ourselves, we can choose to let go of the false beliefs and fears holding us back and adopt an assertive approach to life. When we make that commitment, it's time to take an honest look at where our relationships are right now and what we can expect as we become more assertive.

Taking Responsibility

Your first step—painful as it may be—is taking responsibility for the way other people are treating you. If your life is full of people who impose on you, it's because *you've been giving them the results they want.* (Ouch!) And they may not like it when you decide to change the rules of the game.

In fact, the rewards for saying "no" and sticking to it are often delayed. That is, people who've gotten what they want because of your lack of assertiveness aren't likely to jump for joy when you decide to speak up. It's pretty common for people to initially react with anger and disbelief—and do *more* of whatever has worked in the past. For example, a spouse who has used guilt to get you to back down is likely to use more guilt when you start to set limits. That's a normal reaction from anyone who is facing a new set of rules; you don't have to judge this, but you certainly don't want to give in to it.

However, over time you'll reap many rewards for asking for what you want and setting limits about what you don't. People will respect you more. Those who truly care about you will adjust. If someone leaves, so be it; they may not have cared about you, just what they were getting from you.

STRESS RELIEF

Consider posting a list of your strengths in a place you can see easily. Organize them into three categories: *I have* (strong relationships, structure at home, role models); *I am* (a hopeful person, a caring person, proud of myself); and *I can* (ask for help when I need it, solve problems). These words can constantly remind you that you have what it takes.

Practicing How to Say No

In addition to anticipating some resistance, you can also practice how to say "no" with grace and confidence. Here are some of my favorite guidelines.

Say, "No." Say, "I'm sorry, I can't." Say, "No, thank you." But however you say it, don't elaborate. Get comfortable with the word *no* through practice, and use it as a complete sentence whenever you can. Don't volunteer a reason, especially when you're dealing with people who chronically impose upon you. To these folks, offering a reason is like raising a target for them to shoot down.

If it's too uncomfortable not to give a reason, just give one deal-killer rather than a bunch of little ones that can reduce your resolve. "I have other plans" and "I've decided not to take any more projects until June" are examples. "I don't want to" is another one; no one can logically argue that one away.

When dealing with an especially persistent person with whom you don't have an ongoing relationship (for example, a telemarketer who keeps calling or an overly enthusiastic salesperson), adopt the broken-record technique. In a calm and pleasant tone, keep repeating what you have already said. It won't take long for them to realize they've hit a dead end.

Let them have their feelings. People are allowed to be disappointed and frustrated when you tell them "no." You are not responsible for making them feel better; don't even try.

When You Have a Request

What if *you're* the one asking for something? The first step is to prepare yourself mentally. Remember your assertive stance: "I matter, and you do, too." You have every right to ask for what you want, and others have every right to answer however they please.

Before you speak up, be very clear in your own mind about the difference between how you feel and what you want. For instance, I might feel overwhelmed by all the things I have to do today. However, if I just talk about my feelings, I may get sympathy but no offer of assistance. On the other hand, if I'm specific about what kind of relief I need, I might get some real help. Think about how differently you might respond to your spouse's venting ("I'm so stressed about all the kids' Valentine's parties") versus your spouse's request ("Will you go to one of the kids' parties tomorrow? I've got a proposal that needs to be out by the end of business Wednesday.")

If the attitude is right but you still aren't sure about the skill part, practice with a friend or in front of a mirror. You can use the mirror to practice relaxed, confident body language. And your friend can help you create a realistic conversation. In this conversation …

- State your problem and what you need from the other person. ("I'm distressed because of X, and I would like you to do Y to help me solve that problem.")

- Deal effectively with distracting responses. ("If you'd like for me to take out the trash more often, I'm happy to talk about that later. Right now, I need to address X. Are you willing to do Y?")

- If you meet objections, listen to the other person's point of view with respect. See whether you can work out a solution that works for both of you.

- Stay focused on clear, honest communication.

- If applicable, agree to get the help of a third party if the two of you can't come to an agreement.

- If what you need to ask for is nonnegotiable (for example, fidelity, nonviolence, or fair pay), be polite but clear about what the consequences are if the need is not met. Say what you mean, and mean what you say.

Delegation

Many anxiety sufferers have an excessive sense of responsibility. (We talk more about anxiety-prone personality traits in Chapter 10.) They feel like no one can do things as well as they can. They've got to oversee everything to make sure it's done right. Why delegate when they'd wind up worrying about it so much that they might as well just do it themselves?

The Cost of Not Delegating

When people are unable to delegate, they wind up shooting themselves in the foot. If you feel compelled to do everything yourself, your to-do list will always be endless. Dangling to-do's create stress and worry, which can exacerbate anxiety. With some advance preparation, you can delegate tasks in such a way that you don't wind up obsessing endlessly about how well things are being done.

 STRESS RELIEF

"We are what we read"? True or not, it sure doesn't hurt to borrow courage and inspiration by reading biographies about people who have faced obstacles and been successful.

Delegation Guidelines

The following guidelines can be useful in knowing when, to whom, and how to delegate effectively—and peacefully:

- **Develop some delegation "rules of thumb."** *Don't* delegate tasks that are enjoyable and meaningful to you. *Do* farm out tasks that someone else can do better, that you dislike the most, or that are overly time-consuming in comparison to the value they bring you.

- **Choose and train the right person.** A 7-year-old is probably not capable of successfully cleaning the bathroom; most 11-year-olds can. Skills and abilities also vary with adults; even if it's a task any human could do, take nothing for granted, and spend the up-front time interviewing and training.

- **Alleviate worries (and glitches) by creating feedback loops.** Set mini-deadlines if the situation warrants. Create a proactive system for handling the unexpected; for example, put the responsibility on the delegate to come to you with any problems or questions well before the agreed-upon deadline.

- **Delegate the authority, not the methods.** If your spouse agrees to comb your daughter's hair, keep your mouth shut if it's not in a French twist. Focus on the bigger goal (getting help from your spouse) rather than the immediate outcome (a particular hairdo). Otherwise, the "you're not happy with how I do it anyway" excuse can rear its ugly head.

You can't—and wouldn't want to—delegate everything. When you're first starting out, delegate to the edge of your comfort level and no further. When you gain confidence in your ability to manage tasks—rather than always do them—you'll feel freer to tackle more important items, such as the activities that you've been procrastinating on.

Procrastination

Procrastination isn't a bad word. It's simply the act of putting off doing something until later. Sometimes procrastination is appropriate and even valuable; for example, you have a job to do that will take a couple of hours, and you're starving. Putting off work until after you've eaten is probably the best decision, especially if you want to think clearly while you work.

The reason "procrastination" has a bad reputation is that it can become a way to avoid any task that is stressful or anxiety-inducing. You need to prepare for that business talk, but just the thought of getting up in front of those people makes you anxious. So instead of preparing extra hard for it—which would be a great anxiety-relieving strategy—you avoid even the thought of it. As time gets closer, and you're still unprepared, your anxiety escalates. And you've still got to give the talk!

 ON THE CUTTING EDGE

Researchers studied the effects of procrastination on health and stress levels among college students. Although those who procrastinated began the semester with lower stress levels than non-procrastinators, they ended up with worse stress levels and health by the end of the semester.

What Procrastinators Fear

Procrastination is often rooted in fear, which can manifest in several ways. We can fear one or more of the following things:

- **Failure.** This can be paralyzing for anyone with an anxiety disorder. It's so easy to believe that failing at even a small task would be devastating.

- **Success.** For those of us prone to anxiety, success just ups the ante. "What if they expect too much of me in the future?" "What if I do so well I get a promotion, and I don't like that job as much as I like this one?"

- **Imperfection.** Your motto might be "If something's worth doing, it's worth doing perfectly." The problem with that is that perfectionism is a tyrant that won't allow you to let go of a task after you start. In an effort to avoid imperfection, you avoid the task.

- **Being overwhelmed or trapped.** There's nothing like seeing the entire list of semester assignments on the first day of class to get the adrenaline flowing. Anxiety can make it difficult to see that you can break down large tasks into smaller, easily managed ones. As a result, you wind up thinking you have to swallow the elephant whole rather than taking it one bite at a time.

- **Abandonment or isolation.** Getting things done can mean giving up your hyper-vigilant attention to people and relationships, and feeling disconnected from others raises your anxiety level.

- **Being controlled by someone else.** If you resent someone's authority over you, you may find it hard to get going on projects assigned to you. Unfortunately, you only punish yourself by procrastinating.

Overcoming Procrastination

Fortunately, some powerful tools can help you overcome procrastination and address the fears underneath. Start by taking inventory of all the undone tasks and unresolved matters that clutter your mind and stress you out. This is not a to-do list! This is just an exercise in self-exploration.

Start with a piece of paper split into two columns with the following headings.

Action	Obstacles

On the left, list every task that needs doing or that you find yourself putting off. Write down small tasks, such as household errands, as well as big goals you've always had but never accomplished. Just get it all down on paper and out of your head.

On the right, across from each task, write down any obstacles: fears, worries, or other negative things that come up. For instance, maybe you've promised to do something for someone you feel resentful toward; the promised action would be on the left, and the anger and resentment would be on the right.

 MYTH BUSTER

> *"When I feel better, I'll do it."* Nine times out of ten, our feelings change *after* we take action, not before. You may need to take very small steps, but don't let that keep you from taking any steps at all.

Don't consider anything off limits. Your procrastination may have nothing to do with the actual task, so just write what comes to mind. When you finish, look for any patterns that emerge. Do you put off things that you're afraid of? Angry about? Ambivalent toward? As you become acquainted with the thoughts and feelings that feed your procrastination, you can choose the most workable methods for dealing with it.

Most often, these strategies involve better use of your mental space or wiser use of your time.

Mental Space

Perhaps as you perused your list you noticed that your feelings get in the way of your accomplishments. Every time you sit down to do the put-off task, you feel anxious and nervous and wind up finding reasons to delay it again. The following tips are some ways you can create "space" between yourself and your anxiety symptoms:

- **Do calming activities first.** We discuss specific relaxation techniques in the self-help chapters in the next section. For now, though, try listening to calming music or taking a leisurely walk before you tackle a daunting task.

- **Give yourself an "out" that allows you to stay "in."** Give yourself as much control over the process as possible, but don't let yourself quit. For example, if you feel anxious, take a break and focus on your breathing; inhale deeply while counting five heartbeats, and then exhale as you count five more. Make deals with yourself; work on it for 15 minutes, and then stop for a little while.

- **Bookend the scary stuff.** When you feel afraid to face a task alone, call up a friend right before you do it. Tell her what you're about to do and that you'll call her right after you do it. You'll get support and feel more accountable at the same time.

Time Management

"It's not mental space I need, it's an extra hour in the day." If those were your thoughts reading the preceding section, take heart.

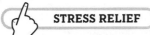
STRESS RELIEF

Dr. Steven Covey's *The Seven Habits of Highly Effective People* is excellent in terms of "putting first things first." Consider reading it—or rereading it if it's been a while.

Here are some logistical tools that can help you plow your way through a confusing, undifferentiated mass of to-do's. They can help you make time your ally, not your tormentor. Use only those tips that seem doable. If a system seems too complicated, it might be difficult to stick with it.

- **Prioritize your to-do list.** List items either by their importance or the date they are due.

- **Jog your memory.** Get yourself the right "tickler" system, such as a calendar that has room for notes, a planner, or a simple spiral notebook. Your tasks will go into the calendar.

- **Get a quick fix.** Schedule one or two quick tasks to be done every day. That will give you some relief and get the ball rolling.

- **Be disciplined.** Tackle one piece of a larger task each day. If you're trying to plow through a packed closet, schedule 30 minutes a day to chip away at it, preferably at the same time each day. Be just as diligent about not overdoing it as you are about sticking to your commitment. If you start out with too much effort, you can become overwhelmed before you get to the heart of the task at hand.

- **Schedule breaks.** Make room for pleasurable activities such as hobbies or outings with friends. Schedule them as seriously as you would any other item; these daily uplifts are what help us stay balanced and focused.

- **Under-schedule.** Leave spaces in your calendar for the unexpected. When asked to do something next week, ask for a day to think about it. Assume you will be as busy next week as you are this week.

As you've seen, a lack of assertiveness and procrastination both involve avoidance, either of conflict or of tasks. They also both have a complicated relationship with anxiety; fears can underlie passivity or procrastination, and either of them can cause you to feel anxious. We've also talked about how you can get active to stand up for your rights and get the job done.

But what if your struggle is mainly internal, in the form of negative thoughts or chronic worries? In the next chapter, we take a look at how you can take control of your thoughts and use them to soothe—rather than feed—your anxiety.

ANXIETY ATTACK

If you find yourself automatically saying "yes" to every request (and later regretting it), start saying, "Let me think about it and get back to you." This delay will buy you some time to evaluate whether the task or activity is really in your best interest.

The Least You Need to Know

- Conflict avoidance fuels procrastination by overloading our schedules and tempting us to use others as an excuse for putting things off.
- Procrastination and interpersonal passivity are often used to avoid discomfort but actually make us more anxious in the long run.
- Assertiveness is both an attitude and a skill. It carries the message "I matter, and you do, too."
- Delegation is a way to be responsible without getting overwhelmed.
- Procrastination can be a result of mental barriers or poorly used time.
- Mental aids in the war against procrastination can include getting support and encouraging others to hold us accountable; time boosters can include prioritization, under-scheduling, and balanced to-do lists.

Taming Those Alarming Ideas

Behind every painful emotion is a dysfunctional thought. Generalized anxiety sufferers, in particular, are susceptible to thinking errors that magnify uncomfortable feelings and physical sensations.

This part explores the iceberg of cognition, starting with the negative automatic thoughts that surface every day and moving deeper to uncover, and correct, dysfunctional core beliefs. Finally, we look at the relationship between personality traits and anxiety disorders, detailing how you can embrace your natural temperament and still relinquish self-defeating habits.

Taming Your Thoughts

Too much anxiety might be bad for a person but good for business. A typical marketing strategy is to create mild anxiety in potential customers and then offer a product or service to manage that anxiety. Several years ago, a popular clothing company introduced "anxiety zones" as a way to classify all of their women's swimsuits. (Worried about your too-big tummy? Buy this suit! For your too-small bust, buy this other one!)

Similarly, television news programs use careful wording to conjure up fears that need to be tamed with further viewing. Gavin de Becker identified some of these phrases: "Officials are worried," "We've identified a new threat," "Disturbing new questions are being raised," and "Many Americans think that X will happen," for example.

American popular culture is permeated with such messages of fear. For some of us, everyday life can be like this, too. Some of us seem to have an inner monologue stuck on alert, constantly monitoring our environment for threats and having "what if" conversations in response to the slightest worry. Without question, being prepared for trouble can be helpful. However, when our inner voice is too quick to jump to conclusions, we can find ourselves plummeting deeper and

In This Chapter

- Discover how actively we produce our inner dialogue
- Investigate the relationship between thoughts and feelings
- Discover how to correct the thinking errors that fuel anxiety
- Learn how to make pessimism work in your favor

deeper into an anxious state of mind. Small fears can become huge catastrophes merely in response to what we tell ourselves.

In this chapter, we discuss the relationship between our thoughts and our feelings. Specifically, we investigate thinking styles that have a calming effect as well as some common thinking styles that magnify anxiety. And you'll find out how to think in a more helpful way.

Thinking About Thoughts

In many ways, it's hard to think about thoughts. By the time we're adults, they happen so automatically that they seem to be the correct "take" on reality, or at least a central part of who we are. How often do you think of yourself as the author of your thoughts? Unfortunately, most of us feel more like an audience member than an author.

In reality, though, we are the authors of our internal play. We write the script and develop the characters. More and more, psychologists and psychiatrists consider thoughts to be mental behaviors, perhaps to emphasize how actively we participate in them and how much we can change them. Just as we can quit a bad habit such as smoking or overeating, we can get rid of self-defeating or counterproductive mental habits.

But how can we tell whether a thought is "bad" for us? Often our feelings provide the clues. For example, if we heard a celebrity warning people about how much sugar is in our usual breakfast cereal, we might think, "Too much sugar is bad for me, and my health will suffer from it." If we made a mental note of it and decided just to buy a different cereal next time, no harm done. On the other hand, if these thoughts resulted in sleepless nights and crippling anxiety about how much sugar we had already eaten in the old cereal or how much might still have been lurking in the new cereal, perhaps our worries were obsessive.

Many anxiety sufferers have a habit of making mountains out of molehills, getting so caught up in what-ifs that they lose the ability to enjoy the here and now. For example, pretend you just found out that you didn't get accepted to your number-one college choice. Here's your reaction: "Oh, my god. I didn't get into NYU. This is *terrible!* I was sure I would be accepted—the admissions director told me I was just the kind of student she was looking for! What if I don't get into *any* of the colleges I applied to? I bet I won't. I should have applied to more! Why was I so lazy?"

As you can see, negative thinking can take hold and snowball. What starts as a simple disappointment can turn into a cascade of worry and defeating ideas. Imagine the anxiety we might feel—rather than normal sadness or disappointment—if we view one incident as a sign that all is lost, or the future is doomed. Our thoughts have a profound effect on our anxiety.

STRESS RELIEF

Keep a journal! Research shows that people who write down their anxieties in a journal are healthier and better able to cope with stresses. As an experiment, write for 20 minutes a day for four consecutive days about your deepest thoughts and feelings concerning the most stressful aspects of your life.

Thinking Errors

In the previous example, we turned disappointment over one college's rejection into worry and fear by imagining the worst-case scenario—that we might not get accepted by *any* college. This is an example of a *cognitive distortion,* a faulty thinking pattern that distorts the reality of a situation. Cognitive distortions have a certain logic, but they do not take into account all of the facts. They can also create a lot of unnecessary anxiety and worry. In fact, by learning to identify the distortions or mistakes in our thinking process, we can combat anxiety by recognizing that what we are afraid of is unlikely, and the reality is not that bad.

For example, you have to give a presentation to a group of potential customers next week. You're presenting on a new product line, so the content of your talk is new to you. Cognitive distortions could make your life miserable before ("I'm not a good presenter, I know I'll bomb this"), during ("Look at that guy's frown; I know he thinks I'm an idiot"), and after ("I can't believe I forgot to show that last slide"). The problem is that our anxiety or stress level may have no connection to the reality of the situation.

Almost everyone automatically generates cognitive distortions at times. They are particularly rampant in those who struggle with anxiety. On the bright side, they're so prevalent that psychologists have made tremendous strides in identifying them and devising ways to overcome them. We briefly covered some of these in Chapter 3; let's take a closer look at how you can prevent them from impacting you on a daily basis. Some of the most common cognitive distortions follow:

- **Catastrophic thinking** happens when we turn a molehill into a mountain. For example, individuals with panic attacks often believe they are dying, having a heart attack, or going "crazy." Although panic symptoms *feel* dangerous, they really aren't. *Believing* they're dangerous, though, makes it harder to cope with them.

- **Black-and-white thinking** is when we think thoughts such as "If I'm not perfectly safe and totally free from harm, then I'm in utter danger and completely vulnerable to harm." This kind of thinking operates in extremes; it's all or nothing. In reality, most situations are somewhere in between completely safe and too dangerous.

- **Disqualifying the positive** happens when you reject the positive experiences you've had (they don't count) or ignore the good feedback you get. "He only said I did a good job on that presentation because he feels sorry for me."

- **Emotional reasoning** happens when you decide that what you feel must really reflect reality. "I feel like I'm going to crack up!" means I'm really out of my mind. The reality: feelings often overwhelm our ability to see things objectively.

- **Fortune telling** happens when you act as if your worst fears will certainly come true. "I just know I'll have a panic attack while I'm driving—I'll have a wreck and maybe kill someone. So I don't drive." Reality check: plenty of people drive while they're anxious, and panic attacks don't usually cause wrecks.

- **Labeling** is a form of all-or-nothing thinking applied to ourselves. It occurs when we give a global label to ourselves (for example, telling ourselves "I'm inadequate!" instead of seeing an obstacle as a challenge—and recognizing that we've faced challenges before).

- **Mind reading** is when we assume that others are reacting negatively to us—even when we have no evidence. ("Everyone can see how nervous I am at this party.")

- **Magnification/minimization** happens when we distort the significance of particular events. For example, we focus on all our minor mistakes but ignore our accomplishments/successes.

- **Overgeneralization** happens when one negative event means that nothing will go well. ("I had another panic attack. I'll never get better.")

- **Personalization** means relating negative events to oneself even when there is no basis. For example, the CEO doesn't speak to us when we encounter her in the hall, and we automatically interpret this as a snub. In reality, she may have been preoccupied about something else or not felt well.

- **"Should" statements** are when we tell ourselves that things should be the way we hoped or expected them to be rather than accepting what is. ("I shouldn't feel so anxious and afraid; no one else feels this way." "I shouldn't have made so many mistakes.")

Having thought "conversations" with ourselves is pretty normal; in fact, we all do it. But if we let our thoughts take on an unhealthy attitude, one that is working against us rather than for us, it's time to turn our internal conversation back to reality rather than let it engage in a running, negative commentary.

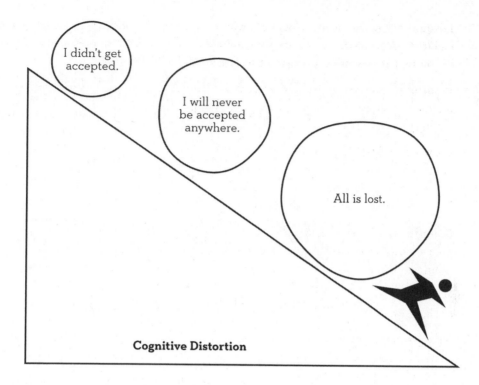

Cognitive Distortion

Restructuring Thoughts

So how do we catch those negative thoughts and turn them around? Obviously, we have to start by paying attention to our thoughts. Thought awareness is the first step in managing negative thoughts; we cannot manage thoughts we are unaware of.

The words we use to talk to ourselves can provide valuable clues about how productive—or not—our thinking is. For example, "what if?" is often the first sign that we are making negative predictions about the future. One what-if thought can quickly lead to another, resulting in a spiral of worry. Other examples of negative thoughts involve putting ourselves down, doubting ourselves, expecting failure, and criticizing our mistakes. The accompanying self-talk often involves phrases such as *I should, I never,* or *I always.* Negative thinking damages confidence, harms performance, and paralyzes mental skills.

Catching negative thoughts takes conscious effort. In fact, in the beginning, it helps to write them down. By logging our negative thoughts for a reasonable period of time, we can start to identify negative thinking patterns. This process also slows down automatic thoughts and allows us to take the role of observer (or investigator) rather than participant. It can also help us see the link between our emotions and our thoughts; in fact, when we start tracking our negative thoughts, we may initially start with "bad" feelings and work our way backward. It can be surprising to find that negative thoughts often lead to upsetting feelings rather than the other way around.

When we start analyzing and understanding our counterproductive thoughts and their sources, the real work begins. We have to put them "on trial," gathering evidence that both supports and disputes these thoughts.

For example, Sara lost her father to cancer when she was 10. As an adult, she is terrified of getting sick; whenever she has *any* physical symptoms, she finds her thoughts spinning out of control. "I feel dizzy. Maybe it's a brain tumor."

She's diligent about getting it checked out, but finds it hard to accept her doctor's reassurance. "Maybe she missed something. Maybe the MRI scan is wrong." Not surprisingly, her worry and anxiety actually increase her physical symptoms, which, in turn, increase her worry and anxiety.

For Sara, doing a reality check meant taking an objective look at the evidence. Her dizziness, she found, increased when she was under stress. Over time, Sara began to see the role her misinterpretation of anxiety symptoms had in perpetuating her fear and was able to substitute more realistic thought processes. She also became better at observing her thoughts, much like a friend would listen to someone's fears and concerns. "There are those anxiety thoughts again," she would tell herself, instead of interpreting those thoughts as real or letting them control her mood.

Cognitive restructuring requires us to develop a greater awareness of our thoughts and our moods. It also involves replacing counterproductive thinking with realistic thoughts. This is not a "look on the bright side" panacea. It's impossible for most of us to go from fearful to optimistic thinking. Sara couldn't just tell herself, "There's no way I have brain cancer." But she *could* take a realistic look at the evidence and begin to replace her catastrophic thoughts with balanced ones. Often this requires us to get at the core beliefs underneath our worries. In Sara's case, she believed the following:

If my father had cancer, I am destined to have it.

Reality: Heredity is rarely destiny. Although some illnesses have a genetic component, the fact that a parent has a life-threatening illness does not automatically mean a child will get it.

Physical symptoms are always a sign of serious illness.

Reality: The average person experiences about two or three inexplicable twinges, pains, aches, or odd symptoms every day.

If I do have cancer, it is sure to be inoperable and fatal.

Reality: Many cancer patients recover. In fact, overall, 50 percent of cancer patients eventually die of something else.

If my doctors couldn't find anything wrong with me, it was because they missed something.

Reality: The odds of a neurological exam, MRI, and complete physical workup missing a brain tumor are astronomically in Sara's favor. In this day of proactive medicine (and malpractice lawsuits), doctors are more likely to rule out any diseases that can kill the patient first and then work their way down to less serious diseases.

Use the thought restructuring worksheet to identify and start to correct your own cognitive errors. Feel free to make as many copies as you'd like! To practice, fill in the first copy with information about Sara's provoking situation, emotions, automatic thoughts, cognitive distortions, and more adaptive alternative thoughts.

Thought Restructuring Worksheet

Situation	Emotion(s)	Automatic Thought(s)	Cognitive Distortion(s)	Alternative Thought(s)
(Events, stream of thoughts)	*(Nervousness, fear, panic)*	*(Resulting thoughts, images)*	*(Specify from list)*	*(More accurate or helpful)*

ANXIETY ATTACK

Having trouble telling moods from thoughts? Moods can usually be expressed in one word: happy, sad, mad, or anxious. But thoughts are more complex, needing several words to express them (I'll never get that promotion; he's saying that because he knows it gets to me).

By discovering the basic belief that underpins a negative thought and then challenging that belief, thinking can return to a more objective, reasonable style. One way to uncover these beliefs is to ask yourself questions such as "Where does this thought come from?" In fact, we can use what-if thinking in our favor. Try this technique to find the core beliefs underneath your worries. Write down your what-if thought. Then ask yourself, "What if that did happen?" Write your answer. Then ask again, "What if that did happen?" Write it down. Keep going until you find your core belief, the belief that is at the root of your fears. For most of us, we uncover a deep-rooted fear of being rejected, hurt, or unloved. (We discuss how to deal with these in the next chapter.)

Defensive Pessimism: Preparing for the Sky to Fall

Cognitive restructuring, as discussed previously, involves challenging negative or counterproductive thoughts and replacing them with more rational, less anxiety-producing ones. Certainly, always seeing the dark clouds instead of the rainbow can take its toll on our mental disposition and, according to some studies, our physical health. However, according to Dr. Julie K. Norem, not all forms of pessimism are equal. Those of us who use our what-if thinking to *prepare for* upcoming events, for example, are just as successful as optimists.

Joni has a long-standing coping strategy—she imagines worst-case scenarios and makes plans to avoid or prevent them. If she had to give a speech, she would automatically imagine potential problems: *perhaps I won't be able to see my notes, what if I forget my opening lines, what if I suddenly lose my train of thought in the middle?* In response to these anxiety-producing thoughts, she would overprepare and memorize her opening lines; she even had a joke prepared just in case she drew a blank.

MYTH BUSTER

"What-if thinking is always bad." It's true that getting stuck in what-ifs is counter-productive; however, imagining worst-case scenarios can be useful if we then switch into planning mode and take action to prevent them.

Putting Worries to Good Use

Dr. Norem calls this strategy *defensive pessimism* and says it's a common strategy for anxiety sufferers who don't see life through rose-colored glasses. It's an adaptive way of going with our natural flow, by putting our worries to good use. In other words, by imagining potential problems, we can develop strategies for dealing with or preventing negative outcomes.

For those of us who are natural worriers, this strategy can give us a sense of control over uncomfortable circumstances. We use our thinking to prompt creative problem-solving, rather than cause an anxiety buildup. Sometimes, lowering our expectations and preparing for the worst allows us to tackle potential challenges without the stress of high expectations.

Defensive pessimists take *action* to keep anxiety from leading to avoidance or self-sabotage. An avoider does not figure out how to plan for and overcome something that makes him feel anxious. As a result, he does not learn how to reduce his anxieties except by avoiding situations that lead to anxiety. Self-handicappers tend to procrastinate in response to anxiety; they are least likely to work on what is most important. Defensive pessimism does not simply mean having a bad attitude, such as "This job sucks."

ANXIETY ATTACK

One way of controlling your amount of worry is to set aside a daily worry time. Give yourself 20 minutes a day to worry about anything and everything. When worries hit at any other time, tell yourself "stop" and remind yourself that you can deal with it at worry time.

Are You a Defensive Pessimist?

So how do you know whether you're a defensive pessimist? Think about how you tend to approach a new situation or challenging situation. Do you naturally ...

- Lower your expectations to protect yourself from disappointment?

- Make a point of not being overly confident in case you miss something or underprepare?

- Prefer to prepare up until the last minute rather than relax or do something else?

- Automatically imagine all the things that could go wrong?

- Think through every possible glitch or problem?

- Develop contingency plans for problems?

- Drive optimistic friends batty with anticipatory troubleshooting?

If you find yourself chuckling as you read these, the odds are you have a defensive coping strategy. You've developed a way to manage your anxiety in a way that keeps it from interfering with what you need to do. You've learned to tolerate anxiety in order to get things done.

However, it's possible to go overboard with defensive pessimism. As with everything, taking it to extremes can be detrimental. Existential philosophers and psychologists remind us that persistently focusing on the past or attempting to control the future (busily anticipating disaster) can breed unhappiness. To maintain personal well-being and healthy relationships, we also need to be present in the moment.

Optimism

Optimism is not all bad. In fact, optimists tend to experience less stress and more positive emotions than pessimists. Arguing *for* negative thinking as a way to manage anxiety and prepare for worst-case scenarios is very different from arguing *against* positive thinking.

To some degree, optimism seems to be an inborn trait. It runs in families, although research has yet to shed light on what genes or brain chemistry is responsible.

ON THE CUTTING EDGE

Aiming for high self-esteem? Research suggests that perhaps we should strive for a happy medium. Although low self-esteem can be associated with depression and anxiety, high self-esteem is more common among people who treat others badly, such as committing violent crimes and fraud.

Still, the thinking habits we learn and cultivate are important. For instance, when faced with challenge or novelty, optimists set high expectations, and they actively avoid thinking about unpleasant possibilities; in fact, when forced to do so, their anxiety goes *up*. Optimists and pessimists also tend to explain problems to themselves in different ways. Optimists usually think of problems as temporary, external ("It's not my fault"), and impacting a relatively small part of their world. Pessimists, on the other hand, more quickly conclude that problems are their fault, that they're irreversible, and that they will have a major impact on their day-to-day lives.

The Pros and Cons of Optimism

There's a trade-off with each viewpoint. Pessimists may have a more accurate view of situations and a clearer picture of their strengths and weaknesses. However, their realism may lead them to aim for easier-to-achieve goals. The optimist is more likely to persevere in the face of defeat and ultimately overcome problems. In addition, in situations where we have to "fill in the blanks," or where there's more than one possible explanation, pessimists may naturally gravitate toward the most devastating and the most personal story. Relationship breakups are but one example where there are often multiple causes and different perspectives; if we automatically assume blame and feel devastated every time a relationship ends, we may be less willing to take chances with future relationships.

So which is the best strategy? Do we accept our defensive pessimism and applaud ourselves for the productive avenue into which we're channeling our anxiety? Or do we keep striving to be more upbeat and positive?

The best solution may be somewhere in the middle. First of all, optimism may come more easily as we overcome our anxiety; as long as we're caught up in our symptoms, looking on the bright side may be difficult. At the same time, we *can* watch carefully to make sure our pessimism is *strategic*, that we're using our what-ifs to make a plan, limiting our negative thoughts to events or situations (not ourselves), and controlling the amount of time we spend worrying about things.

Guidelines for Balancing Optimism and Pessimism

Here are some guidelines that might help:

- Don't beat yourself up over negative thoughts; instead, mine them for useful information.

- Stop critical thoughts about yourself. When you find yourself putting yourself down, argue as forcefully against those thoughts as you would while defending a friend who was under verbal attack by your worst enemy.

- Separate feelings about a setback or mistake from the thoughts about it. Allowing yourself to feel the feelings (disappointment, worry, or sadness) can help prevent the catastrophic thoughts that often happen when thoughts and feelings get mixed up.

- Practice interpreting setbacks or mistakes as temporary difficulties that can be overcome.

- Immediately after a disappointment, do something pleasurable. Wait to think about your problems until you're in a more positive frame of mind.

In this chapter, we've discussed the role our thoughts play in shaping our feelings and guiding our behavior. We've seen how automatic thoughts can fuel our anxiety without our even being aware. We've also investigated common thinking errors that tend to plague anxiety sufferers and how we can develop more realistic and useful thoughts.

Changing "bad" mental habits is hard. However, by paying attention to our inner conversations, we can become more aware of their power and evaluate the truth in what we tell ourselves. What can be harder to detect are the core beliefs that shape how we view ourselves and the world. Core beliefs lead us down certain daily thinking paths. In the next chapter, we examine core beliefs we've developed (often in childhood) and how to change problematic ones.

 MYTH BUSTER

"Seeing the glass as half-empty means you can't have a good life." Although it's great to see things in a positive way, there are some advantages to seeing life's problems and challenges. Society needs people who know how to use caution in judgment—as long as your view of things leads to a positive outcome, such as safer driving or carefully planned business decisions.

The Least You Need to Know

- Our thoughts are mental behaviors that we can learn to change.
- Certain thinking habits distort reality and raise anxiety levels.
- By paying attention, we can learn to replace negative thoughts with realistic or more helpful alternatives.
- Defensive pessimism can work for us if we use it to overcome anxiety and make a plan for worst-case scenarios.
- Optimism seems to run in families but can be developed through practice, especially when we're less anxious.

Understanding Core Beliefs and Their Impact

A second spouse should be better than his predecessor. A new spouse should be able to step right into the role as parent to her stepchildren.

Imagine the pressure you would put on a remarriage if you automatically expected it to be better than the first, or if you assumed a step-parenting role should be effortless. Odds are this attitude would make it much more likely you'd wind up divorcing again. On the other hand, if you recognized that your past relationship history is less important than building a strong relationship with your new partner, or if you expected it to take some time for family members to adjust with a new stepparent, you'd be off to a better start.

In the preceding chapter, we discussed how your everyday thoughts can get off track and raise your anxiety level. These mental behaviors are shaped by your core beliefs about yourself and the world around you. Often, at an early age you develop theories about how life works and what it takes to survive and thrive. In this chapter, we examine beliefs that can make life harder than it has to be—and how you can replace dysfunctional assumptions with empowering ideas.

In This Chapter

- Discovering your hidden assumptions
- Getting to the core of your "self"
- Finding out how believing affects seeing
- Identifying dysfunctional beliefs that cause anxiety
- Resetting your core belief system

Beliefs

A belief is something that you *assume* to be true. It's different from a fact, which can be objectively verified. For instance, if you drop an apple from a tree, it will fall to the ground. This is a fact that can be observed and repeated. It doesn't matter what kind of tree you have climbed or the size or color of the apple. On the other hand, you could have different *beliefs* about why this is. You could subscribe to the most popular explanation—gravity—or you could come up with another theory.

Beliefs come from two sources: your own experience and reflections, and from what other people tell you. Either way, beliefs serve an important purpose. They anchor your understanding of the world around you, giving you a sense of predictability and control. They drive how you behave and influence how you feel. By the time you're an adult, you have multiple beliefs that affect your sense of reality. If you believe that people are basically good, you are likely to be trusting and trustworthy. This may make it easy for you to develop friends and close relationships. On the other hand, if you assume that this is *always* true, you may be taken advantage of.

 MYTH BUSTER

"Beliefs shouldn't change." Whereas some beliefs may be sacred, others, such as a person's political views or beliefs about himself or his capabilities, change with time. In fact, it's natural to modify your beliefs whenever you receive more information.

When you form a belief, you often stick with it despite contradictory evidence. For example, in one research study, participants were told to find certain letters (B, E, and R) and certain numbers (5, 6, and 8). In phase two, they were told to find certain letter-number combinations with the instruction that B and 6 would never occur together. When questioned later, 40 percent said they had doubted the honesty of the researcher's instruction. These participants were significantly more likely to report seeing the "B-6" combination *even though it was not there.* Seeing isn't just believing; rather, beliefs affect what you see.

From this perspective, the visible aspects of your daily life—the things you think, the feelings you have, the things you do—are the part of the iceberg that is above the surface. What lies below your thoughts, feelings, and actions are your core beliefs. Whether they are stated or unstated, whether you are conscious of them or not, your core beliefs are principles you live by that affect your thoughts, feelings, and actions.

STRESS RELIEF

Ask yourself, "What do I believe is true even though I cannot prove it?" That's a good way to get at some of the core beliefs that shape your perceptions and responses in your everyday life.

Core Beliefs

I have to be perfect in order to be loved. I must be liked by everyone I meet. I can't take care of myself. If I show vulnerability or weakness, I will be rejected.

Imagine the anxiety these beliefs can generate. And yet many of us have at least one of these lurking in our psyches. Just as you develop strong beliefs about the world around you, you develop some pretty fixed ideas about yourself. A child whose parents are overwhelmed may feel like the only way to get approval is to be "strong" or "tough." Another who faces frequent criticism may come to doubt her ability to make sound decisions, ultimately concluding that she can't trust her own instincts or judgment.

Unfortunately, as we've seen, you can fail to challenge or reexamine assumptions about yourself or the way the world works, even when these assumptions are causing you worry and anxiety. Instead, you may continue to draw false conclusions about yourself and selectively "tune in" any data in your environment that supports these assumptions—however negative or self-defeating they may be.

Examining your core beliefs about yourself is perhaps the most important step in reducing anxiety and leading a happier life. Dysfunctional self-beliefs cause you to misinterpret what happens to you, block you from achieving your goals, create extreme negative emotions, and can lead to counterproductive behaviors. In fact, one definition of a dysfunctional belief is any belief that makes life harder, limits your options, and/or magnifies negative emotions.

ON THE CUTTING EDGE

Studies suggest that some of our beliefs are influenced by our culture. For example, American culture values uniqueness and individualism; not surprisingly, Americans tend to take personal credit for their successes and to see themselves as exceptional. In Asian countries, on the other hand, loyalty to family and relationships is vital; as a result, individuals are more likely to believe personal success comes through strong affiliation with one's group, teamwork, and collaboration.

Common Beliefs for Anxiety Sufferers

Those of us with anxiety often have core beliefs about perfectionism, approval, and control. Based on these beliefs, we've developed a personal code of conduct—unwritten rules that you must live by in order to feel loved and accepted by yourself and others. Although these probably served you well at some point in your life, it's easy to get stuck in them and live by them long after their usefulness has expired. See whether some of these beliefs resonate with you:

- I must worry about things that could be dangerous, unpleasant, or frightening; otherwise, they might happen.

- I must always have the love and approval of those around me.

- I must "earn" the love of others through success and accomplishments.

- I cannot make a decision without the approval of the people around me.

- I should be upset by other people's problems.

- It is better to avoid conflict or tension than to face up to it and risk rejection.

Another problematic belief system that plagues many anxiety sufferers has to do with our beliefs about our feelings. Beliefs that negative emotions are bad, destructive, or intolerable often have a boomerang effect. Rather than help you avoid unpleasant feelings, these beliefs can increase your anxiety. Believing that *feeling* out of control means you *are* out of control can quickly increase your anxiety.

 ANXIETY ATTACK

Want to discover your basic beliefs about yourself? Write out your life story. What are the themes in your story? What kind of "character" are you? Do you describe yourself as competent or incompetent, trustworthy or untrustworthy, lovable or unlovable?

Common Dysfunctional Beliefs About Emotions

One clue that your core beliefs about emotions are working against you is when you find your emotions snowballing in response to your thoughts. You may have negative emotions, become concerned about them, and then feel worse. Some of the most common dysfunctional beliefs about emotions include the following:

- Fear is a sign of weakness.

- It is wrong to feel angry at the people I love.

- Feeling bad means my life is out of control.

- I *can't stand* feeling uncomfortable or anxious.

- If I feel guilty, I must be guilty.

- I should always be in control of how I feel.

Just as we discussed in the last chapter, changing core beliefs requires insight and realism; it's not a blindly optimistic approach to life. For example, everyone feels fear, anger, and guilt; the trick is to use these feelings as signals to make your life better or take a different path. You can start reducing their power by reframing beliefs as preferences. It would be *nice* to never feel angry at the people you love. You would *prefer* to always be in control of your emotions. It would be *great* if everyone always loved and approved of you. *But it's okay if things don't always work out that way!* Because they won't.

What core beliefs do you have about yourself? Are they working for you? If you often find yourself bogged down by disappointment or self-criticism, perhaps it's time to look deeper at your beliefs about yourself.

 MYTH BUSTER

"I can't change who I am." You can change what you do. In fact, many people find that changing their behavior results in unexpected benefits, including calmer emotions, higher self-esteem, and more positive thinking.

Effects of Core Beliefs

Two core beliefs about yourself, in particular, predict how happy and how successful you will be. These beliefs have to do with how lovable and how capable you believe you are. Clues about these core beliefs can often be found in memories of your early childhood, especially when you examine how you learned to gain acceptance and attention. What were you taught about being lovable? Did you get love through self-sacrifice or by denying negative or painful emotions? What messages did you get about being powerful and responsible? Were you encouraged to take ownership for mistakes, to blame others, or to punish yourself for minor errors?

For better or worse, these early messages often solidify into core beliefs and can guide the way you approach most situations. For example, beliefs about competency and ownership might lead to very different attitudes, feelings, and behaviors. Seeing yourself as competent is likely to lead you to take on new challenges, to try new things, and to have confidence in yourself. On the other hand, seeing yourself as incapable is likely to lead to a self-defeating approach whereby you either avoid new situations or quickly give up when faced with setbacks or challenges.

Beliefs About Others

We've already seen how core beliefs about yourself can either cause you needless suffering or help you withstand the ups and downs of everyday life. So, too, can your core beliefs about others.

For instance, support from friends and family can play a critical role in recovering from an anxiety disorder. And yet many anxiety sufferers have core beliefs about relationships that prevent them from getting the support they need. You may hide your symptoms for years, putting on a false front that hides your loneliness and pain. You may lie to avoid a threatening situation because you don't trust the other person to "handle" the truth or accept you the way you really are (even if they already know and do accept you the way you are).

Or you may go to the other extreme, depending upon your support person so much that you never have the chance to work through your fears and recognize your own strength. Relying exclusively on one person to support your recovery is likely to lead to disappointment on your part and resentment on the part of your support person. You may pull your family into spending too much time trying to help you, failing to see any progress. You may blame yourself instead of realizing that you have picked a person who is unavailable or unwilling to accept you; a good support person is someone who will help you in a productive way while also encouraging you to be responsible for your own emotional well-being.

As you begin to examine how you see other people, bear in mind that your beliefs, even those that are deeply held from infancy, are only beliefs. They are assumptions you work with until you know better. Then you can change them.

The Need for Control

One of the deepest needs we humans can have is the need for control. We long for consistency, understanding, closure—anything that will give us a feeling of predictability. In fact, feeling out of control can be one of the scariest experiences a person can have. When you think about life stressors, it's the feeling of powerlessness, of being unable to do anything about what's happening, that is often the most difficult part to handle.

However, for those of us who are anxiety-prone, the need to be in control can mask a deep-seated fear of losing control. This fear can take many forms: fear of losing control to illness, fear of being dominated or controlled in a relationship, or fear of acting weird or embarrassing oneself during a panic attack. It's amazing how skillful some of us can become at *acting* in control when we are intensely anxious.

What kind of core beliefs might contribute to these fears? They may relate to beliefs about your vulnerability. Deep down, you may question your ability to handle life's unexpected challenges, in spite of evidence that you have done so on many occasions. *I couldn't handle that,* you think as you worry about some possible catastrophe. *I would just die,* you think as you imagine yourself screaming and running out of a place where you've just had a panic attack. *I don't know what I'd do,* you think as you imagine someone ridiculing your social discomfort or laughing at your public-speaking anxiety.

Underneath are core beliefs that tell you (1) you are vulnerable, and (2) the world is dangerous, and you have to be on your guard. Challenging these core beliefs is an important part of increasing your sense of personal safety. As anxiety sufferers, you can—and you have—handled tougher times than many people ever will. You don't have to put up emotional roadblocks to protect yourself from the possibility of rejection or from being dominated by others; you can set limits or reevaluate your relationship status at any time. You also need to remind yourself of all the things you have accomplished at the same time you have been riddled with anxiety; a friend of Joni's told her recently that during the friend's worst bouts with generalized anxiety, she threw two of her sons' birthday parties, was room mother for both boys, and had a successful part-time business!

Challenging core beliefs may mean rethinking your ideas of what "handling" means. For example, it doesn't mean you don't have painful feelings about problems or upsetting events. Few people sail through life without some degree of emotional pain; perhaps "handling" should mean you continue to do the things you need and want to do *in spite of* how you feel.

Core Beliefs Are Persistent

At the beginning of the chapter, we reviewed some core beliefs about remarriage that could make it harder to stick with a new partner during normally tough times. We also saw how hidden these core beliefs can be, superficially revealing themselves through painful feelings or negative thoughts. And yet if you focus solely on changing the surface, without addressing the rest of the iceberg below, you're likely to develop new versions (thoughts, feelings, or actions) of the old problem (fundamental beliefs about your lack of worth or capability).

Negative core beliefs are most likely to pop to the surface when you're feeling the worst. What are the things you tell yourself when you're feeling your worst? You're not looking for the things you think you *should* believe about yourself, but what you really *do* believe about yourself when things look darkest—things such as *I'm never going to be a success. No one will ever love me. There's something wrong with me. I can't seem to do anything right. People will take advantage of me if you don't watch them very carefully. Women always leave me in the end. No one cares about me. The world is dangerous and unpredictable.* These statements are big clues to what these negative core beliefs are.

Another shortcut to identifying these beliefs is to look at what is happening in your life. What results are you getting? If you have a string of disappointing romantic relationships, you may have a core belief about women or men that is clouding your judgment about who you get involved with or how you handle relationships. If you put off getting professional assistance even though you've tried several self-help strategies, and anxiety is still causing lots of difficulty, you may have negative core beliefs about asking for help and/or trusting others. Remember, you may be attracted to people and situations that fit with your core beliefs.

 STRESS RELIEF

For those of us who have a need for control, anger can be seductive because it makes us feel powerful. Take some time to look underneath the anger; the feelings and thoughts you uncover can provide valuable information about your core beliefs.

They're Only Thoughts

Being able to change your thoughts and your responses to them is perhaps the very essence of being in control of yourself. No one can take that away from you. No matter how hard it is to believe, you do choose your beliefs, and at some point in your life they may have served you well. They may have protected your self-esteem, and they may have provided you a sense of predictability and certainty. But they may have outlived their usefulness.

However, until named, negative core beliefs are often experienced as "feelings." Worriers, for instance, are often responding to a number of beliefs that cause you a lot of anxiety. *If I think it, then it must be true* is a common belief in response to a frightening thought or scary possibility. In reality, of course, all of us have occasional irrational thoughts. And that's all they are—just thoughts.

I have to be in control to be safe is an underlying belief that exacerbates fear in the face of unpredictability or uncertainty. Again, in reality, how you play the hand you're dealt is the best predictor of happiness and success. You often aren't the one dealing the cards.

 ANXIETY ATTACK

Another way to get at your core beliefs is to complete the following sentences: *I am _____. People are _____. The world is _____.*

Correcting Core Beliefs

Your core beliefs weren't born yesterday, and they won't go away tomorrow. It takes a lot of energy and work to challenge some fundamental assumptions about yourself and the world around you. In the midst of your anxiety, you may not have the internal resources to tackle a longer-term project such as this one; what you can do, though, is to start paying attention to the core beliefs that rear their heads during your toughest times.

As you feel calmer and more secure, you can begin to actively challenge your unhelpful core beliefs. You can remind yourself that your beliefs are merely assumptions you have made about the way things are. You can acknowledge that your core beliefs may have helped you make sense of your world but are no longer helpful. You can look at what you want out of life and come up with core beliefs that would help you get it. *I am worthy of love. I deserve to be treated well. I am a strong, capable person. I can make my own decisions. I can handle tough times and unpleasant emotions.*

Several strategies can help you tackle dysfunctional core beliefs; many of them are discussed in this book. Keeping your values up front (see Chapter 4) can give you the motivation to keep at what seems like a daunting task. You can use the restructuring tips we discussed in Chapter 8 to help you replace negative core beliefs with more realistic ones.

STRESS RELIEF

Ask questions that cause you to rethink your assumptions. Is the problem really a problem? Is what I am doing or thinking working for me? What should I stop or start thinking or doing to change my situation?

The overall message in this chapter is that you do have control over what's really important—your thoughts and your actions. No matter how firmly entrenched your thought patterns, or how deeply ingrained your behavior, you can steer yourself in a different, more peaceful direction. In fact, new research shows that even personality traits, once believed to be "set" by an early age, are more malleable than you once thought. In the next chapter, we take a look at anxiety-related personality traits and how you can let go of perfectionism and the need for approval.

ANXIETY ATTACK

When you feel a negative emotion rising, ask yourself, "What could I be telling myself that causes this feeling?" When you identify the self-talk, ask, "What assumption or belief would have to be in place to support this kind of talk?" You can then begin to tackle the core belief.

The Least You Need to Know

- Beliefs are assumptions you believe to be true.
- Everyday thoughts, feelings, and actions give you clues about your core beliefs.
- Dysfunctional beliefs limit your options and cause unnecessary stress and anxiety.
- Anxiety sufferers often have negative core beliefs about their self-worth and ability to handle life's ups and downs.
- You can learn to identify negative core beliefs by paying attention to what you tell yourself when you are feeling down and by examining counterproductive patterns of behavior.

Personality Traits and Anxiety

Considerable research suggests that certain personality traits and anxiety often go hand in hand. Personality traits—unique patterns of relating to the world around you—are thought to emerge from genetic predispositions, life experiences, and learning. Depending on the circumstances, personality traits can be helpful or a burden.

This chapter takes a look at the link between personality traits and anxiety. We cover how certain personality traits can predispose you to tension and worry. You'll have the chance to see whether you're a "highly sensitive person." And we cover some strategies for tackling two traits that are common in persons prone to anxiety: perfectionism and the need for approval.

In This Chapter

- How personality experts view personality traits
- Defining the "anxiety-prone personality"
- Finding out whether you're a highly sensitive person
- Discovering strategies for tackling perfectionism and the need for approval
- Learning how to gracefully handle criticism

Personality Traits

"It's just in her nature to help others." "We have such different personalities." "He's just a difficult person." Many of us have made these statements, and it shows that, on some level, we are aware that we are not all built the same. Your personality influences how you tend to think and feel and what choices you tend to make.

Each personality is made up of several traits, stable characteristics that influence an individual's thoughts, feelings, and behaviors. Someone with a "difficult" personality, for example, might be described as argumentative, closed-minded, and irritable. On the plus side, this person might also be described as ambitious and self-reliant.

A person with detail-oriented personality traits might choose an accounting profession, using his or her personality strengths to excel in the workplace. But this same attention to detail might make it hard for the person to make everyday decisions in a timely manner. What works in one situation may not work in another.

Instead of labeling personalities in terms of categories, personality experts are recognizing that personality traits fall on a spectrum, like height or intelligence. For example, we humans vary in how comfortable we are in social situations. Some of us "have never met a stranger," whereas others consider ourselves shy or reserved (that is, introverted—whether or not we are also prone to negative emotions). Someone who is shy may feel more uncomfortable meeting new people than you or I yet genuinely desire to make friends and join the group. In addition, a shy person may succeed in social situations in spite of discomfort; the desire to connect may be strong enough that the anxiety is ignored.

 STRESS RELIEF

Don't confuse personality with skill. The abilities to network effectively or stand up for yourself are communication skills that can be learned by anyone.

Context

Of course, whether your personality traits cause problems for you doesn't just depend on where you are on the spectrum; context is also important. Tendencies rewarded in some contexts can be problems in others.

A person with dependent personality traits may be a loyal, cooperative member of a work team, yet falter when forced to lead. Many police officers are discerning, observant, and suspicious, personality traits that allow them to thrive in an environment where caution and wariness are rewarded.

On the other hand, a conscientious, detail-oriented employee may become quite distressed when faced with a disruptive corporate transition or sudden change in his work duties. The extrovert may thrive in sales or public relations but have great difficulty when put in an isolated work environment requiring sustained attention. Clearly, the "fit" between your personality traits and your environment can either be good or a source of considerable stress.

If you think of your personality traits as neutral, this frees you up to examine how effectively you are using your natural strengths and how often you choose situations that complement your natural attributes. Can you, for example, meet a deadline even though you're obsessively thorough? Can you stand up for yourself when you're being taken advantage of, even though you're naturally agreeable? If you have a strong need for independence, do you take jobs that allow you to flourish?

"I depend on close relationships for emotional support" is a belief that many of us could find useful. It could serve as a powerful motivator to develop and nurture the kind of social support that research consistently shows buffers you against life stress. "I can't tolerate being alone" or "I can't take care of myself," on the other hand, are beliefs that can lead you to chronic self-doubt and low self-esteem. These beliefs may also lead you to make poor relationship choices or stay in interpersonal situations that are abusive or unfair. Rather than change your personality, you can recognize your strengths and weaknesses and make choices that capitalize on your strengths.

The Anxiety-Prone Personality

We're all born with certain *temperaments,* innate characteristics that influence how reactive we are to our environment and how intensely we express these reactions. Research shows that babies who are highly reactive to environmental stimuli tend to become children who cry, try to avoid, and show distress in the face of unfamiliar objects, people, and events. Not surprisingly, babies who are highly reactive are also more likely to develop anxiety disorders as adults.

Of course, babies may be born with a propensity to over-excitability, but parenting practices and other life experiences may determine whether such infants become fearful of unfamiliar people and events later in childhood. In particular, parents who respond to a child's sensitivity with overprotection may unwittingly reinforce their child's fears by never giving him or her a chance to learn how to handle stress or challenging situations.

As adults, certain personality traits often coexist with anxiety disorders; so much so, in fact, that it's not unusual to see researchers use terms such as "anxious personality traits." Avoidant personality disorder, dependent personality disorder, and obsessive-compulsive personality disorder are often called the "anxious triad," not because most anxiety disorder sufferers have personality disorders, but because we often share similar personality traits. It's unclear whether these personality traits predispose you to anxiety or are part of the same developmental pathway.

 ON THE CUTTING EDGE

> An Italian study found that patients with panic disorder who were treated with the antidepressants Paxil and Celexa showed more than just a reduction in panic symptoms. They also experienced a reduction in dependent, paranoid, and avoidant personality traits, suggesting that these may have been influenced by panic attacks, rather than being an enduring part of the patients' personalities.

For example, anxiety sufferers often describe themselves as perfectionistic, emotionally sensitive, and highly self-conscious. Those of us who experience anxiety can be highly sensitive to a wide variety of stimuli, ranging from physical sensations to the feelings of others. On the downside, we may at times feel like emotional tuning forks, picking up on others' distress even when we don't want to.

In addition to emotional sensitivity, many of us acknowledge a strong desire to be in control of ourselves and our surroundings, especially when we are in the company of others. Stoicism may have been a family value. On the plus side, this need to be in control often gives us tremendous self-discipline; on the down side, our ability to conceal our anxiety symptoms (and other emotional pain) may leave us feeling lonely and isolated. Our need for control may also mask our underlying fear of losing control.

Another commonly shared trait is high performance consciousness. Many anxiety sufferers are hyperaware of their performance on any given task, particularly when our performance is being evaluated. We have a strong drive to avoid failure, or at least avoid looking like a failure to others. On the plus side, many of us are highly conscientious; a potential trap is placing excessive pressure on ourselves and giving others undue power over how we view ourselves.

As you can see, traits such as emotional sensitivity, a strong need to control, and high performance consciousness can be both blessings and curses depending on how much you have them and how you express them. The more extreme these traits are in your own personality, the more prone you are to experiencing anxiety.

High Sensitivity

At 18, Joni represented her junior college in the Miss Alabama beauty contest. What she remembers most clearly from that experience was how differently it affected her in comparison to the other girls. After the pageant, she was totally and completely exhausted; while most of the other girls were gathering to have fun and socialize, all she wanted to do was go back to her hotel room and get some peace and quiet. It wasn't the first time she'd noticed that she seemed to be more drained after emotion-charged events than most people, but it was the first time she clearly remembers thinking, *What's wrong with me?*

Many of us have found it helpful to learn of research psychologist Dr. Elaine Aron's research on the "highly sensitive" person. Just as dogs are able to hear whistles that humans can't hear, the highly sensitive person processes sensory information more deeply and thoroughly than most of the people around her.

This biological sensitivity, which Dr. Aron believes is inborn like other personality traits, brings gifts and causes challenges. On the plus side, our highly developed emotional tuning fork allows us to feel deeply, to have a keen imagination and a rich inner life, and to easily pick up on the moods of the people around us. On the down side, we can't turn our emotional radar off. As a result, environmental stimulation that wouldn't faze the average person—noises, bright lights, crowds, intense movies—may feel overwhelming to the biologically sensitive person.

This biological sensitivity doesn't just apply to the world around us, though; it also applies to our internal world. Highly sensitive persons often have a high sensitivity to pain and can feel overwhelmed when dealing with time pressure, sudden changes or transitions, or multiple demands. "Don't be so sensitive" is a mantra many of us with this biological temperament have heard since childhood, often in response to our distress over other people's moods or comments or because we "overreact" to minor annoyances. It's like we have the proverbial "thin skin" that leaves us vulnerable to all sorts of stimuli.

 MYTH BUSTER

"People who are 'emotional' make poor decisions." The truth is, used wisely, your emotions can help you make very good decisions because you can appreciate certain nuances.

The highly sensitive person is not necessarily always anxious but is *at risk for* anxiety. For example, because they pick up so much from the world around them, they are more prone to overstimulation and quicker to feel stress, especially when they can't retreat to a quiet room or place of solitude to get some "down time." Also, recent research suggests that they are more impacted by life experiences. For instance, researchers found that individuals with this biological sensitivity were three times as likely to suffer from shyness, anxiety, and depression if they had a troubled childhood compared to persons without this trait. As adults, the highly sensitive person is also more likely to be negatively affected by a bad life experience. However, it's important to remember that you can learn to adapt your strengths and weaknesses to your advantage and take care of yourself.

So how do you keep the gifts your emotional sensitivity gives you and minimize the intrusions? On a practical level, you can do the following:

- Make sure you have plenty of solitude and down time, especially when you are going through a stressful period.

- Quit comparing yourself to other people who seem less drained or bothered by the world around them.

- Take extra steps to guard your physical health; hunger and lack of sleep can make you even more prone to overstimulation and fatigue.

- Intentionally put yourself in calming environments when you can, whether it's a quiet room at home or a beach or mountain vacation.

- Develop ways to create inner calm, such as through yoga or meditation.

- Learn to say "no" even if this triggers negative emotions.

- Break down big goals into small steps, and create your own deadlines.

- Take new relationships *slowly*. Because of the tendency to feel deeply, you can jump in and get hooked into a relationship before you have the chance to evaluate whether it's good for you.

 MYTH BUSTER

Research suggests that highly sensitive people with a good childhood are no shyer, more anxious, or more depressed than others.

Perfectionism

As you've seen, having finely tuned emotional radar can predispose you to both empathy and anxiety. It can work for you, but at times it takes some work to keep it from stressing you too much. It's both a blessing and a curse. On the other hand, perfectionism—another personality trait many anxiety sufferers share—rarely does you any good at all. In fact, it can keep you from experiencing joy and pleasure even when you deserve it.

Ever feel like nothing you do is good enough? Is it hard to be satisfied with your efforts? If you meet a goal, do you push yourself harder rather than take time off to appreciate what you've done? If you answered "yes" to any of these questions, welcome to the perfectionist club.

Perfectionism may have its roots in childhood, when the message "I love who you are" somehow gets confused with "I love what you do." When a child feels that acceptance and love are conditioned upon success, she or he naturally tries to earn it. In adults, perfectionism is often expressed through exceedingly high standards. High standards are not necessarily problematic; they can be extremely valuable, of course.

What does cause problems is when, no matter how successful you are, you never feel like it's good enough. For example, imagine that your daughter comes to you, stressed out because she's convinced that she needs an A+ on a final exam; she believes her chances of getting into a good college will be dramatically reduced if she doesn't get an A in this class. After a week of stress, cramming, and snapping at you, she comes home with her grades. She did it! An A+! However, instead of patting herself on the back, she glumly tells you that she'll never be able to handle college if she has to study so much to ace a stupid high school course. In other words, if she were perfect, she *should be* able to do it more easily.

 ON THE CUTTING EDGE

Research suggests that first-borns may be more likely to be perfectionists than later-born children, perhaps because first-time parents might reward "eager beaver" behavior.

As you can see, there's a difference between the desire to succeed and excel and the desire to be perfect. It's the combination of high expectations plus dissatisfaction with your performance, no matter how stellar it actually is, that causes the pain of perfectionism. The greater the discrepancy between your performance and your satisfaction with it, the more likely it is that you are caught in perfectionism's trap.

The attitudes and beliefs underlying perfectionism fuel anxiety by creating a constant sense of time pressure coupled with a rigid, unforgiving standard of performance. There's no room for mistakes. "I'm a loser unless I reach my ideal. I don't have value unless I'm successful. I should be able to do it better, faster, easier ...." In reality, no one can always get everything done on time and perfectly. Stuff happens. Glitches pop up. It's like there's a taskmaster inside you that you just can't escape, one who is never satisfied and waiting to pounce on your slightest mistake or setback.

 STRESS RELIEF

Keep a daily journal of everything positive you do to shift the focus from what you haven't done (or why it wasn't good enough) to what you have.

Antidotes for perfectionism often involve an attitude adjustment to catch self-defeating or irrational thoughts, such as the cognitive restructuring strategies discussed in the last two chapters. You can use feelings of anxiety and worry as opportunities to ask yourself if you have set up impossible expectations in your current situation and explore the fears behind the feelings. In addition, you can intentionally remind yourself that few things really are "all or nothing." For example, you can do the following:

- Focus on the process of doing an activity, not just on the end result. Evaluate your success not only in terms of what you've accomplished, but also in terms of how much you enjoyed the task. Recognize that there can be value in the process of pursuing a goal.

- Read biographies of famous people who failed often (Thomas Edison, for example) or stories of mistakes that turned into accidental discoveries (penicillin, x-rays).

- When you make a mistake, ask, "What can I learn from this experience?" More specifically, think of a recent mistake you have made and list all the things you can learn from it.

- Rank your goals and tasks according to how important they are to you. On less important tasks, decide how much is "good enough."

The Need to Please

We've talked about the kind of perfectionism that drives you to overwork and chronic dissatisfaction with your efforts. But another kind of "perfectionism" can complicate your relationships and diminish your sense of self-worth. This perfectionism is socially prescribed and often takes root in the belief that others will only value you if you are perfect. This kind of social perfectionism has been linked to both anxiety and depression, not to mention a chronic sense of loneliness and insecurity. This kind of perfectionism can tempt you to put on a mask with others, hide any fears or problems, and focus on pleasing others rather than standing up for yourself.

There is nothing wrong with wanting to make other people happy; it's an endearing trait. However, when you get stuck in people-pleasing mode, you may deny, hide, or suppress your own emotional needs because you believe it is the only way to gain the acceptance and approval of others. Normal feelings of anger or irritation can be threatening and, as a result, cause anxiety; after all, how many friends and family members are pleased when you're angry with them?

There's another link between anxiety and people-pleasing. Recent research suggests that children who felt unsure of the availability of their primary caretaker, especially those who felt emotionally abandoned during times of distress, are more likely to develop anxiety than children whose attachment was more secure. In addition, these children were more likely to try to hide their emotions and appear neutral, even when experiencing pain and distress. In addition, many had greater trouble tolerating separation from the primary caregiver than children more securely attached.

 **MYTH BUSTER**

> *"Personalities don't change."* Wrong! In fact, research suggests that, after age 20, most of us become more conscientious, agreeable, and emotionally stable.

As discussed at the beginning of this chapter, personality traits, in and of themselves, are neutral; it's when you do not recognize and adapt to them that they can become problematic. Chronic people pleasers tend to have an *excessive* need to seek approval to avoid anticipated rejection, abandonment, or disapproval. You work too hard to keep the peace, do anything to avoid hurting someone's feelings, and often have a problem letting others know how you really think and feel about things. In return, you give too much power to others' opinions about you and, at times, expect others to take care of your feelings.

Owning Your Self-Esteem

Those of us with a strong need for approval work hard at being good in the various roles in our lives—and we are good at them. Unfortunately, though, we may wait for others to give us recognition or credit rather than honor ourselves. This dependence on others to boost our self-worth can create a constant state of tension; after all, we have no control over what others say and think about us.

Inevitably, this takes a toll on our relationships. The people who love us may treat us with kid gloves, trying their best to reassure us and boost our self-esteem. They may become overly protective, not telling us the truth for fear of hurting our feelings or damaging our egos. They may also feel resentful and overwhelmed by the need to "be there" for us. If we have the misfortune to get involved with someone who feels the need to exert power over someone, she or he will gladly take advantage of our need for approval, either using it to manipulate us to carry more than our share in the relationship or taking delight in wielding power over our self-esteem. Most of us know a friend or acquaintance who stays involved with a critical partner and are driven batty as we see a decent human being believe—and tolerate—a bunch of manipulative bull.

Ultimately, if you're an approval seeker, no one else can satisfy the deep need to be accepted that you desperately pursue. You've got to confront your fears head on. You've got to find security and trust in yourself. When you start identifying and restructuring your irrational beliefs about rejection, neglect, abandonment, and disapproval and uncover where these fears came from, you can get to the root of your need for approval.

 STRESS RELIEF

Religious or spiritual beliefs can be a powerful antidote for perfectionists, especially when they find it difficult, if not impossible, to forgive themselves when they have made a mistake or done wrong.

A first step is to ask yourself what you really gain by trying to please everyone in your life. What do you give up when you keep your opinions and feelings to yourself or when you can't make a decision without consulting someone? What are the taboo subjects that limit your intimacy with your partner? Taking a small risk—by saying "no," by sharing a problem, or by giving honest feedback—can be a giant step in providing evidence that you can please people by being yourself. In fact, one of the biggest benefits of an anxiety support group is sharing feelings and thoughts that many attendees have never disclosed to anyone—and never imagined they could.

As discussed in this chapter, personality traits are neither good nor bad; they only become problematic when they don't fit the situation. This chapter has also explained how certain personality traits and anxiety often go hand in hand; they can push us in the direction of anxiety, exacerbate an existing anxiety disorder, or, in excess, cause anxiety themselves. Reducing the role perfectionism plays in your life, or tackling an excessive need for approval, can help us address some of the underlying thoughts and feelings that increase your stress level and create tension and worry.

The Least You Need to Know

- Personality traits are neither good nor bad; they may help you or cause trouble, depending on the context and how much you allow them to influence your behavior.

- Anxiety sufferers often share certain personality traits such as perfectionism, a high level of emotional sensitivity, and a strong need for approval.

- Highly sensitive people have built-in emotional radars that pick up data most other people would miss, ignore, or not care about.

- Tackling perfectionism and the need to please others often involves addressing underlying fears of rejection, abandonment, and disapproval.

Boosting the Mind-Body Connection

This part focuses on how you can build a physical foundation that promotes peace of mind. Starting with the myths and realities of what exercise can do for anxiety, we then turn our attention to diet and sleep. Finally, we outline the stress-management tools that can prevent the buildup of daily hassles that can eventually lead to clinical distress.

Getting Help from Exercise and Breathing

We all know exercise keeps us strong, builds our endurance, and helps with weight loss. But with society's emphasis on the physical-health benefits, not to mention physical appearance, it can be easy to lose sight of the mental-health benefits. Can a workout really boost your mood and reduce your stress? And can regular exercise cure depression and anxiety?

In this chapter, we take a look at exercise and mental health. We look at what exercise can do for you and what it can't. And, of course, we focus on the fascinating link between exercise and anxiety: what exercises promote calm, what exercises can stir things up, and how simple breathing and meditation techniques can soothe a troubled mind.

In This Chapter

* Finding out what exercise can—and can't—do for your state of mind
* Developing a strategy for successful workouts
* Uncovering your motivation for regular exercise
* How breathing can help with anxiety
* Exploring some at-home breathing strategies

The Mental Health Benefits of Exercise

Ann was diagnosed with panic disorder and depression two years ago. She would often isolate herself and stay home, feeling unable to face work or enjoy social outings. She sought help from her general practitioner, who prescribed an antidepressant and recommended psychotherapy. Ann started feeling better; she returned to work and made more of an effort to get together with friends. However, she still felt exhausted by the demands of a stressful job.

At her doctor's insistence, Ann began to exercise, starting out slowly just by walking and gradually increasing her workout routine. She also found a walking buddy, which made her feel less isolated and gave her an extra incentive on the days she felt too tired or stressed to move. Within three weeks, her energy level improved. She also began to appreciate the calm she felt after her workout. When Ann felt ready to discontinue her medication 14 months later, she upped her exercise routine a bit, and she found it helped her with the anxiety she felt over discontinuing her medication.

An increasing number of health professionals are prescribing exercise as an add-on to other treatments when helping an emotionally distressed patient. It's no magic bullet (what is?), but a growing body of literature suggests that increasing physical activity is a positive and active way to help manage anxiety symptoms—*and* boost self-esteem.

But how can physical exercise have any effect on the mind or mood? Let's take a look at what we know about the mental benefits of physical exercise—and what we don't.

ON THE CUTTING EDGE

Research has found that levels of phenylethylamine, a feel-good hormone, are lower in people suffering from a mental disorder; exercise seems to boost its production.

How Does Exercise Help?

We don't fully understand how exercise improves emotional health, but we've got some pretty good ideas. For example, on a physiological level, exercise may positively affect the levels of mood-enhancing neurotransmitters in the brain. The increased body temperature may also have calming effects. In addition, physical activity may boost feel-good endorphins, release tension in the muscles, help you sleep better, and reduce the stress hormone cortisol.

MYTH BUSTER

"Exercise can cure anxiety or depression." Physical activity cannot cure clinical levels of anxiety or depression, but it can provide psychological and physical benefits that alleviate symptoms and can be an important part of the recovery process.

Exercise also seems to have a number of direct and indirect psychological and emotional benefits when you have depression or anxiety. These include the following:

- **Confidence.** Engaging in physical activity offers a sense of accomplishment. Meeting goals or challenges, no matter how small, can boost self-confidence at times when you need it most. Exercise can also make you feel better about your appearance and your self-worth.

- **Distraction.** When you have depression or anxiety, it's easy to dwell on how bad you feel. But dwelling interferes with your ability to problem-solve and cope in a healthy way. Dwelling also can make depression more severe and longer lasting. Exercise can provide a good distraction. It shifts the focus away from unpleasant thoughts to something more pleasant, such as your surroundings or the music you enjoy listening to while you exercise.

- **Interactions.** Depression and anxiety can lead to isolation. That, in turn, can worsen your condition. Exercising can create opportunities to interact with others, even if it's just exchanging a friendly smile or greeting as you walk around your neighborhood.

- **Healthy coping.** Doing something beneficial to manage depression or anxiety is a positive coping strategy. Trying to feel better by drinking alcohol excessively, dwelling on how badly you feel, or hoping depression and anxiety will go away on their own aren't helpful coping strategies.

It appears that your body—and your mind—will always reward you for taking good care of them.

ANXIETY ATTACK

Aerobic exercise was the top-rated "treatment" for generalized anxiety disorder and second for panic disorder by consumers on an independent remedy-finding website.

Exercise Is Rewarded by Your Body

It's great that our bodies have a built-in mood-improving system. For example, our brain's pituitary gland produces beta-endorphins, which can attach themselves to the same receptors that morphine uses, producing some of the same pleasant feelings. Another chemical, phenylethylamine, is produced during exercise and is related to amphetamines, but without the long-term side effects. These chemicals may also contribute to the calm you experience when you exercise.

Some studies have shown that these chemicals are released whenever you take action to get your needs met. Apparently, it's your body's way of saying, "You've done well. Do more of this." It's also one of the reasons some people seem to get "hooked" on exercise, and why athletes often describe the "buzz" of a workout as a "natural high."

ANXIETY ATTACK

It may take at least 30 minutes of exercise a day for at least 3 to 5 days a week to see an improvement in anxiety symptoms. However, even 10 to 15 minutes of exercise can improve mood in the short term.

Motivation to Exercise

You may be convinced that exercise might be a good idea. However, many of us make New Year's resolutions that involve exercise—and few of us keep them. To improve the odds that you'll stick with it, take some time to prepare yourself by doing the following:

- **Get your doctor's advice.** Your doctor or other health professional may have some excellent exercise plans and advice. Use their support to talk over your thoughts and concerns.

- **Go with your natural flow.** Start with things you like to do, perhaps activities you've enjoyed in the past or new things you'd like to try. If you're a people person, find an exercise buddy. If childcare is a problem, involve your kids. Don't plan to exercise at the crack of dawn if you're a night owl.

- **Do an attitude adjustment.** Keep track of the immediate benefits of exercise, such as a calmer state of mind and better sleep. Give yourself credit for every step you take, and use setbacks as an opportunity to learn. Set realistic goals, and go at your own pace.

- **Reframe your motivation.** Don't let exercise be a burden; instead, think of exercise as your own private therapy session or personal meditation time.

STRESS RELIEF

Exercise builds up your stress tolerance as well as your muscles. Exercise buffs with anxiety say their workout routine serves as a form of controlled stress that supplies a kind of "vaccination" against uncontrolled stress.

Try an Exercise You Enjoy

The following table lists some exercises you can consider taking part in.

Indoor	Outdoor
Yoga	Bicycling
Aerobic dance	Skating
Jumping rope	Fitness walking
Stair climbing/steppers	Running
Ski machine/elliptical	Swimming
Aerobics/water aerobics classes	Gardening
Working around the house	Mowing

Aerobic exercise involves continuous low- to moderate-intensity exercise involving the heart and lungs. Examples include walking, running, biking, swimming, skiing, and many other exercises. Aerobic exercise is great for reducing tension and improving mood.

ANXIETY ATTACK

Some people worry that exercise might trigger an anxiety or panic attack—sometimes the normal feelings from working out such as breathlessness and a faster heart rate can feel similar to some of the early signs of a panic attack. It's best to start slowly—take a little walk at first, and then build up.

Long-Term Motivation for Exercise

Here's Gary's story:

At first I found it hard to get excited about any exercise. I used to enjoy mountain biking, so I thought I would try that. I found a route that would give me opportunities to stop—I'm not as fit as I used to be. But once I cleaned up my old bike, I just let the days go by without doing anything, until one day I was talking to my friend. He saw my bike sitting out and offered to go riding with me. We went. It was tough, but it felt great to be out again.

Gary got the push he needed from a friend; luckily, he noticed some benefit from his first outing. What gets you out there, though, may not always keep you going. For example, over time, he may get bored with biking and need to vary his activities. If he's not too confident about biking alone, he may not always be able to rely on his friend to be available. Also, biking is a seasonal activity in many areas.

 ON THE CUTTING EDGE

Some research suggests that yoga, with its focus on mind-body harmony and breathing techniques, can lower anxiety levels. Regular practitioners report better concentration, improved perception, and an enhanced ability to calm themselves.

You can boost your long-term commitment to exercise by doing the following:

- Varying your activities; have two or three alternate exercise options
- Including a friend
- Starting off gently and building up slowly
- Setting a specific time of day to exercise and sticking to it
- Preparing for setbacks
- Not giving in to counterproductive thoughts

If It Seems Impossible

When Kirsty's therapist suggested exercise, the first thing she thought was, "What has that got to do with anxiety? Between work and family, I'm already stressed enough." She listened to some exercise suggestions, but she couldn't find anything that suited her. She works long hours and doesn't have access to a gym or exercise equipment.

However, after several stops and starts, she decided to fit it in wherever she could. She took the stairs rather than the elevator. She walked to work twice a week and went for a walk during her lunch hour. By breaking up exercise throughout her day, Kirsty was easily able to achieve her goal of 30 minutes of physical activity per day.

The key is to be flexible and have a backup plan. If your last workout was too much, scale it down. If you're bored, try something else. See obstacles as hurdles rather than defeat.

In addition to tackling your exercise routine stumbling blocks, focus on the opportunity. What *will* happen if you exercise regularly? So you're only able to fit in 10 minutes of jogging; you *will* feel better than if you did nothing.

Play games with yourself. For example, keep track of the number of steps you take, or try to walk a little faster than you did yesterday. Use humor; keep track of all the creative excuses your mind comes up with and post them somewhere in your house.

The Benefits of Breathing

Your breathing is an amazing barometer of your mental state. For instance, when you're stressed, your breathing tends to become shallow and rapid. Very rapid breathing can cause you to feel lightheaded and give you tingling sensations in your arms and legs.

How you're breathing also influences how you feel. For example, it's hard to feel calm and relaxed when you're hyperventilating. Noticing the feedback loop between breathing, feelings, and physical sensations, mental-health professionals began teaching effective breathing as a way to control arousal and reduce anxiety.

 MYTH BUSTER

"Isn't yoga a religion?" No! Some simple yoga techniques include breathing exercises and simple stretches. In fact, the first principle is learning how to relax your body and mind.

It may sound silly to say you need to learn how to breathe, but many of us breathe in a non-relaxing way; specifically, we expand our chest or raise our shoulders when we breathe in. This may be helpful in certain circumstances, but not for relaxation.

Instead, for relaxation, you need to shift your breathing down into your diaphragm. This fills your lungs from the bottom up. Here's a quick lesson:

> Lie down on your back, place your hands on your stomach, and loosely interlock your fingers. As you breathe in, your stomach should rise and your fingers become separated. If you can, breathe in through your nose and out through your mouth. When you've gotten the breathing down, capitalize on your physical calm using your mind. You might try mentally repeating *My toes are relaxed; I can feel my toes relax. My calves are relaxed; I can feel my calves relax* and working your way up through the rest of your body.

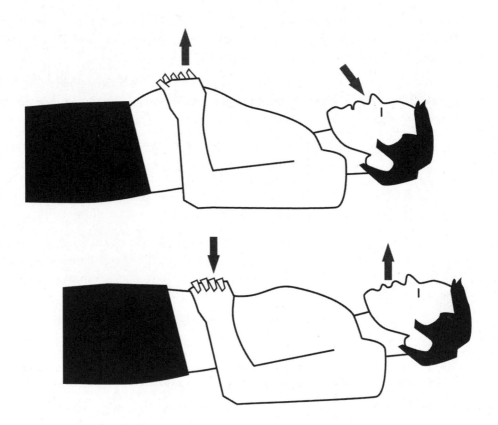

The more you practice deep breathing when you're already relaxed, the easier it will be to achieve when you're under pressure. Advanced students are able to do it wherever they are—even when they're about to give a speech or face a scary medical procedure. Just as it's hard to relax when you're hyperventilating, it's hard to feel terror when you're breathing slowly and calmly.

After you've gotten the basic breathing technique down, you can add extra impact to your deep breathing by doing some of the following:

- Control your exhale—a longer "out" breath activates the parasympathetic nervous system, your built-in relaxation mechanism.

- Address anxious feelings by mentally repeating, "I feel scared/anxious/vulnerable" while breathing in and welcoming relaxation by thinking, "I'm letting these feelings go" as you breathe out.

- Consider occasionally adding meditative qualities to your breathing by fasting (no food or drink) for a couple of hours, but time this around your workouts so you're not depleting yourself of needed water or energy.

- Don't give up! Many people find it difficult to get the hang of it at first (or stop because they think it's pointless). In reality, the ability to control your breathing can help you reduce the physical effects of stress and regain a sense of control when anxiety overwhelms you.

Two physical activities—exercise and proper breathing—can play a powerful role in boosting mood and reducing tension. In the next chapter, we examine how other ways of taking care of your body—through good nutrition and the right amount of sleep—can improve your mental well-being and lower anxiety.

 ANXIETY ATTACK

Curious about using yoga but don't know where to start? Check out life.gaiam.com/ article/beginners-guide-8-major-styles-yoga, which gives you a rundown of different types of yoga you can use.

The Least You Need to Know

- Aerobic exercise can reduce anxiety by stimulating natural painkillers, boosting your confidence, and distracting you from worrying thoughts.
- Regular exercise provides immediate benefits (a mood boost) and long-term rewards (a sense of calm).
- Getting the most benefit from aerobic exercise requires 30 minutes of activity a day.
- A regular exercise routine requires motivation, flexibility, and a willingness to overcome external and internal obstacles.
- Learning to control your breathing can be a powerful step in soothing troubling physical symptoms and taming fear and anxiety.

Eating and Sleeping

In the preceding chapter, we discussed how exercise can boost your mood, improve your health, and help you relax. However, you can do even better if you take care of your body in other ways. For example, it will be harder to remain peaceful after a yoga session if you haven't slept properly and you drink a double shot of espresso on the way home.

Nutrition has often been a focus for those looking for better physical and mental health. Recently, the role sleep plays in the quality of your waking state is gaining attention, perhaps because many of us get too little of it.

In this chapter, we examine the roles nutrition and sleep play in your mental well-being and how what you eat and how much you sleep can influence your level of anxiety or calmness.

In This Chapter

- Finding out how food affects your mood
- Discovering and eliminating anxiety-provoking foods
- Learning which foods promote calm
- Investigating the relationship between anxiety and insomnia
- Strategies for better sleep

Foods and Anxiety

We've all heard it: you are what you eat. Every day, you take in fuel to keep your body functioning and rebuild worn-out cells and tissue. An increasing body of evidence tells us that the quality of your nutrition can impact your emotions. Also, think about how irritable you can get when you're hungry; it's easy to see the link between mood and food. The stress you feel when you need food is your body's way of telling you that your nutritional needs are not being met.

ON THE CUTTING EDGE

Some recent research suggests that mood can be affected by nutrition. For example, a 2011 study found that healthy adults given omega-3 supplements for three months showed a 20 percent decrease in anxiety symptoms compared to those given placebo pills.

But the key isn't just eating *enough* food; it's eating the *right* foods and avoiding the wrong ones. Let's take a look at two different lists of foods—one anxiety-provoking, the other anxiety-reducing. See which most closely resembles your daily intake.

Foods and Substances That Can Make Anxiety Worse

Here are some things you take into your body that increase anxiety:

- Caffeine

- Nicotine

- Stimulant drugs

- Sugar

- Alcohol

High amounts of caffeine can trigger feelings of anxiety and nervousness in most of us. It can also extend the time necessary to pass through the early stages of slumber into deep sleep. Not surprisingly, individuals with agoraphobia and panic disorder reported significantly more anxiety, nervousness, fear, nausea, heart palpitations, and restlessness, depending on caffeine intake, sometimes after as little as one cup of coffee.

Smokers often reach for a cigarette when under stress and say that nicotine helps them calm down. In reality, though, nicotine can be both calming and stimulating. Recent research suggests that cigarette smoking may increase the risk of anxiety disorders during late adolescence and early adulthood; in other words, smoking seemed to come before anxiety, not the other way around.

Some over-the-counter and prescription drugs contain caffeine and/or amphetamines, which can induce anxiety. Recreational drugs such as cannabis and cocaine can also raise anxiety levels.

Consuming large amounts of sugar and sweets can put your body on a roller coaster between feeling weak and feeling high-strung and jittery—your body's response to changes in blood sugar.

Alcohol is tricky when it comes to anxiety. In the short run, it reduces anxiety, which is one reason why anxious people are at risk for alcohol problems. In the long run, though, alcohol use can stress the nervous system, worsen anxiety symptoms, and significantly disrupt sleep cycles.

Situation: Invited to an office party for my husband's new job. He says it's important that we both go.

Anxiety: Tension, thoughts that everyone will see how nervous and shaky I am— and that this will not be good for my husband.

Relief: My anxiety decreases, and I end up enjoying myself. My husband is thankful that I came and stayed.

I drink wine: One glass before we leave home and two glasses at the party.

ANXIETY ATTACK

A magnesium deficiency can cause anxious feelings, so make sure you're eating enough magnesium-rich foods, such as nuts, cereals, and certain fish such as halibut. Talk with your health-care provider if you think you might not be getting enough magnesium.

Foods That May Improve Mood

Now that you've seen what can increase your anxiety, take a look at vitamins that seem to buffer physical and mental stress, how they do it, and what foods have them.

Nutrient	What It Does	Where to Get It
Magnesium	Regulates blood-sugar levels, normalizes blood pressure, keeps heart rhythm steady, supports immune system	Green vegetables, beans, peas, nuts, unrefined whole-grain foods
Vitamin B_{12}	Maintains healthy nerve cells and red blood cells	Fish, meat, poultry, eggs, milk and milk products
Niacin (vitamin B_3)	Maintains normal nervous system function, blood pressure, mental alertness	Liver, chicken, tuna, eggs, milk, broccoli, tomatoes, sweet potatoes
Glycine	Reduces the release of anxiety hormones	Gelatin, fish, meat, beans, dairy products
Folic acid (vitamin B_9)	Helps proper nervous system function	Leafy vegetables, citrus fruits, dried beans and peas
Thiamine (vitamin B_6)	Supports nervous system function	Pork, soybeans, peas, liver

So a mood-improving grocery-shopping excursion could have you buying healthful foods such as lean meat, fish, whole grains, vegetables, and fruit. These foods are also good for general health.

ON THE CUTTING EDGE

Preliminary studies suggest that low blood sugar can increase anxiety symptoms. When you're in a hypoglycemic state, the tissues in your body, including your brain, aren't getting enough energy to work properly. Building your diet around lean protein, "good" fats, and slow-burning carbs like whole grains can help you maintain a steady supply of energy without the extreme highs and lows that can cause problems.

Thinking About How You Eat

Taking the time to focus on your food (whenever possible) can not only ease your digestion; it's also a chance to improve your general health. Some suggestions:

- Don't do anything else (such as read, watch TV, drive, or even stand up) while you eat.

- Chew at least 15 times per mouthful.

- Take periodic breaks to give your stomach time to tell you whether it's full, satisfied, or still hungry.

- Eat regularly (at least every five hours) to keep your blood sugar at a reasonably normal level.

Supplements and Herbal Remedies

Much has been written about the pros and cons of taking herbal and other dietary supplements—so much, in fact, that it's hard to separate the wheat from the chaff. On the one hand, many experts say that the best way to make sure your body gets the right nutrients is through a balanced, healthful diet. Many physicians note that vitamin supplements aren't necessary for those who eat such diets. On the other hand, if a food source isn't particularly appealing, supplements can be a good way to ensure that you get vital nutrients.

Some people adopt a "belt and suspenders" approach to vitamins and nutrients, either taking more than the recommended amount or taking vitamins when they are getting everything they need through their meals. If vitamins and nutrients are good for you, you might think that more is better.

Unfortunately, this is not the case. Vitamin toxicity is becoming increasingly common in developed countries because of the popularity of vitamin supplements. Taking too much of some vitamins can have a toxic effect. In fact, megadoses of vitamin D, vitamin A, and vitamin B_6 can be fatal. For that reason, it is important to discuss with your physician whether or not to take a supplement.

Herbal Supplements

Many herbal supplements—such as passion flower, skullcap, kava kava, chamomile, mugwort, and valerian—are available for anxiety and stress. Each has its loyal supporters, but the jury is still out for many of these proposed remedies.

Just because herbs are promoted as "all-natural" alternatives doesn't mean they aren't potent; many of them are as powerful as prescription drugs.

What's more, herbal medications do not have to meet the same federal regulations as other drugs do—meaning the potency, purity, and safety can vary from brand to brand. The bottom line: do your homework, check carefully for interactions with other medications, and always ask your doctor.

Trouble Sleeping

What do Madonna, Abraham Lincoln, and George Clooney have in common? They've all suffered from insomnia.

Sleep problems are amazingly common. At any given time, one out of every eight Americans is struggling with insomnia, and in one survey, 60 percent of respondents said they had some trouble getting to sleep the previous week. Life events such as moving, the birth of a child, or the loss of a loved one can be particularly difficult times.

 ANXIETY ATTACK

Our bodies use tryptophan to make serotonin and melatonin, two brain chemicals that aid sleep. Tryptophan is plentiful in oats, bananas, dried dates, milk, cottage cheese, meat, fish, turkey, chicken, and peanuts. These foods, eaten a couple of hours before bedtime, may help you feel sleepy.

Anxiety and fear can impair your sleep cycle. Research has consistently shown that worries tend to delay the onset of sleep. Even worse, the fatigue from lack of sleep—or the worry about another sleepless night—can increase your anxiety during waking hours and make it more difficult to fall asleep. This can be another vicious cycle. Let's take a look at what happens when you sleep and how you can sleep better.

MYTH BUSTER

A recent clinical trial of herbal remedies provided evidence that kava kava and valerian were no more effective than an inactive placebo.

Sleep Stages

The first phase of sleep is a light slumber, during which your mind begins to free itself of waking concerns. It is possible to dream during this phase, but the dreams are easily broken by sudden jolts of mental activity, known as spikes. The next phase is a deeper sleep where your brain activity slows down. Dreams are rare during this phase. After you're refreshed with slow-wave sleep, the rapid eye movement (REM) stage begins. This is when you tend to dream most.

Research suggests that both depression and anxiety disrupt sleep, making it harder to fall asleep and sleep deeply. As a result, sufferers may find sleep nonrestorative even if they get eight hours of it.

One way to improve sleep is to lower worry levels during the day—this will make your mind more able to relax as you drift off.

STRESS RELIEF

Studies have shown that a cooler body temperature can help you get to sleep. Allow at least three hours between exercise and bedtime, and keep your bedroom cool and dark. Spend no more than 20 minutes lying in bed trying to fall asleep. If you haven't drifted off, get up and do a relaxing activity until you feel sleepy again. Repeat this process until you fall asleep.

Improving Sleep

In general, most healthy adults are built for 16 hours of wakefulness and need an average of 7 or 8 hours of sleep a night. However, to some extent this varies by age.

Sometimes it seems that the more you need sleep, the harder it is to get it; stress is an important cause of short-term sleeping difficulties.

Often, sleep problems pass when a stressful situation gets resolved. However, if short-term sleep problems aren't handled properly from the beginning, they can persist long after the original stress has passed. Worrying about lack of sleep, for example, can make it even harder to relax at night, exacerbating insomnia.

 MYTH BUSTER

Think TV, video games, or social media can help you relax? Actually, bursts of light and sound from an electronic device can activate the attention-focusing part of the brain usually reserved for activities such as crossing a busy road. If you want to do something to help you fall asleep, do something boring!

The first step in improving sleep is developing good sleep habits. For example, here are some basic bedtime rules:

- Lower caffeine intake during the day, and avoid it altogether for four to six hours before bedtime.

- Avoid alcohol, nicotine, and heavy meals before bedtime.

- Go to bed and get up at the same time every day, and avoid naps longer than 20 minutes.

- Try to wake up without an alarm clock when possible.

- Minimize non-sleep-related activities such as TV watching or computer or phone use in the bedroom.

- Remove or minimize distractions. Use eye shades, ear plugs, or "white noise" if needed.

- Don't do anything too mentally or physically stimulating in the few hours before bedtime.

When Sleep Is Disrupted

Basic bedtime rules help you get ready for sleep. However, despite your best efforts, you will have the occasional bout of sleeplessness. During these times, the trick is to take some additional steps to promote sleep without panicking in the process:

- If you've had trouble falling asleep, don't let yourself sleep later or spend more time in bed. These strategies usually backfire.

- Let go of catastrophic thoughts such as "I'll get sick if I don't get enough sleep" or "I won't be able to function."

- Incorporate relaxation techniques into your bedtime routine. Consider listening to a relaxation CD before bedtime.

- Keep a sleep diary for a week, keeping track of what time you go to bed, what you're doing in the hour just before going to bed, what time you wake up, how often and how long you wake up after falling asleep, how long you slept, and how good it was. Tracking sleep in this way can help you become aware of your habits and see which ones might be worth changing. You might also notice positive patterns you can build on. If nothing else, having to write this all down helps remind you of your commitment to taking care of yourself by sleeping well.

As you can see, getting good sleep can be a challenge. On the one hand, there are many reports about the dangers of sleep deprivation: drowsy driving, less motivation, and more irritability. On the other hand, just because you need seven or eight hours of sleep doesn't mean you can always get this amount. And stressing about your lack of sleep—when it's stress that's causing your sleeplessness in the first place—can add fuel to the fire!

 STRESS RELIEF

Research shows that just *believing* you slept badly will affect you negatively the next day. One or two nights of bad sleep won't hurt the work performance of the average person on the average day, so keep that in mind.

In this chapter, we've explored the relationship between what you ingest and mood/anxiety. We've also explored the importance of sleep, how to develop good sleep habits, and what to do when sleep eludes you.

We've seen that poor nutrition and lack of sleep can make anxiety worse, and stress can make it harder to get enough sleep or make the right food choices. We've spent the last two chapters looking at how you can address this—that is, how you can strengthen yourself through exercise, relaxation, healthful eating, and adequate sleep.

In the next chapter, we shift our focus to exploring how life stressors affect you, how to evaluate your stress levels, and what coping strategies can restore your mental equilibrium.

The Least You Need to Know

- Your diet can impact your mood and anxiety levels.
- Most of us get adequate nutrition through our meals and don't need vitamin supplements.
- Investigate vitamin supplements and herbal remedies carefully before use; they can be as powerful as prescription drugs.
- Developing good sleep habits is vital.
- Stress is the number-one cause of short-term insomnia. The way you handle restless nights can either minimize their impact or contribute to a growing problem.

Reducing Stress

Monday—I'm stuck in traffic on my way to work. I'm running 15 minutes late. I can feel my heartbeat speeding up and my chest tightening. The minute I get to work, the boss dumps a ton of work on my desk and—oh great, my computer has crashed!

I try taking some deep breaths, and it helps a little. I have to keep taking breaks during the day because it's hard to concentrate.

Home isn't much better. My kids are unusually demanding, making a seemingly endless number of requests of me. My chest is very tight; I feel like screaming. I'd love to go for a long walk to calm down, but I can't leave the kids. I settle for a handful of cookies instead.

I know all this stress isn't good for me. I've read that it can put a strain on your heart and lower your immunity. But how do I manage my stress when I don't even have time to take a walk?

In This Chapter

- Learning the definition of stress
- Recognizing the symptoms of stress
- Taking an inventory of your coping mechanisms
- Buffering yourself from stress
- Finding out how severe traumas can affect you

Most of us have experienced some version of this. We all feel stressed at times; the daily hassles pile up, we suffer a major life event, or we just run out of the emotional resources to cope. Of course, some of us work best "under pressure," thriving on the "buzz" of energy we get from life's unexpected challenges. One person shines when her back is up against the wall; another says stress destroyed his marriage and sabotaged his career.

How much stress is too much? In this chapter, we look at what stress is and isn't, what is most likely to cause an unhealthy level of stress, and how to keep stress from getting the better of you.

What Is Stress?

"I'm so stressed out." Most of us have said this at some point. But what exactly *is* stress? Is it having a really bad day? Having too much to do? Dealing with a difficult person?

Actually, these pressures can build up and cause stress, but they're not "stress" in and of themselves. Stress is what you experience when you start feeling like the demands life is placing on you are greater than your resources for coping with them. A pending layoff might cause most of us to worry (and polish up a résumé); however, your level of stress will probably vary, depending on how easily you think you can get another job, how much your self-esteem is tied to your career, and how much savings you have in the bank.

Your stress level isn't just impacted by the immediate resources you have at your disposal. Positive habits you develop to take care of yourself—humor, self-awareness, relaxation, creating pleasurable experiences, exercise—can reduce stress. These daily uplifts can build up your mental reserves, making it easier to marshal your coping mechanisms when faced with a tough life circumstance.

 ON THE CUTTING EDGE

New research suggests that people who respond poorly to stressful situations are likely to have higher-than-normal levels of cholesterol, which have been connected with heart problems.

Symptoms of Stress

As you've seen, stress is what you experience when you feel overwhelmed by what you have on your plate. Not surprisingly, the belief that you don't have the resources to cope with life's demands is likely to cause symptoms of stress. Some of the most common stress symptoms are included in the following table.

Physical Symptoms	Psychological Symptoms	Behavioral Symptoms
Muscle tension (clenched jaw, grinding teeth, tight shoulders)	Sensitivity to criticism/being critical of others	Insomnia
Increased blood pressure	Moodiness (tension, irritability)	Appetite changes
Restlessness, fidgeting	Concentration problems	Withdrawing from others
Headaches, stomachaches, indigestion	Indecision	Less self-control (smoking, drinking, overeating)
Shallow breathing	Rigid thinking, no sense of humor	Verbal outbursts

As you look through these, perhaps you notice that, although unpleasant, some of these symptoms can serve a useful purpose. Essentially, they reflect a narrowing of your focus and energy to the threat at hand. However, it's the side effects that you have to watch out for. For example, because it's so all consuming, stress can adversely impact your ability to communicate clearly, to control your behavior, or to be sensitive to others. In addition, your mental attention gets locked on your problems, and you can become rigid in your decisions, despite the facts.

 MYTH BUSTER

"No symptoms, no stress, right?" Well, perhaps. Some medications can mask the symptoms commonly associated with stress. Be sure any prescription medication isn't covering up stress symptoms. And remember, stress affects us all differently—your symptoms won't exactly match someone else's.

The Right Amount of Stress

We all know that sometimes a little stress helps us get things done. Deadlines can provide the adrenaline boost you need to finish a daunting task. In moderation, stress is a motivator; it can rally your resources, wake you up, and get you moving. The trick is to find the balance between too little stress and too much. No one ever made it to the Olympics without performance stress; on the other hand, too much pressure leads to mistakes, not medals.

As we noted in Chapter 1 in discussing the Yerkes-Dodson findings, researchers have found that the relationship between arousal (or anxiety/stress level) and performance is like an inverted U: too little or too much and you can't focus properly. If you feel motivated *and* able to concentrate, focused on the task at hand but able to retain a sense of composure, and open to broader thinking and different ways of accomplishing the task, then you're in the peak performance zone.

But if you cross over the stress threshold, your performance deteriorates. A bank robber was once caught red-handed simply because he couldn't open a door. Loot in hand, he repeatedly tried to push the door—even though the sign "Pull" was clearly visible. It was as if his mind "froze," and he kept pushing and pushing the door—until the police arrived.

 ON THE CUTTING EDGE

Stressful situations can interfere with mental agility. Studies at The Ohio State University have found that stressed research subjects were less capable of solving problems and word puzzles than those who were at ease and calm.

A Coping Inventory

Celebrities are known to suffer from more than their fair share of stress. Busy work schedules, little privacy, numerous critics, and the unpredictability of the public are great potential stressors. But celebrities are not the only people who experience substantial stress. Ask yourself the following questions to see how well you are coping with your stress:

- **How would you summarize your friendships?** A supportive network of friends and acquaintances is one of the most powerful buffers against stress. It's not just the number of friends, though; it's how available they are, how often you contact them, and how much you can trust and confide in them.

- **How do you use your free time?** Having hobbies and outside interests is a great way to keep active and emotionally fit. However, if they leave you with no "downtime," they themselves can cause stress. Consider leisure activities that balance your life: an exciting activity like bungee jumping might liven up a boring work routine; a reading group might be a relaxing break from a high-stress job.

- **Have you experienced significant changes in your life over the past year?** Any significant life event will stir emotions. Don't overlook the stress of positive changes. A wedding, for instance, can cause tremendous stress. And be especially tuned in to the stress of loss, which can overwhelm many of us. Acknowledge the normal emotional wear and tear following a loss, and give yourself time to recover.

- **How are things at your job?** Too much responsibility (work overload, unrealistic expectations) in combination with too little control (demanding boss, conflicting or unclear communication) is a poisonous combination influencing work-related stress. And work stress can be particularly hazardous because most of us spend more time there than anywhere else during our waking hours.

- **How do you feel at the end of the day?** Do you dwell on all that's happened? Can you unwind, or do you feel tense yet exhausted? Your ability to unwind at the end of the day is a powerful indicator of how your coping mechanisms are working.

 ON THE CUTTING EDGE

Recent research has produced the first-ever visualization of psychological stress in the brain. During a "stress test," MRI scans showed increased blood flow in the prefrontal cortex, an area long associated with anxiety and depression as well as working memory and goal-oriented behavior. Interestingly, the blood flow continued even after the test was completed.

Buffers Against Stress

After five years working nights with a demanding boss and trying to raise a family, Sarah decided enough was enough. She quit. Within three weeks, she found a new job with better hours and a better boss, and it was closer to home. Her lower stress more than made up for the slight reduction in pay.

When Bill's father was diagnosed with cancer and had to move in with him, it brought their longstanding relationship problems to the fore. Bill struggled with often feeling angry and short-tempered with his father—and then feeling guilty about it. When a friend commented one day that Bill was lucky to have this special time with his father, it gave him some food for thought. He made more of an effort to get to know his father and better understand the choices and actions he had made. It didn't change his father's personality or make up for past tensions, but Bill was surprised that it did take away his resentment and give him a sense of peace.

Greg's world imploded when his daughter died. He felt anger over his loss and resentful toward his friends who had healthy, happy children. Only when his marriage began to deteriorate did he agree to attend a support group for grieving parents. As he listened to parents who had gone through similar experiences, he felt less alone. Three years later, Greg's marriage is great, and he's started a research foundation to find a cure for the illness that took his daughter's life.

Sarah, Bill, and Greg each found ways to channel their stress into positive action. Sarah was able to remove herself from the stressor. Bill and Greg had to first deal with the emotions around their stressful life event before they could decide what to do. You can deal with stress in a lot of ways, and the most effective strategy depends on how much control you have over it and how intense your feelings are about it.

Taking Action

When Sarah couldn't renegotiate her work hours or get transferred to a better boss, she decided to change her situation. This decision didn't come easily; she had to first look at the risks versus the rewards, deal with the fear and uncertainty of potential unemployment, and initially exert more effort (preparing a résumé and conducting a job search) when she already felt exhausted.

When experiencing stress, one of the most useful questions to ask yourself is "What do I have control over, and what can't I change?" For instance, you may not be able to change the uncomfortable physical sensations that accompany panic, but you can change how you interpret them (unpleasant but not dangerous). You can keep them from controlling your life by refusing to avoid situations where you have felt panicked before. Similarly, you can't change a power-hungry manager, but you can "watch your back" by putting everything in writing and figuring out how to defuse his tactics.

Dealing with Uncomfortable Feelings

On the other hand, perhaps—like Bill or Greg—the stressor in your life isn't something you can control. Unfortunately, you can't make a life-threatening illness, the loss of a loved one, or a company merger disappear. During times like these, it's easy to feel helpless and out of control. But even in these situations, there are things you can do. You can change the story you tell yourself about what's happened; you can develop the skills to more effectively manage your feelings; you can surround yourself with caring people; and you can use your grief or fear to get more information or help others.

For instance, imagine how your stress would differ if you interpreted a company merger with a neutral, "let's wait and see" attitude versus a career-threatened panic. It doesn't mean you shouldn't go ahead and polish up that résumé (prepare for the worst) or do some research on the success rate of similar mergers; but you're staying with the facts versus embellishing them with catastrophic interpretations.

ANXIETY ATTACK

Yet another reason to tackle stress: research has found a link between dieting, stress, and overeating. A combination of deprivation (such as dieting) plus stress causes a "hedonic deprivation state," a craving for something pleasurable. "Comfort foods" high in fat and sugar were found to mimic opioids, the brain's natural pleasure chemicals.

Emotion-focused coping, as opposed to active problem solving, is a way to manage the negative feelings toward your stressor. On the positive side, emotion-focused coping strategies such as relaxation and distraction can help you pay more attention to what your emotions are telling you and free you from obsessive worrying. On the other hand, you don't want to use these strategies as a replacement for dealing directly with aspects of your stressor that you can control: crying on a girlfriend's shoulder may make you feel better, but it does nothing to get you out of an abusive relationship.

Even in situations that seem unavoidably stressful, there are often ways to cope. For instance, the book *Full Catastrophe Living* by Jon Kabat-Zinn is highly recommended for people experiencing the stress of chronic pain or illness.

Developing Resources

Imagine you've just found out your life depends on completing a marathon that will take place in four weeks. With that kind of motivation, most of us could muster our way through. But think what an advantage you'd start with if you were already working out.

Developing resources to manage stress is similar. Situational stressors often require tailor-made responses; but living a healthful lifestyle, knowing yourself, and developing an arsenal of coping skills give you a head start when life gets tougher. Studies confirm that people who are clear about who they are and where they want to go are better able to handle stress. In particular, those who take preparation time seriously are less stressed. Researchers at ULCA, for example, found lower levels of the stress hormone cortisol in people who had been asked to think about their values and priorities before being subjected to a stressful experience.

STRESS RELIEF

Use a mental picture as a calming anchor. For example, develop a mental picture of your ideal place (for example, a beach or a mountain scene) and practice conjuring it up at the same time you focus on slowing your breathing; the more detail you can insert, the better. Pair this scene with relaxation often enough, and you can take it anywhere you go.

Create a Stress Journal

In a life filled with daily hassles, it can be hard to keep track of your stressors, the emotional reactions you have to them, and what you do when you encounter them. Keeping a stress diary for a couple of weeks can help you connect the dots between your external reality and internal stress and provide insight into what you're doing right and what's not working. This helps you to separate the common, routine stressors from those that occur only occasionally.

To get started, buy a notebook and record your stress ratings for 14 days. Make a note every hour or so, particularly when you notice stress symptoms.

Here's a typical stress diary entry:

<u>Monday, 10 A.M.</u>

Happiness level: (Scale of −10 to +10) +4

Mood: I feel relieved that I wasn't late for work!

Work efficiency: (0–10) 6

Stress level: (0–10) 3

Most recent stressful event: Thinking about the presentation I need to give next week

Stress symptom felt: Butterflies, sweaty palms

Cause of stress: Worrying I'll look stupid

My chosen reaction: At first I panicked, but then I relaxed my breathing and thought about how to prepare for the presentation. The stress dropped.

After you've collected your 14 days' worth of data, use the following sheet to look for patterns:

Part 1: My Stressors
Most commonly occurring stressful events
Most commonly occurring specific stress triggers
Events rated as most stressful

Part 2: My Reactions
Most common chosen reaction
How well did each chosen reaction in the row above work?
For reactions that did not work well, what could I have done instead?

By the end of this exercise, you'll have a pretty good handle on recurring stress triggers, how they impact you, and how you try to manage them. You'll also get a sense of the effectiveness of your current coping strategies and can begin to think about alternatives that might work better.

 STRESS RELIEF

Believe it or not, for most of us, the daily hassles (work overload, a chronically procrastinating child, an unreliable car) cause more stress than big life events. Don't let these pile up just because they aren't crises!

Communication Under Stress

Given enough pressure, a normally expressive, assertive communication style can turn into quick-tempered explosiveness. Similarly, a normally efficient, bottom-line communication style can transform into a dictatorial style.

Your communication style can change under stress. You respond to internal cues that tell you you're in a crisis and have to do something drastic to "survive." You try to reduce your stress, regardless of your tactic's effectiveness or the feelings of others. In essence, you resort to a fallback mode. Your typical communication style may become exaggerated and inflexible:

- The emotionally responsive, assertive person may become aggressive.

- The bottom-line leader may become controlling.

- The reserved, cooperative person may become overly ingratiating.

- The quiet, analytical person may become avoidant.

This fallback mode is an extreme manifestation of your normal communication style. It is yourself at your most primitive. As you grow and develop, your interpersonal skills are less primitive; you have wisdom and more strategies to choose from; and you're able to respond to the cues of the interpersonal situation you're in. When you experience enough stress, though, you often wind up using old, outdated communication strategies that are ineffective but make you feel safe. This is your fallback communication mode.

As such, although your fallback mode can disrupt relationships, it serves a good purpose by helping to reduce your stress. Thus, it is often not helpful to tell an acutely stressed person to "snap out of it" or point out how ineffectively she is communicating. What *is* helpful is to learn to recognize the signs of a fallback communication mode and develop strategies for minimizing its impact on your relationships.

Keeping Cool Under Pressure

One key to a happy long-term relationship is to learn to recognize stress signals in each other and adjust your behavior accordingly. When you see a work colleague or a loved one losing his or her cool, to avoid becoming equally stressed (and responding with your own fallback behavior), use the following strategies:

- **Don't take it personally.** Remind yourself that a fallback communication mode is a survival strategy rather than a personal attack or a plot against you.

- **Avoid analysis paralysis.** If you're drowning, the last thing you need to do is puzzle over how you fell in the ocean. You need a lifeboat. Avoid theoretical discussions or explanations for how the current situation came about; instead, engage in crisis management by focusing on realistic, short-term goals.

- **Sidestep fallback communication.** Don't waste your breath trying to get someone to stop using a fallback communication style. If they could, they would. Instead, minimize the damage this crisis communication style can have on interpersonal relationships. For instance, if you're a manager, teach your employees to recognize their fallback communication signals, and encourage them to find ways to vent their stress without passing it on to someone else.

Odds are that you, too, will occasionally find yourself in fallback communication mode. When this happens, here are things you can do to relieve the pressure in the short-run without increasing stress over time:

- **Postpone what you can.** When you're operating under extreme stress, you're much more likely to say or do things you later regret. This is the time to reschedule meetings or postpone appointments if possible and avoid making major life decisions.

- **Get feedback from others.** It's hard to see yourself clearly, especially when you're clouded with emotion. Getting a view of yourself from the eyes of the people around you can provide powerful clues for further personal and professional development in the context of stress.

- **Acknowledge that you're in fallback mode.** Without judging it, simply notice it and remind yourself that it's a sign of stress. That can be your cue to slow down, take a breath, and refocus on your goals. In those few moments, you can recommit to mindfully using your intended communication style.

- **Imagine that your fallback communication is being recorded on video.** Is this the side of yourself you want others to see? This outside perspective can make it easier to catch yourself and realign your behavior with your goals.

- **Take a walk.** Even a 15-second walk down the hall and back can help you shake off the intense feeling driving your panicked fallback behavior.

 MYTH BUSTER

"Stress is a sign of spiritual weakness." Although faith can be a source of great strength, it does not make you immune to stress. Stress is a natural motivator designed to help you improve and move you to do better.

Responses to Severe Trauma

If upsetting life events and daily hassles can take such a toll on your mental health, imagine what a catastrophe can do. An extreme emotional reaction to trauma is normal; even the most resilient among us will feel devastated or frightened after a life-threatening or life-altering event. Depending on the nature of the trauma, your exposure to previous trauma, your pre-event mental health, and your internal and external resources, these natural emotions may or may not lead to a clinical disorder.

Within the first month of surviving a violent assault, intense combat, or another severe stressor, a survivor often experiences unwanted memories, emotional numbing, and a sense of danger. Other symptoms can include irritability, sleep problems, and being easily startled.

If the symptoms persist longer than four weeks and are severe enough to interfere with the person's life, a diagnosis of *post-traumatic stress disorder* may be applicable. PTSD is a condition in which a person continues to be affected by trauma even though it may have happened years ago.

Symptoms include the following:

- Having intrusive memories of the trauma, possibly including flashbacks, while awake or asleep

- Avoiding people, places, and things that remind the person of the initial trauma

- Changes in feelings and thoughts—numbness, losing interest in activities, feeling isolated, and feeling that the world is a dangerous place

- Hyperarousal—feeling on guard, overreacting to noise or other environmental cues, and loss of sleep and concentration

Most serious trauma survivors do not develop or have persistent post-traumatic stress disorder. In fact, PTSD is another example of how stress is a result of both what happens to you (the nature and severity of the stressor) and the resources (genetic, social, and so forth) you have to cope with it.

If you are experiencing PTSD or less extreme post-traumatic symptoms, it is important to get help. Researchers have identified several PTSD treatments that are effective across a range of different traumas, such as cognitive processing therapy, prolonged exposure therapy, and eye movement desensitization and reprocessing, which must be conducted by a specially trained therapist. Many people find relief through a combination of talk therapy and medication

The National Center for PTSD (ptsd.va.gov/public) is an excellent source of information about PTSD and learnable skills that can help with everyday living. They offer many free tools for self-help, including a mobile phone app and an online PTSD coach with very short, accessible videos.

Each of us experiences stressors, whether they come as minor hassles, moderate life events, or extreme trauma. How well and how easily you cope with them is a combination of both skill and luck, how resilient your genetic makeup is, how stressful your life experience is, and how well you've built up your resources. In the next chapter, we take a look at an extreme stress response, often without a clear stressor: panic disorder.

The Least You Need to Know

- Recognize your stress levels by being conscious of how narrow your focus is becoming.
- Keep a stress diary to understand your sources of stress and how stress affects you.
- Use three stress-busting tools—taking action, dealing with uncomfortable emotions, and developing coping skills.
- Recognize stressed communication styles in yourself and others.
- Understand that severe trauma can cause serious difficulties, but that this is not inevitable.

Survive-and-Thrive Strategies for Diagnosed Distress

Now that you've strengthened your mental resilience and physical well-being, we turn your attention to three of the "big guns"—the clinically diagnosed anxiety disorders. From panic disorder to social anxiety, we look at the most effective strategies for coping with physical symptoms, disrupting irrational thoughts, and reentering fearful situations. We then consider the evidence on the most effective treatment for anxiety and how you can ensure that your treatment team is up to the challenge.

Self-Help for Panic Disorder

Drs. Jack Loehr and Jack Groppel, founders of LGE Performance Systems, use this story as part of their corporate training: a group of NFL superstars is given a mission. They must follow a wilderness trail for one mile, touch a white fence, and return to the training center in less than 18 minutes. For such elite runners, this should be easy. However, before the run begins, the runners are warned to look out for water moccasins, alligators, and wild boars in the area. "If you see a wild boar," says the instructor, "take appropriate action, but complete the mission!"

The run begins. A staff member is planted in the bushes at the half-mile mark; when a runner reaches this point, the hidden instructor makes the sound of a wild boar. Inevitably, in spite of their instructions and with no visible evidence of a wild animal bearing down on them, the runners panic and sprint back to the starting point. The only explanation offered for the failed mission? "I heard something."

In This Chapter

- Learning about emotional hijacking
- Discovering the difference between a panic attack and panic disorder
- Finding out why panic attacks aren't the real problem
- Developing panic attack coping skills

This same "wild boar" exercise, when given to elite law-enforcement or military units, yields dramatically different results. Trained to respond to threats, these individuals stop, turn in the direction of the threat, and assume a crouched position. As a result, they quickly determine that there is no wild boar and are able to complete the mission.

For panic sufferers, this story makes some powerful points. First, fear can overpower *anyone's* rational thought. Second, there's a difference between being "tough" and being prepared; law-enforcement personnel felt the same rush of adrenaline and fear that the other trainees did. Their training didn't prevent them from *feeling* fear; it just prevented them from *giving in* to it.

For the three million Americans who have panic attacks, "wild boars" can show up anywhere at any time—at the grocery store, in the pediatrician's office, or at work. Suddenly, we experience the terror people feel when faced with life-threatening danger—and the same urge to escape. This chapter is all about training yourself to respond like Green Berets when you face your own "wild boars."

Emotional Hijacking

Panic disorder sufferers have overwhelming anxiety symptoms spontaneously. The *amygdala*, the danger-response center in your brain's limbic system, seems to become activated for no reason. Although the amygdala is a fairly primitive brain structure, it has a very important job: to ensure your survival.

In fact, the amygdala is extremely important. It has the ability to respond directly to input from your senses before your brain's more rational portion—the neocortex—even begins to register this input. For example, your amygdala can spur you to turn the wheel in response to an oncoming car before you have time to think. The limbic system is one of the oldest parts of your brain evolutionarily; what it lacks in rational thinking it makes up for in speed and action.

 **MYTH BUSTER**

> *"I'm having a heart attack!"* A rapid heartbeat might make you think so, but a healthy heart can beat rapidly for a long time without causing any damage.

Dan Goleman, the author of *Emotional Intelligence*, used the term *emotional hijacking* to refer to situations in which your rational mind is taken over by your emotional response. The problem with emotional hijacking is that it doesn't always result in heroics; emotional hijacking can lead to road rage, domestic violence, and countless other harmful or counterproductive acts. And with panic attacks, the alarm signals go off needlessly; there is no real danger you need to protect yourself from.

Panic Attacks and Panic Disorder

Panic attacks have their origins in your brain, but this doesn't mean the symptoms aren't "real." In fact, many panic symptoms are experienced in your body. Common symptoms include the following:

- Racing or pounding heart

- Dizziness or lightheadedness

- Nausea

- Terror or a sense of impending doom

- A sense of unreality

- Fear of dying, losing control, or doing something embarrassing

- Flushes or chills

- Chest pains

- Tingling or numbness in the hands

- Difficulty breathing

Not everyone experiences *all* of these symptoms, but all panic attack sufferers experience some of them. Not only are the symptoms themselves terrifying, they're unpredictable. At first panic attacks often occur "out of the blue," when you're doing something ordinary like driving to work, having dinner with friends, sitting on the sofa watching TV, or even sleeping. Because they are so terrifying and mimic primary physical problems, many people drive themselves (or get a ride) to an emergency room after having their first attack.

Not everyone who has a panic attack develops a panic disorder. A fortunate few experience one panic attack and never have another. Others—up to 10 percent of otherwise healthy Americans—have them occasionally but continue to lead unrestricted lives. In fact, it's not the number of panic attacks that determines whether a person develops panic disorder; *it's the response you have to them.*

For 1 in 75 U.S. citizens, though, the first panic attack sets in motion a vicious cycle. The fear of another panic attack—of having to go through those distressing symptoms again—causes the panic attack sufferer to worry about having another one. You may avoid situations in which you have experienced panic attacks in the past. As a result, even when you are not in the grip of an attack, you're consumed with the desire to avoid one.

MYTH BUSTER

"I'm going to lose my mind!" It is extremely uncomfortable to have a spontaneous panic attack, and panic sufferers rightly note that their emotions are out of control during attacks. But panic sufferers are aware of how irrational the symptoms are; they haven't lost touch with reality.

Others May Not "Get It"

Unfortunately, the people you rely on to help or support you can unintentionally make things worse. Physicians, for example, sometimes do not recognize panic disorder. Many panic attack sufferers see as many as 10 doctors before meeting one who makes the right diagnosis. In the meantime, they've undergone all sorts of unnecessary, expensive, and anxiety-provoking tests!

Then when they finally meet a medical professional who identifies panic disorder, the explanation often sounds as if there is nothing *really* wrong. *"There's nothing to worry about; you're just having a panic attack"* or *"It's just nerves."* Although meant to be reassuring, such words can be dispiriting to the frantic person whose terrifying symptoms keep recurring.

The same can be true of well-meaning friends and family members. People who've never had a panic attack sometimes assume that it's just a matter of feeling nervous or anxious—the sort of feelings that everyone is familiar with. *I was so nervous about that test I almost had a panic attack! I just panicked at the thought of my boss realizing I hadn't quite finished that project.*

A friend and fellow panic attack sufferer once told Joni that, during the worst period of her life, she had disclosed her experience of panic attacks to a work colleague, who responded with something like, "You know, I get pretty uptight about things sometimes. I wonder if I have panic attacks." Joni's friend comically asked her co-worker if she knew of any new mothers who *wondered* whether or not they had experienced labor pains. If you've had them, you know it. If you haven't, there's no way anyone can adequately describe them to you.

Panic, Phobias, and Other Problems

We've already outlined the vicious cycle characteristic of panic disorder: panic attacks trigger intense fears of having others and a strong motivation to avoid panic-associated situations and sensations. If you have a panic attack while in a crowded store, you may avoid the store when it's crowded. If you have two or three panic attacks in stores, you may avoid stores altogether. If your panic attacks begin with palpitations and shortness of breath, you may avoid exercise. Even if you know logically that the situation or sensation did not cause the panic attack, the fact that the two are associated can make you fearful that revisiting the same situation or sensation will bring on another attack. If your fear leads to avoidance of a situation or sensation, you could have a panic-induced phobia.

Of course, people who suffer from phobias can have intense anxiety or even panic attacks in the presence of the feared object or situation. Social anxiety sufferers, for example, might have panic attacks only in distressing social situations. A person who has a spider phobia may be so afraid of them that just seeing a tarantula on TV triggers a panic attack. In these cases, the panic attack did not "cause" the phobia; rather, the irrational fear of the object or situation caused the panic attack. We discuss self-help strategies for phobias in Chapters 15 and 16.

ANXIETY ATTACK

Like many other anxiety disorders, panic disorder seems to be due to a combination of biological vulnerability and life experiences. Panic attacks often start during a stressful period in a person's life.

When panic attacks occur randomly and frequently, you can come to fear any situation in which you can't easily escape. This is called *agoraphobia,* and it affects about one third of people with panic disorder. Other mental and physical conditions that can coexist with panic disorder include the following:

- **Depression.** Affects about half of all panic disorder sufferers.

- **Alcohol and drug abuse.** About 30 percent of patients with panic disorder misuse alcohol; 17 percent misuse other substances.

- **Irritable bowel syndrome.** When someone has IBS, panic disorder may be overlooked as a contributing cause of the symptoms.

- **Mitral valve prolapse.** This is a generally benign heart condition that can lead to chest pain, rapid heartbeat, breathing difficulties, and headache. Some experts think that people with this defect are more likely to develop panic disorder.

Because spontaneous panic attacks are so disturbing, they can quickly take over your life. Not only can they impact day-to-day activities, your attempts to avoid them can create additional problems. The good news is that you can learn to cope with panic attacks. They don't have to lead to panic disorder, depression, or social isolation.

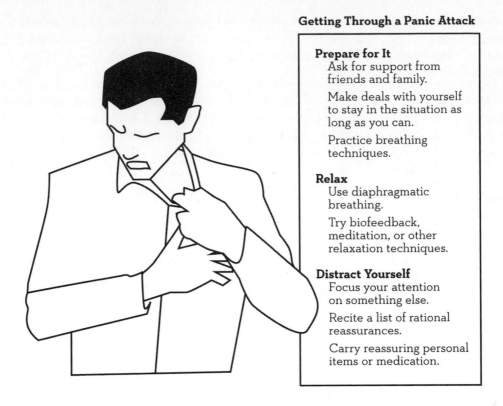

Getting Through a Panic Attack

Prepare for It
Ask for support from friends and family.

Make deals with yourself to stay in the situation as long as you can.

Practice breathing techniques.

Relax
Use diaphragmatic breathing.

Try biofeedback, meditation, or other relaxation techniques.

Distract Yourself
Focus your attention on something else.

Recite a list of rational reassurances.

Carry reassuring personal items or medication.

Preparing for a Panic Attack

Whether or not you get professional help, you can do a lot to overcome your panic attacks. It might be hard to imagine right now, but you can prepare for panic ahead of time, building up your coping skills so that you are able to cope with your symptoms and, over time, reduce the number or severity of attacks you have. Think of it as panic attack training camp, equivalent to the elite military training that enabled the soldiers and law-enforcement professionals to succeed in the story at the beginning of this chapter.

You will also be in charge of how hard you work and how quickly you progress. Before we get to specifics, though, make sure you have the right attitude.

 ANXIETY ATTACK

To jump-start your self-help program, visit panic-attacks.co.uk for a free online course.

Evaluate your progress in terms of what you *do*, not how you *feel*. The more you are able to remain in an uncomfortable situation *despite* anxiety or panic, the more progress you will make in taking away the grip your distress currently holds on you.

Expect the beginning to be the hardest. Why is it that the first 10 minutes of an exercise routine are the hardest? It's true for new exercisers as well as seasoned athletes. The difference between those who stick with it and those who don't is commitment coupled with frequent self-reminders that the initial discomfort will pass, and the end result will be worth it.

Make deals with yourself. It takes a leap of faith to stop running from panic attacks and turn around to face them. You may find a part of yourself "shouting" to get out of there, while another part is struggling to stay put; when this happens, strike a bargain. If your anxiety is a "9/10," try to stay in the situation until it subsides to a "5/10." If you have to leave, go back in when the panic subsides. Feel good about each step forward, no matter how small.

In addition to these empowering attitudes, examine your beliefs about asking for help. You may hide your panic symptoms from friends and family or feel tremendous guilt because your panic attacks are disrupting your home life. As a result, many of us don't get social support that can help us get through the stress and help us stretch ourselves. While you're helping yourself, why not let your family help? They can be valuable cheerleaders, especially when they see you trying hard to overcome obstacles.

Therapists, support group members, and online communities can also be resources, including in the middle of a panic attack. Some panic sufferers carry a list of phone numbers they can call day or night—though they might never have used it. Having outside resources can help you feel stronger; in fact, just knowing you have the option of calling someone at the peak of your anxiety can give you the courage to stay in a frightening situation until the symptoms resolve.

 ANXIETY ATTACK

An additional resource for panic attack sufferers is the National Institute of Mental Health's Hotline: 888-826-9438.

Relaxation

Since panic attacks make you feel so mentally and physically out of control, skills that help you relax are useful. For instance, the hyperventilation that often accompanies a panic attack can be countered—or prevented—by diaphragmatic breathing.

The middle of a panic attack is no time to learn new breathing techniques; but if you practice breathing techniques for five minutes twice a day for a few weeks, you can perform them more easily when you feel the onset of panic symptoms. The kind of steady, consistent breathing practice outlined here will get your body in the habit of always breathing deeply and slowly. This will decrease and may eliminate panic attacks while at the same time reducing your anxiety.

1. Begin by lying flat on your back or standing up straight. You may also sit up straight in a chair, if that is more comfortable.

2. Place your hand on your stomach area.

3. Breathe as you normally would and notice whether your hand rises or your chest rises. To breathe properly, your stomach area must rise as your diaphragm expands.

4. Begin by slowly breathing in through your nose to the count of five while gently pushing your hand up with your stomach.

5. Hold the breath for a count of five.

6. Slowly exhale through your mouth for a count of five while gently pushing down on your stomach.

7. Repeat this process for five minutes.

Any activity (biofeedback, progressive muscle relaxation, meditation) that helps you become familiar with how your body feels when you are under stress can help you consciously relax. Numerous meditation and relaxation exercises are available on CD or video.

Don't get frustrated or impatient with yourself and give up if you cannot do these exercises correctly right away—or if you feel yourself panicking when you try them. They take practice. In the beginning, do them only as long as you are able. Remember that you can stop at any time. Take it slowly if necessary.

If you continue to practice your breathing techniques or other relaxation exercises, you will soon be more naturally relaxed throughout the day. As you gain more awareness and control over your body, you will be able to tolerate daily hassles and minor stressors with a greater sense of calm and peace.

 ANXIETY ATTACK

Because the physical sensations (rapid heartbeat and breathing) during aerobic exercise can closely match those of panic attacks, some panic suffers have trouble with aerobic exercise. Even if intense aerobic exercise seems overwhelming, you can engage in other health-boosting activities, such as leisurely walking or swimming.

Distraction

In addition to bodily discomfort, panic attacks can set off a spiral of fear. Your thoughts begin to race, filling you with dire predictions that you are going to pass out, die, make a fool of yourself, or lose control. The sooner you can interrupt this spiral, the more you can allow your uncomfortable anxiety symptoms to pass through you without overwhelming you.

The best way to control catastrophic thoughts is to focus your attention on something else, something simple enough that you can do it while you're very anxious. This is not the time, for example, to try to rationally combat irrational thoughts. On the other hand, your mental exercise must be complex enough that it requires some effort. Turning your breathing exercise into a mental activity is one idea; you might count each inhale and each exhale. You could perform simple arithmetic (counting backward or reciting the multiplication tables), repeat the words to a favorite song or poem, focus on memorizing the details of your environment, or play simple word games. It doesn't matter what it is as long as it keeps you from "what ifs" and grounds you in the present.

One potentially useful distraction is to repeatedly recite a list of rational reassurances that you have memorized or written down. *These symptoms are unpleasant but they're not dangerous. This is just my alarm system going off. These feelings have passed before and they'll pass again. What doesn't kill me makes me stronger.*

You'll probably find clues to the most effective reassurances by examining the self-talk that typically surfaces during a panic attack. Think back to the automatic thoughts you had during your last panic attack and write out a rational reassurance in response. For example, if one of your thoughts was *"I can't stand this!"* consider something like *"I've been through this before. It's not fun, but I can stand it."*

What personal items tend to calm you? A journal? An MP3 player with a favorite playlist? A rosary? A cell phone? Anything you can carry with you that will help you feel more secure can be helpful. Some people keep an antianxiety medication with them even if they don't really need it. Knowing they *could* take a pill can give extra courage and confidence to keep moving forward.

 MYTH BUSTER

> *"I'm going to pass out!"* A sudden drop in blood pressure is what causes fainting. However, heart rate and blood pressure typically rise during a panic attack, so you are probably not going to faint.

Approach Panic Differently

When Joni was at the mercy of her panic symptoms, she felt like a slave. Her panic attacks would come out of nowhere and "hijack" her feelings and thoughts. All she could do was react; all she could focus on was survival.

However, as she learned ways to prepare for panic, this began to change. Instead of feeling powerless, she began to feel an increasing sense of mastery about what she could do when panic occurred. She and many other panic sufferers have discovered a paradox: the less she feared panic attacks, the less frequent and less intense they were. When she tried to avoid them, they hung on tighter; when she quit fighting, they loosened their grip.

Just knowing this, however, doesn't make it easy. To handle panic in this way is to go against your basic instincts. Logic tells you that, in a situation that feels threatening, you should turn on your emergency responses, tense your body, and get ready to fight or run before you get hurt. What you need to do, though, is turn on your controlled breathing, relax your muscles, not fight your physical sensations, and stay in the situation. Martial artists know these tricks well. Someone who doesn't know how to fight will let his or her anger take over, will wildly attack someone, and will likely end up getting hurt. A trained martial arts expert will stay calm, controlled, and focused—and will be much more likely to win a fight.

Refusing to Give In

With anxiety, the very act of choosing to relax in response to panic helps the neocortex (the rational portion of your brain) to tamp down the alarm from the amygdala.

Refusing to give in to your panic symptoms allows you to think about them differently. Instead of doing all you can to avoid those feelings, you can take an interest in them, even get scientific about them. For example, you can create a worksheet like the following to track your systems. Use a simple symptom severity scale—1 signals complete relaxation, and 10 indicates outright panic. Practice doing this when you have symptoms and when you don't. Notice which thoughts and actions raise or lower the rating. Notice that, even at their worst, panic symptoms actually have a very short life. They can't stay at a very high intensity for more than a few seconds.

Time and Place	Anxiety Level (1 to 10)	What I've Been Doing	What I've Been Thinking	Recent Caffeine Intake	How Long Anxiety Stayed at This Level (for Ratings Over 8)
3:30 P.M. at work	3	Working quietly on a report	*It's been a pretty good day.*	None since breakfast	
9:00 P.M. at home	9	Watching TV	*I should be working on that report due tomorrow* and *I'm having a heart attack.*	Diet Coke at 8:30 P.M.	Less than a minute, then dropped to 8, then 7, then 6

Investigating your symptoms gives your thinking a focus, making it less susceptible to emotional hijacking. If you're busy observing your symptoms, you're not as caught up fighting or escaping from them. In fact, when you learn to observe your panic symptoms without resisting them, you may consider purposefully *increasing* them.

Advanced Training

When you're having trouble tolerating your panic symptoms, it can seem impossible to consider *inviting* them. Yet, when you consider how much the unpredictability of panic attacks contributes to the damage they cause, you can see how empowering it would be to consciously seek them out.

Cognitive behavioral therapists often encourage patients to invite anxiety symptoms in the controlled environment of therapy sessions, so the patients can have the experience that these harmless (but seemingly life-threatening) symptoms don't have to be so frightening. For example, a patient who hyperventilates during a panic attack might be instructed to breathe rapidly; a patient who gets dizzy might be encouraged to spin around and around. A patient may be asked to respond to mild symptoms by consciously attempting to make them worse—letting their anxiety be present until it decreases on its own. All of these exercises allow the panic attack sufferer to start to experience symptoms as they are (harmless), not what they seem to be (dangerous).

Panic disorder develops when you repeatedly try to control or avoid your anxiety—and fail. By embracing your anxiety, you don't set yourself up for failure. As you get better at tolerating your symptoms, you can stay put long enough to calm a bit so your mind can register that there's no real danger in the situation.

Think about any new activity you felt nervous about. Maybe you sang in church or gave a school presentation. Maybe it was asking your girlfriend out on a date or going on your first job interview. It was nerve-wracking at first, but you became more comfortable as you got used to it; your brain recognized you weren't in danger and called off the "red alert." As a result, your butterflies subsided and your heart quit beating so fast.

 MYTH BUSTER

> *"I might lose control during a panic attack."* Some people with panic disorder are afraid they'll either become totally paralyzed or run around wildly, yelling obscenities and hurting other people. But these are cognitive distortions due to intense anxiety symptoms.

Here's another analogy. Imagine a new security system installed in your house has a bug in it. As a result, it occasionally triggers a false alarm. Imagine the police showed up in response—and you tried to keep them out of the house, shouting, "There's no danger!" through the door. Without question, they would insist on coming in to make sure you're safe. The tighter you held the door shut, the more insistent they'd become. On the other hand, if you sheepishly invited them in and assured them you had no emergency, they'd look around the house and leave. If this happened often enough, they might just call to ensure it's a false alarm.

Practice

Initially, as you learn to stay put in panic situations, the goal is to keep your discomfort zone from spreading. Make a pact with yourself that you *will not* leave a situation until your anxiety subsides. If the anxiety is intense, give yourself a small but manageable goal: "I will leave in 20 seconds" or "I will go down one more aisle and then leave." The idea is to delay your exit long enough for the panic to subside—and it *will* subside; the most frightening part of a panic attack rarely lasts longer than 10 to 20 seconds.

When your goal is met, leave if you have to. But go back to the situation as soon as possible. The longer you delay returning, the harder it will be. Spend as much time as possible in the anxiety-producing situation; the more time you spend, the easier it will become. Be prepared to backslide occasionally; don't beat yourself up if you give in once in a while.

But what if you've developed panic-induced phobias? It is very common to develop strong mental links between your panic attacks and certain situations. A couple of panic attacks on the road can trigger a driving phobia, or a panic attack at the mall can lead to a fear of crowded places in general. In Chapters 15 and 16, we examine self-help strategies for phobias—panic induced or not.

For now, focus on setting up small goals that force you to stay in situations. Every time you attempt to master your response to panic symptoms is a step in the right direction. Hold yourself accountable, but don't judge yourself too harshly. Replace any harsh self-talk or discouragement with this truth: "I am working to rewire a complex system. I don't have to do it perfectly. As long as I keep practicing, I'm going to get where I want to go." And give yourself permission to bring in professional help if the going gets too hard.

In this chapter, we've explored panic disorder. We've seen how your brain's misfiring results in a terrifying cascade of symptoms that traps you in an endless cycle of anxiety and avoidance. We've also seen how the best way to deal with them is *exactly the opposite* of what every fiber of your being tells you to do. By accepting (rather than fighting) your symptoms and staying in (rather than fleeing) the situation, you ultimately regain your sense of mastery and power.

The Least You Need to Know

- Panic disorder starts in the brain, but the symptoms are very real—caused by the misfiring of your brain's alarm center, the amygdala.
- Left untreated, panic disorder can become complicated by phobias, depression, and other disabling conditions.
- The fears that are typical during panic attacks, such as fears of dying or losing control, are cognitive distortions in the context of intense anxiety.
- Panic disorder can be successfully treated with cognitive-behavioral therapy, medication, or an intensive self-help program. Most often, it is through a combination of some or all of these.
- Tried-and-true self-strategies center on breathing/relaxation techniques, distraction strategies to stop fearful thoughts, and practice sessions that require staying in an anxious situation until the symptoms subside.

Self-Help for Phobias

Howard Hughes grew up during a time when mothers didn't let their kids play in rain puddles because of fear of the polio germs they thought might lurk there. His mother was especially cautious; she constantly worried about Howard's exposure to germs, was extremely careful about what he ate, and checked him daily for symptoms of disease.

Howard's fear of germs grew throughout his life. As an adult, he once wrote a manual on how to open a can of peaches. The manual included instructions for removing the label, scrubbing the can down to its metal, washing it again and pouring its contents into a bowl without letting the outside of the can touch the bowl.

Howard Hughes was creative and brilliant. He grew up to be an acclaimed airplane pilot, a movie producer, and a billionaire business tycoon. And yet, as anyone who has seen the movie *The Aviator* can attest, Howard Hughes is often remembered as the fear-controlled recluse who spent the end of his life in darkened hotel rooms.

In This Chapter

- Learning to recognize phobias and how they interfere
- The difference between simple and complex phobias
- The role of body and mind in maintaining phobias
- Using systematic desensitization to cure phobias

Howard Hughes's problems were complex; he had chronic pain, an addiction to codeine, and apparently severe obsessive-compulsive symptoms. Yet his fear of germs powerfully illustrates how strongly a phobia can grip a person. In this chapter, we explore phobias: how they develop and what you can do to overcome them.

Phobias Are Common

A simple phobia is an irrational fear of a situation, event, or object coupled with a strong need to avoid whatever it is. Most of us know someone who is deathly afraid of spiders or who can't stand high places. Some of the most common simple phobias are of closed spaces (claustrophobia), heights, water, snakes, or lightning.

A phobia is different from panic disorder (discussed in Chapter 14), even though you may experience panic when faced with the thing you fear. With panic disorder, the fear is of *the anxiety symptoms themselves* or of losing control. In phobia, it's the actual object or situation that you judge to be dangerous, *even when you know it's irrational or out of proportion.*

Faced with a "danger," it makes sense that you'd want to avoid that which you fear might harm you. Unfortunately, this avoidance only strengthens the connection between your fear and the object of it and, depending on how often you need to encounter it, can significantly disrupt your life.

Imagine you get a big promotion at work, but this means you'll need to fly frequently, and you've developed an aversion to flying after a harrowing experience on a red-eye flight. Canceling an important trip at the last minute may seem reasonable at the time, but it can lead to your being considered unreliable at work.

Specific or simple phobias such as these may develop rapidly or build up over time. A car accident can suddenly trigger a driving phobia, particularly in a victim who was genetically or environmentally predisposed to anxiety. It's probably no surprise that flight attendants are more likely to develop a fear of flying than someone who rarely flies; fly often enough, and you're bound to encounter some scary (although usually not dangerous) turbulence. Phobias may also develop gradually from learning and observation, as in Howard Hughes's mother's fanatical focus on the avoidance of germs.

SITUATION: I need to fly across the country to represent our company at a trade show.

ANXIETY: Although I was mildly nervous about the trip beforehand. I am overwhelmed with fear as I approach the airport.

I make an excuse and cancel my trip.

RELIEF: My anxiety decreases, and I tell myself it's not that big a deal that I'll miss the trade show.

Complex Phobias

Whereas a simple phobia has just one object—such as insects, dentists, or heights—complex phobias are made up of multiple fears. For example, agoraphobia involves a whole network of them. There is the fear of entering shops, crowds, and public places. There may be fear of traveling alone in trains, buses, or planes. On top of all this is the fear of what might happen if you are unable to get yourself to safety (home) right away. The more this phobia develops, the easier it seems to just stay home.

Social phobia is another complex phobia, marked by fear of performance or interactional situations. However, this might include any number of situations and fears. You might be afraid of embarrassing yourself or of someone else humiliating you. You might worry that you'll forget how to talk or behave. Some people with social anxiety have trouble eating in front of others; others shy away from parties and public speaking. So even though there is the general fear of social situations, what this means for each social anxiety sufferer can differ. In extreme cases, people can end up in almost complete social isolation.

Even seemingly straightforward phobias are often complex. The fear of flying, for instance, almost certainly involves the fear of crashing. However, it can also involve a fear of closed spaces (you can't walk off an airplane at 30,000 feet when you feel closed in) or be part of a more general fear of heights. Part of the treatment for complex phobias involves peeling away the onion: uncovering and addressing all the underlying fears that make up the phobia.

 MYTH BUSTER

"My phobia will just go away on its own." Whereas childhood phobias often disappear over time, only 20 percent of adult phobias fade without any direct steps to tackle them.

What Causes Phobias?

We don't know exactly why some people develop phobias and others don't. According to genetic research, though, it seems likely that some of us are genetically predisposed to intense, irrational fears.

For those of us who have this built-in sensitivity, certain circumstances make developing a phobia more likely. Most phobia sufferers can identify at least one of following.

A Frightening Experience

Maybe you got bit by a spider and were sick for a few days. Maybe you suddenly felt dizzy while looking at the view from the Willis Tower. Maybe your childhood pediatrician didn't realize that a 12-year-old girl would be humiliated because her father saw the rash on her chest. People who can identify a specific incident that either triggered their phobia or made it worse consistently describe it as personally threatening (although not necessarily dangerous) and as feeling out of their control.

Observation

Elizabeth was 6 when her 3-year-old brother was hospitalized for suspected leukemia. To keep him from walking on his stiff leg, nurses placed him in a playpen with a net on it. She vividly remembers seeing her beloved brother screaming to get out and clawing at the top of the net; while her fear of doctors did not peak until she went through a period of stress as an adolescent, she traces the seeds back to this memory.

For Howard Hughes, his mother's fears and their impact on her parenting appear to have contributed to his developing a full-blown germ phobia. Your brain often can't tell much difference between what you experience and what you *imagine* experiencing, a blessing when you start curing your phobias but a curse when you imagine the worst.

Other Problems Linked to the Feared Object/Event

It wouldn't take many panic attacks while driving to become afraid of getting behind the wheel. Individuals with panic attacks often develop fears of the situations in which they happen. This is probably particularly true for situations from which it's difficult to escape (for example, driving on busy interstates without anywhere safe to pull over).

A Stressful Time

A fearful thought or event packs a bigger wallop if it occurs during a stressful period. Not only do traumatic events often trigger the development of specific phobias (of specific locations, objects, or situations), but stress can make phobias worse or harder to address.

Reinforcement by Physical Symptoms

So what tips the scales from a normal level of distress to a full-blown phobia? First of all, with a genuine phobia, the fear you feel is far out of proportion to the reality. For example, it's normal to feel some anxiety when driving late at night on a foggy, unfamiliar road. On the other hand, if I'm so afraid of driving through a tunnel or over a bridge that I would drive miles out of the way to avoid one, the fear is out of proportion to the risk.

> **ANXIETY ATTACK**
>
> Phobia sufferers often pay attention to information that reinforces their fears and overlook contrary data. One way to counteract this tendency is to study accurate information about your fear: How often do elevators really fail? What are their safety standards and emergency procedures?

Another difference between normal fear and a phobia is the way the body reacts to what you're afraid of. If you're like many with phobias, you experience the same "fight or flight" response you would if you were in a life-threatening situation. Your adrenaline rushes, your heart pounds, and you wind up feeling panicked.

Perhaps in response to the unpleasant physical and emotional symptoms, you then find yourself worrying about any possible encounter with the feared object—or anything associated with it. For example, a person with a fear of dogs may become anxious about going for a walk because he or she may see a dog along the way.

Unfortunately, this becomes a vicious feedback loop. When you remember a bad experience you had with a mean dog, your body can trigger the same emergency signal as when you were running from the dog. Your alarm goes off when you worry about it happening again. In fact, your mind often retrieves past events associated with strong negative emotion; even if you're taking a leisurely bath in the comfort of your own home, if you start "seeing" yourself around dogs, your body will produce anxiety symptoms. In other words, your body responds to that imagery almost as if the event were happening again.

 ANXIETY ATTACK

If the slightest phobia-related thought sends you into a panic, or if your phobia is causing significant disruptions in your life, it may be time to seek professional help.

Reversing the Vicious Cycle

So how do you turn this energy-draining cycle around? One way is through a process called *systematic desensitization*. Systematic desensitization was developed in the 1940s by a clinician named Joseph Wolpe, who found that he could use relaxation techniques to change his patients' responses so that they no longer experienced irrational fear when faced with certain situations. Although initially used with the help of a therapist, Wolpe's method has proven to be a very effective self-help strategy for phobia sufferers.

Systematic desensitization is a process whereby you *gradually* expose yourself to the things or situations or events you fear the most. The thinking behind it goes like this: a phobia is basically an irrational fear you have developed because you have *learned* to associate something bad (pain, fear) with the object of your phobia. Why not learn something else by pairing a different response (relaxation) with the phobia?

On a practical level, this involves three steps:

1. Becoming good at relaxing—for example, practicing breathing techniques until you feel confident that you know how to calm your body down.

2. Creating an anxiety hierarchy, making a list of frightening situations related to the phobia and ranking them in order of how frightened you would be facing them.

3. Gradually progressing up the ladder, starting with a less frightening situation and, over time, making your way to the top.

With sufficient repetition through practice, an imagined situation loses its anxiety-provoking power. At the end of training, the real thing will also have lost its power to make you anxious. In this chapter we focus on imaginal exposure (systematic desensitization), but note that the same principles work for exposure in real situations (if practical).

 ON THE CUTTING EDGE

New research suggests that phobias can be successfully treated with internet-guided self-help. Successful help most often includes guided exposure exercises with backup telephone assistance from a clinician.

Overcoming phobias is not easy. Remember us talking about motivation in Chapter 4? The hardest step in overcoming a phobia is the first one: developing the commitment to see it through. To develop that kind of commitment, your determination must be voiced in terms of what you hope to get out of it.

It's often not helpful to tell yourself things like "I don't want to be afraid of heights anymore." That is, there's a lot more power in focusing on what you do want. If you have a phobia of flying, think about what you have to gain by overcoming this fear. If flying is a necessity in your profession, there are financial and career incentives. You can take faster, more exotic vacations if you travel by air. You can even focus on the increased safety of flying over other forms of transportation; it's the safest way to travel. Steadily focusing on the positives—and developing concrete rewards as you succeed—can help you take the first step up the desensitization ladder.

Let Anxiety Come

When you resist anxiety symptoms, they often persist. For example, when your internal alarm system goes off as if it is needed to protect you, struggling against it only increases the symptoms you want to let go of. Instead, when possible, you should welcome them. Your body and emotions will acclimate to the situation.

You might tell yourself, "It's okay I'm feeling this way. In fact, I expect to be nervous right now. I can handle this." The point is not to talk yourself out of your feelings, but rather to just let them be there. Don't hold them at bay, and don't obey them, either. Just notice them and remind yourself that it's okay to feel nervous. Feeling nervous is uncomfortable, but it won't actually harm you.

Then while you allow your feelings just to be as they are, you move on to the next step. You breathe.

ANXIETY ATTACK

Regaining a sense of control is critical in dealing with many phobias. If you have a dental phobia, for example, select a dentist who will go slowly, offer treatment options, and allow you to call for a break at any time.

Allow Yourself to Relax

"I was in the dentist's chair for three hours. If I hadn't had my breathing exercises … I would have jumped out of that chair or had a panic attack. I did not have a panic attack, and I was so much more comfortable when I had something to do."

We all have a tendency to hold our breath when we're frightened. In fact, many of us are in the habit of breathing more shallowly than our bodies would like. The problem is that shallow or erratic breathing can feed anxiety. Conversely, learning to breathe properly can be a valuable tool, especially as we work up our nerve and begin to approach our fears.

Learning to breathe properly, and practicing various relaxation methods, is like the training before a marathon. It's what gives many of us the courage to sign up for the "big race," it helps us stay in tough situations during the process, and it helps us regroup after a practice session.

There is a ton of relaxation and breathing exercises; it doesn't matter which ones you choose as long as you stick with them. Here are a couple to get you started.

MYTH BUSTER

"Systematic desensitization works equally well for any phobia." In fact, systematic desensitization is more effective for simple phobias than for more complex ones like social phobia or agoraphobia.

Calming Counts

This breathing technique takes about 90 seconds to complete, during which time you should focus on counting. In addition to giving your mind a break, your body has a chance to relax.

1. Sit comfortably.

2. Take a slow, deep breath and exhale slowly while saying the word *relax* silently.

3. Close your eyes.

4. Allow your body to take 10 easy breaths. Count down with each exhalation, starting with 10 after the first breath, 9 after the second, and so on.

5. While doing this comfortable breathing, become aware of any tension in your body and imagine it loosening.

6. When you say "1" on the last long, deep breath, open your eyes.

ANXIETY ATTACK

Learning to control your breathing is one of the best ways to relax.

The Ten-Second Grip

This is a relaxation technique that helps you let go of tension in your muscles. When you tense your muscles on purpose, it's easier to let the tension go.

1. While seated in a chair with arms, grab the armrests and squeeze them as hard as you can to tighten your lower and upper arms. Tense your stomach and leg muscles, too.

2. Hold that contraction for about 10 seconds, still breathing.

3. Let go with a long, gentle, calming breath.

4. Repeat steps 1 through 3 twice.

5. Now loosen by moving around in your seat. Shake out your arms, shoulders, and legs, and gently roll your head around.

6. Close your eyes and breathe gently for 30 seconds. Enjoy letting your body feel warm, relaxed, and heavy.

These skills work to the degree that you concentrate on them. The trick is to stay in the present moment, concentrating on the breathing exercise, and replacing any negative thoughts with thoughts of counting and loosening.

Arrange Your Fears in Order

Let's say you're motivated, accepting, and able to relax. Now it's time to begin dissecting your phobia by developing a "hierarchy of anxiety." Start by listing 15 to 20 scary but objectively safe situations related to your phobia, then rate them from 1 (relaxed) to 100 (terrified) in terms of how scary they are. Finally, reorder them so that the most frightening situations are at the top of the hierarchy.

The situations on your list will most often be those that you have actually experienced. However, they can also be situations that you're afraid of even though they have never actually happened to you. For example, you may want to include "Having to wear the oxygen mask during a flight" even though this has never actually happened to you. The important point is that items included in an anxiety hierarchy describe situations that produce varying levels of anxiety, some more fear-inducing than others; this is what we mean by the term *hierarchy*.

 STRESS RELIEF

If you have a fear of plane crashes, limit your news watching and newspaper reading. Media coverage of airline crashes and catastrophic car collisions can skew your sense of the relative danger involved in these modes of transportation.

Describe the items on your anxiety hierarchy in sufficient detail to enable you to vividly imagine each one. It might be sufficient to say, "Standing in line at the ticket counter," but it might be more graphic to say, "Standing in a long line at the crowded ticket counter, with nothing to do but wait to get my luggage checked." Remember that items are most effective if they can help you experience the event in your imagination, not just describe it.

The following is a sample hierarchy worksheet to help you develop your own hierarchy. Your items should, of course, be more fully detailed. For the sake of convenience, these items are ordered temporally in terms of what might happen for a particular flight, not by what would be most anxiety provoking.

Anxiety Hierarchy Worksheet

(1 = least anxiety-arousing; 100 = most anxiety-arousing)

4	Thinking about/deciding to travel by plane
12	Booking a flight online
8	Packing
16	Traveling to the airport
20	Arriving at the airport
24	Checking in
32	Going through security
28	Going to the gate
36	Boarding the plane
44	Seeing/hearing the doors close
40	The safety drill
48	The plane taxis on the runway
80	Takeoff
64	Climbing/gaining altitude
68	Changes in plane speed
84	Changes in engine noise

continues

Anxiety Hierarchy Worksheet   (continued)

(1 = least anxiety-arousing; 100 = most anxiety-arousing)

52	The plane's maneuvering
96	Experiencing turbulence
100	Emergency landing
72	Beginning descent
88	Final approach
92	Touchdown
76	Decelerating
56	Doors open
60	Getting off the plane

As you start listing your feared situations, it's normal to feel some unease. Just remember that you can let these feelings be what they are and practice your new breathing skills, even as you move forward in this next step.

To create the actual anxiety hierarchy, re-order the items so that the most anxiety-provoking one is on top, and the least anxiety-provoking is at the bottom. The following anxiety hierarchy could be used for imaginal systematic desensitization, moving from the bottom of the hierarchy to the top. For this particular phobia, exposure in imagination is more practical than exposure in real life (that is, you may never experience an emergency landing, and you can't actually land before taking off).

Anxiety Hierarchy

(1 = least anxiety-arousing; 100 = most anxiety-arousing)

100	Emergency landing
96	Experiencing turbulence
92	Touchdown
88	Final approach
84	Changes in engine noise
80	Takeoff
76	Decelerating
72	Beginning descent

68	Changes in plane speed
64	Climbing/gaining altitude
60	Getting off the plane
56	Doors open
52	The plane's maneuvering
48	The plane taxis on the runway
44	Seeing/hearing the doors close
40	The safety drill
36	Boarding the plane
32	Going through security
28	Going to the gate
24	Checking in
20	Arriving at the airport
16	Traveling to the airport
12	Booking a flight online
8	Packing
4	Thinking about/deciding to travel by plane

 ANXIETY ATTACK

As a general rule, systematic desensitization practice sessions should last no more than 30 minutes and should tackle no more than three items on your list.

The Three R's: Reintroduce, Refocus, and Repeat

Self-administered systematic desensitization consists of seven steps. These steps should be repeated—in order—for each item of your anxiety hierarchy:

1. Use your favorite relaxation technique to create a state of calm.

2. Read the appropriate item from your hierarchy. (In the first session, this is the bottom item in the hierarchy. In all other sessions, this is the last item from the preceding session.)

3. Imagine yourself in the situation for a tolerable time. (Start out slowly and work your way up until you can tolerate at least 30 seconds of exposure. This might take more than one practice session.)

4. Stop imagining the situation and determine the level of anxiety that you are experiencing (on a 0–100 scale). Reestablish your relaxation again and relax for about 30 seconds.

5. Reread the description of the situation. Imagine yourself in the scene for a tolerable time.

6. Stop and again determine your level of anxiety. If you are still experiencing anxiety, return to step 2. If you feel no anxiety, go on to step 7.

7. Move on to the next item of your hierarchy. Repeat the above procedure for this next item, beginning with step 1.

Experiment with your hierarchy, fine-tuning the level of anxiety each item generates to make it challenging enough but not overwhelming. If your first few items don't cause any anxiety at all, perhaps you're not imagining the situation vividly enough or for a long-enough time period, or perhaps the situation would not be particularly anxiety provoking in real life. If an item is still terrifying after several cycles, maybe this item should come later in the hierarchy and be assigned a higher anxiety rating.

It may be tempting to rush up that list, but stick with each item until you're comfortable with it. End each session with several minutes of relaxation. This process is not complicated, but it requires persistence. When you become bored or discouraged, it's okay to take a break, but aim for a minimum of two practice sessions a week.

 ANXIETY ATTACK

Be practical. If you have a rational fear of crashing your car, lower your odds of having an accident or getting hurt in one by driving a car known for safety. If you fear poisonous snakes, keep an emergency or poison control phone number handy.

In this chapter, we've discussed an effective phobia self-help technique. Developing strong relaxation skills and slowly pairing them with the feared object or event can help you face long-avoided situations. But what if the object of your fears isn't so simple? In the next chapter, we explore the most common complex problem, social phobia, and how you can use what you've learned in this chapter to get a leg up in reducing your social anxiety.

The Least You Need to Know

- A phobia is an intense, irrational fear coupled with a strong desire to avoid the object or situation that triggers the fear.
- Phobias can develop suddenly, often after a bad experience with the feared object or situation, or they can be learned gradually.
- Simple phobias involve only one fear, whereas complex phobias involve a collection of related fears.
- People are more likely to develop a phobia during periods of prolonged stress, especially if they already have a built-in sensitivity to fear.
- Systematic desensitization involves learning to associate a relaxation response with the object of your phobia.

Self-Help for Social Anxiety

Jack used to feel self-conscious walking down the street, dreading the possibility of running into someone he knew and being forced to say hello. Nancy hated to stand in line at the grocery store; although she knew it wasn't actually true, she couldn't shake the feeling that everyone was staring at her. Every time she had to deal with the grocery store checkout, she started sweating and her mouth felt like it was full of cotton. "I'm making a total fool of myself," she thought.

Jennifer once agonized over returning a phone call from a new work acquaintance inviting her to an informal get-together. Maybe she'd call at the wrong time—the other person would be busy and wouldn't want to talk to her. It was unbearable to feel rejected, even over the phone, even from someone she barely knew. After the call was made, Jennifer didn't feel any better. She endlessly analyzed what she said, how she said it, and what the other person likely thought about it. And the party she was invited to? Forget it; as lonely as Jennifer felt, she couldn't imagine walking into a room full of people.

In This Chapter

- Discovering the difference between social anxiety and just butterflies
- Understanding the complexity of social anxiety symptoms
- Learning how to recognize you're not in the spotlight
- Identifying your self-help plan of attack
- How the internet can help—or hinder—social anxiety relief

Granted, meeting a crowd of new people, giving a speech, or going on a job interview can make many of us nervous. However, what Jack, Nancy, and Jennifer experience far surpasses the butter-flies in the stomach or performance jitters that afflict most people now and then. Nancy, Jack, and Jennifer have social anxiety, a disorder in which the sufferer is plagued by such an excessive fear of embarrassment in social situations that it interferes with his or her life.

Here's a list of just a few things we've seen people do—people who were once almost completely inhibited by their social anxiety: give a presentation, join a drama club, go out to a nightclub, make good friends, and be the center of attention at a birthday party. Some of these courageous individuals did it with the help of medication or formal psychotherapy; others did it without either of these. In this chapter, we take a look at the best self-help weapons against social anxiety—and how to use them.

Feeling Scrutinized

Ever walked up to a group of people who suddenly stopped talking? Or made a late entrance to a party and found yourself confronted by a roomful of strangers? All of us have been under the social microscope at some point, and it can be darned uncomfortable. We might have put on a brave face, but underneath, the alarm bells might've been ringing. *Why did they stop talking? Were they talking about me? Who are all these people and why are they staring? What are they thinking about me?*

Social anxiety sufferers feel this way much of the time when they're around others. Some of us may be anxious in one or two situations, such as when we have to give a speech or when we ask someone out on a date. This is often referred to as a *specific,* or *discrete,* social phobia. Those who are afraid of and avoid many or even most social situations suffer from generalized social anxiety disorder.

Regardless of the number of situations that trigger it, the symptoms—racing heart, trembling voice, shaky hands, and rapid breathing—are similar. Many of them are shared by panic-attack sufferers; we discussed ways to handle these symptoms in Chapter 14.

As if these physical sensations weren't bad enough, they are magnified by your fear that others will notice and judge your emotional distress. As a result, some social anxiety sufferers become so afraid that they actually feel paralyzed—as if they are unable to move. Not surprisingly, it doesn't take too many negative experiences to try to find ways to avoid stressful situations and, when that's not possible, to worry long before the event, suffer through it, and "obsess" about it afterward.

ON THE CUTTING EDGE

Research has shown that people suffering from generalized social phobia have more amygdala activity when confronted with threatening faces or frightening social situations. We may ultimately be able to use brain imaging methods to help assess the severity of a person's social anxiety and evaluate the effectiveness of treatment.

Throughout this book, you've seen how anxiety can lead to vicious cycles. As a social anxiety sufferer, you can get stuck in your own fear of ridicule or humiliation, too. You worry about the possibility of doing something embarrassing, which makes you anxious. The more anxious you become, the more likely you are to tremble, blush, or make abrupt, clumsy movements. Your fear of disapproval, more than your fear of the actual situation, is what's responsible for your anxiety.

But why are you afraid in *social situations?* Why does your anxiety center on fears of embarrassment or humiliation instead of snakes or spiders? Let's take a look at the unique factors that can lead you down this particular path.

Risk Factors for Social Anxiety

In the movie *The Perfect Storm,* George Clooney and his supporting cast encounter a merging of weather conditions that collide to form a catastrophic storm. Had even one of them been missing, the result might have been vastly different. A similar conclusion might be drawn for the development of social anxiety disorder: an accumulation of risk factors adds up to tip the scale from shyness to social phobia.

Risk factors for social anxiety disorder include the following:

- **Gender.** Men are about two thirds as likely as women to have social anxiety disorder.

- **Family history.** Some research indicates that you're more likely to develop social anxiety disorder if your biological parents or siblings have the condition.

- **Environment.** Your environment may influence the development of social anxiety disorder in a number of ways. Some experts theorize, for instance, that social anxiety disorder is a learned behavior. That is, you may develop the condition after witnessing others with symptoms. In essence, you may be learning social anxiety disorder by example. In addition, there may be an association between controlling or protective parenting and social anxiety disorder in children.

- **Negative experience.** Children who experience high levels of teasing, bullying, rejection, ridicule, or humiliation may go on to develop social anxiety disorder. In addition, other negative events in life, such as family conflict or sexual abuse, may be associated with social anxiety disorder.

- **Temperament.** Children who are shy, timid, withdrawn, or restrained when facing new situations or people may be at greater risk of social anxiety disorder.

- **New social or work demands.** Meeting new people, giving a speech in public, or making an important work presentation may trigger the signs and symptoms of social anxiety disorder. These signs and symptoms usually have their roots in adolescence, however.

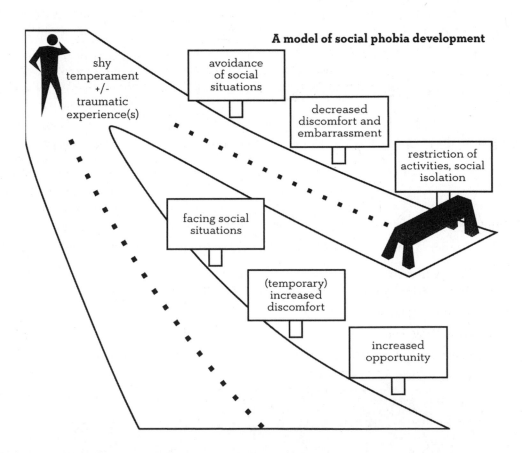

A model of social phobia development

As you can see, a number of things can contribute to the development of social anxiety. And, like a perfect storm, it's often a matter of certain risk factors converging: biology (anxiety in general has a genetic component); temperament (some people are just more inhibited in social situations than others—this is also influenced by genetics); and life experiences (a humiliating event, the parenting style you grew up with, and other situational experiences). For instance, a shy third grader "freezes" when called on in class and, as a result, is reprimanded by her teacher and teased by her peers.

When you begin to feel socially anxious—often as a result of a stressful event or period in your life—the fear usually doesn't go away on its own. The good news, though, is that social anxiety, like other forms of anxiety, is treatable.

ANXIETY ATTACK

Many people think that having a drink before an experience that makes them nervous is a good way to calm down. However, there's a strong link between social anxiety and alcohol use disorders; self-medicating with alcohol or drugs (recreational or prescription) can easily become a "crutch" and may lead to substance problems.

Social Fears

Social anxiety is complex; not everyone is afraid of the same situations. I may be petrified about speaking in public. You may be nervous about eating in a restaurant. Underlying each situation are fears of scrutiny (criticism or ridicule arising from attention or evaluation from others), humiliation (being rejected), or embarrassment (from making a mistake or appearing foolish). Here are some common anxiety-provoking situations; check the ones that consistently make you nervous:

- ❏ Acting, performing, or giving a talk in front of an audience
- ❏ Talking to people in authority
- ❏ Expressing your opinion
- ❏ Interviewing for a job
- ❏ Voicing disagreement
- ❏ Speaking at a meeting
- ❏ Responding to criticism

- ❏ Giving a report to a group
- ❏ Giving and receiving compliments
- ❏ Eating out in public
- ❏ Asking someone out on a date
- ❏ Drinking in public places
- ❏ Answering personal questions
- ❏ Using a public restroom
- ❏ Meeting strangers
- ❏ Being the center of attention
- ❏ Getting onto a crowded elevator
- ❏ Calling someone unfamiliar
- ❏ Entering a room when others are already seated
- ❏ Returning items to a store
- ❏ Going to a party
- ❏ Making eye contact
- ❏ Giving a party
- ❏ Resisting a high-pressure salesperson
- ❏ Joining a conversation already in progress
- ❏ Making mistakes in front of others
- ❏ Participating in small groups
- ❏ Taking a test
- ❏ Bumping into someone you know
- ❏ Writing while being observed
- ❏ Talking with people you do not know very well
- ❏ Working while being observed
- ❏ Initiating conversation with someone you're attracted to

Many of these activities are things a lot of us do regularly. Many of them are also vital to your career success and personal relationships. As such, untreated social anxiety can wreak havoc on virtually every aspect of your life. On the positive side, when you decide to face your fears, you have a lot of opportunities to practice. And practice you must if you're going to overcome your social fears. This practice involves changing your mental behaviors as well as your outward ones.

> ### ON THE CUTTING EDGE
>
> New research indicates that one of the most stressful situations for those of us with social anxiety is meeting people we consider "authority figures," whether that's a boss at work or our future in-laws.

Fear of Negative Evaluation

Most people consider the term *performance* to mean some type of formal presentation or event. Those of us with social anxiety can feel performance pressure in the simplest social interaction; shaking someone's hand or greeting a stranger can feel like a test. In fact, one of the hallmarks of social anxiety is the tendency to misinterpret neutral social cues as evidence that others are negatively evaluating you. People who suffer from shyness or social anxiety often believe other people will think badly of them or people will judge them. Because of their vulnerability to rejection and disapproval, they also tend to be overly concerned with making a positive impression on people.

In Chapters 8 and 9, we examined the link between negative automatic thoughts, irrational beliefs, and feelings of anxiety. For instance, we discussed how negative thinking (*"What if I lose it?"*) in response to an uncomfortable feeling (fear) or unpleasant physical sensation (dizziness, rapid heartbeat) can worsen your anxiety. With social anxiety, your automatic thoughts and irrational beliefs center on social situations, the opinions of others, and your sense of your own competence/lovability as influenced by interpersonal interactions. In other words, your fear about what others are thinking is often a reflection of what you believe about yourself. It's these thoughts and beliefs that you have to change.

ANXIETY ATTACK

If your social anxiety causes severe physical symptoms, use the panic-attack survival strategies discussed in Chapter 14.

You can start by catching your negative automatic thoughts and slowly beginning to replace them with realistic, rational ones. You can easily get so caught up in the anxiety and dread around stressful situations you don't pay attention to the negative conversation you're having with yourself. To get used to this process, think back over three or four actual occasions you found difficult over the past month and try to recreate your thoughts before, during, and after these occasions. Create something like this:

Situation: Giving a presentation.

Thoughts beforehand: Man, I dread that talk next week. I don't know what I'll have to say. Maybe I'll go blank; I'm going to make a total fool of myself.

Thoughts during: Oh, man. I'm sweating. I know the boss can see how nervous I am. She must think there's something wrong with me.

Thoughts afterward: Well, I blew it again. How could I have missed that statistic?! John does these kinds of things like they're a piece of cake.

Conclusions: I can't handle things the way other people can. Some people have it and some people don't; I don't.

Now, keep a social anxiety diary over the next two weeks. Write down what situations you felt anxious in as well as the thoughts, feelings, and physical sensations you experience before, during, and after. As you journal, begin using the strategies we discussed in Chapters 8 and 9 to counter your social-anxiety-specific thoughts and beliefs. Remember, the trick is to recognize the thinking errors that are common in social anxiety—catastrophizing that a minor faux pas is a major disaster, personalizing reactions from others without any concrete evidence, focusing only on what you did wrong and ignoring situations you handled well—and begin to make them more rational and neutral. The more you consciously practice and repeat this process, the more automatic it will become.

In addition, as people become well acquainted with the negative thoughts that plague them, they often discover dysfunctional beliefs that form the core of their social anxiety. *"I just can't handle rejection. If someone criticizes me, it means I am a bad person. I just can't fit in with other people. No one likes people who are weak or make mistakes. If others don't think I'm worthy, I must not be."* These kinds of beliefs have often been around for a while and take time to correct. By paying attention to and correcting the conclusions you draw about your social anxiety, you can begin to chip away at these core beliefs. *"I can't tolerate rejection"* gradually turns into *"I don't like to be rejected, but I can handle it. And it doesn't say anything about my value as a person."*

ANXIETY ATTACK

Volunteer work naturally focuses on helping others and, as such, can be a great way to practice letting go of the "spotlight" effect.

The Spotlight Effect

One of the cognitive distortions social anxiety sufferers tend to share is sometimes referred to as the "spotlight effect," the excruciating sensation that all eyes are on you and that you are being judged. You tend to *consistently* overestimate the degree to which other people's attention is focused on you, how much they remember about what you said or did, and how much importance they attached to it. It's not that you're self-centered; it's just that you're so self-conscious in social situations that you can't help but think others see—and judge—what you're doing. In fact, research suggests that at the root of the "spotlight effect" is your excessive self-processing in anxiety-inducing social situations. This means that you do the following:

- Zoom in on what is happening inside your body, especially anxiety symptoms like shaking, sweating, redness of the face, and difficulty speaking

- Focus on the negative images and thoughts that are swirling around in your head

- Are less able to pay attention to, and evaluate, the reactions of others

- Easily interpret ambiguous responses (body language, unclear comments) as confirmation that you are being rejected or ridiculed

In other words, you are likely to see what you already believe. However, understanding the reason for the spotlight effect doesn't make it go away. What can help, though, is to *plan out* ways to shift the focus from yourself to others. In fact, this is an excellent strategy.

For example, at a small gathering, you might make a goal of helping another person feel more comfortable. You might decide to find out three things about another person in the room and prepare questions that another person would enjoy answering. You can practice being a good listener, making a point of reflecting back what you are hearing to ensure that the other person feels heard.

You can look around the room and see if anyone else seems nervous. Social anxiety disorder affects 13 percent of the U.S. population; the odds are good that someone else in the room has some degree of it. Can you spot who it might be? If you can't, the odds are that *no one can spot you, either.* But what if you do spy someone who seems unsure or anxious? How would you feel toward that person? Would you instantly dislike him or her and direct the rest of your time and attention to negatively critiquing him or her? *No?* Then why would anyone do that to you?

STRESS RELIEF

As part of an experiment, students wearing what they believed to be embarrassing T-shirts were sent into a room of their peers. Although the students were convinced (and mortified) that almost everyone would notice the T-shirts, fewer than 50 percent of their peers actually remembered them.

When you shift your focus in social situations, you begin to see that you are not, in reality, the center of anyone else's attention. In social situations where you're feeling especially vulnerable, you can be skeptical of what your thoughts are telling you.

Changing Behavior

It's possible, though, that you're putting the cart before the horse; maybe you don't go into social situations at all. Many people who have suffered from social anxiety for years have become exceptional escape artists, learning to either avoid a threatening situation altogether or to use enough "tricks" while in one that they never truly engage. Unfortunately, learning to think new thoughts isn't going to get you very far if you don't engage others.

Changing your behavior is just as important in conquering social anxiety as changing your thoughts. In fact, in the long run, changing what you *do* is probably the most helpful way to overcome social anxiety. Many of the strategies we discussed in the preceding chapter are extremely relevant to social anxiety; you need to develop an anxiety hierarchy where you list your feared social situations, ranking them from most frightening to least. Then start at the bottom of the hierarchy and work your way to the top.

ON THE CUTTING EDGE

Although social anxiety disorder is highly treatable, most people who have it never seek professional help.

Because social anxiety is so complex, it may be useful to develop different hierarchies for different situations. For example, a fear of speaking in front of a group can be broken down into various steps, starting with an easy one and moving up to a challenging one. The same can be done for going to a party or interviewing for a job. A social anxiety hierarchy for fear of talking in front of a group of people might look something like this:

Most Stressful

Giving a formal presentation

Leading a team discussion in front of a boss

Asking a question or giving input during a staff meeting

Joining a group of co-workers already sitting at the lunch table

Engaging in casual conversation with strangers in the elevator

Going with a friend to a party where I don't know many people

Bumping into a couple I don't know very well

Least Stressful

As we discussed in the preceding chapter, the goal is to gradually tackle each item on the anxiety hierarchy. However, unlike some simple phobia situations that you can avoid altogether, you may find that you actually have to do a few of the items on this list on a regular basis. As such, you need to also take an honest look at ways you escape mentally while you are in an uncomfortable situation and gradually eliminate these, too.

For instance, you may go to a party but sit in the corner, say little or let someone else do the talking, or stay close to a safe person. These "safe" behaviors allowed you to stay in a stressful situation, but now you need to move beyond merely surviving your social anxiety. You want to overcome it!

In between practice sessions when you focus specifically on the items in your hierarchy and on restructuring your negative automatic thoughts, countless opportunities exist for you to boost your social self-confidence. Some of these need last only a few seconds or a few minutes at most. For example:

- Return a greeting from a neighbor or co-worker.

- Say hello to a neighbor or co-worker without waiting to be greeted first.

- Ask a clerk where to find something in a store.

- Ask a stranger for directions.

- Accept an invitation to lunch with a small group where other people will do most of the talking.

- Accept a compliment with a simple thank you.

- Give someone else a compliment.

- Respond to a simple question with a brief answer if you have one.

- Respond to a question you honestly can't answer with a simple admission that you don't know.

You will gradually learn that you can cope and feel comfortable in social situations. It is worth remembering that many other people feel anxious in social situations, too; it just doesn't show. You are not the only one.

ANXIETY ATTACK

Medication by itself may not be effective in alleviating social anxiety altogether, although it can help make taking social chances easier. Across studies, half or more of social anxiety sufferers report significant improvement from cognitive-behavioral psychotherapy.

Practice

To manage your recovery from social anxiety, you need to consistently and repeatedly practice your newfound skills. There are several issues to keep in mind as you do this:

- **Divide and conquer.** It can be daunting to think of all the skills you need to work on to conquer social anxiety—dealing with the uncomfortable physical sensations that occur, challenging negative thought patterns, and socializing with other people at the same time. Instead, look at your recovery as a three-pronged approach and, in the beginning, work on them individually.

- **Schedule practice sessions.** Don't wait for situations on your hierarchy to appear before you start working on them. If nothing's coming up on your schedule, create situations that will force you to practice: go to the grocery store, ask a friend to look over your shoulder while you're writing, or go out to eat in a restaurant.

- **Expand your social skills.** You can learn how to join in, listen, make memorable presentations, and communicate effectively. Build your social confidence by acquiring knowledge in which you feel lacking; this could include reading columns like "Miss Manners" or books like *How to Win Friends and Influence People.*

- **Consider seeking professional help.** Studies suggest that as many as 70 percent of social anxiety sufferers also suffer from other challenges such as agoraphobia, panic disorder, or depression. And approximately 20 percent of those with social anxiety use alcohol to ease their fears. If you are experiencing other difficulties in addition to social anxiety, consider seeking professional help.

STRESS RELIEF

The first few minutes of a presentation are usually the most anxiety provoking. You can plan ahead for this by memorizing the first few minutes of your talk, getting to the room early and meeting everyone there, and asking the audience several questions to shift your mental focus from yourself to others.

Virtual Help or Avoidance

Virtual reality can be used to help people overcome debilitating fear; for example, people who are too terrified of flying to make the leap between visiting an airport and actually taking a flight can benefit tremendously from therapy that includes a simulated airplane ride. Could the internet provide a "virtual" social setting, a safe place where a severe social anxiety sufferer could jump-start his or her recovery?

The answer appears to be a qualified "yes." There are wonderful online support groups for all anxiety disorders, including social anxiety. Some of these are filled with good tips, warm support and encouragement, and touching personal experiences. Chat rooms or discussion boards can be a great way to "put one's toe in the water" and try out social contacts with which you're less comfortable in the "real" world.

For example, research in 2013 showed that the more one felt connected to others on Facebook, the fewer symptoms of anxiety and depression they reported. A 2014 study showed that among people with high social anxiety, feeling connected to others on Facebook was related to higher well-being regardless of how connected they felt to people in the offline world. Findings were the opposite for people low in social anxiety—it was the offline connections that mattered more, with Facebook connectedness adding little.

On the downside, you can't allow online relationships to substitute for "real-world" ones. Posting and commenting on Facebook is no substitute for face-to-face interaction. Allowing the internet to become one's entire social network is not a therapeutic use of virtual reality. When it comes to social anxiety, the internet best serves as a stepping stone; you try out your new skills with your online contacts and then take them out into the real world.

ANXIETY ATTACK

Not sure if your internet use is too much? Ask yourself whether your relationships have improved or deteriorated since you went online and whether you spend more or less time interacting with others in real life.

In the last three chapters, we've looked at what self-help has to offer to help you overcome your anxiety. In these chapters, we've reviewed strategies for recognizing, and slowly tackling, the distressing thoughts, feelings, and physical symptoms that plague anxiety sufferers. We've also reviewed systematic desensitization, a way you can gradually train yourself to face situations you've been avoiding.

These self-help techniques work as long as your psyche is ready and able to use them. The reality is that many of us anxiety sufferers have struggled for years with our fears and have developed fairly ingrained habits of "survival." Or we find ourselves battling more than one problem; perhaps an additional anxiety disorder, a secondary depression, or excessive drinking.

Overcoming an anxiety disorder should not be thought of as something one has to do on one's own. In the next chapter, we explore state-of-the-art anxiety disorder treatments and how "self-help" can include finding the right assistance.

The Least You Need to Know

- People suffering from social anxiety disorder fear ridicule, rejection, or embarrassment to such an extent that they avoid social activities that are essential to professional success and personal satisfaction.

- Social anxiety is often a result of a biological vulnerability (shy temperament, family history of anxiety) interacting with certain life experiences (critical parenting, humiliating social experiences).

- Social anxiety is a complex phobia. The fear of public humiliation and scrutiny can generalize to many different situations.

- The most effective self-help for social anxiety incorporates strategies for managing physical symptoms, restructuring dysfunctional thoughts and beliefs, and gradually introducing social situations. Boning up on your social skills can also increase your interpersonal self-confidence.

Getting Professional Help

Taking that first step to get help might be difficult but might end up being one of the best things you can do for yourself. Good for you! Many people who could benefit from professional help don't get it, for a variety of reasons.

Not only should you bring motivation and openness to your professional's office, you should also come armed with knowledge—accurate information about your symptoms and also an awareness of what treatment is likely to work best and what kind of clinician you're looking for.

In this chapter, we take a look at how you can get the most benefit from anxiety treatment. Especially if you have social anxiety, the process of reaching out to a stranger may seem like the last thing you want to do. Pat yourself on the back for exploring this possibility.

In This Chapter

- Learning what's "state-of-the-art" in anxiety treatments
- Discovering what the best anxiety treaters do with their patients
- Considering a "background check" on a prospective clinician
- Knowing when to seek a new treatment angle
- Evaluating the risks and rewards of medication

Sarah's Story

"I first started having anxiety symptoms about 10 years ago. After several trips to the ER and numerous visits to my general practitioner, I decided perhaps it was time to find a specialist. My health insurance company hooked me up with a psychiatrist, who put me on an antidepressant. It took a while to get the right dose, but I finally started feeling better.

"After a while, though, my anxiety got worse again. When I called my doctor, he upped the dose and offered to give me a note so I could take a few weeks off work. Okay, I thought, I can sure use the time off. The problem was, this 'treatment' continued for seven years. I would feel better for a little while, my anxiety would come back or get worse, and my doctor would add medications and tell me to take some time off. Not only did I start feeling like a zombie from all the drugs, I felt increasingly depressed and hopeless.

"The last straw came for me when my doctor told me he thought I needed to go on disability. I'm 32 years old, for God's sake. I guess that was a wake-up call that my doctor had given up on me; he didn't think I would ever get better."

Sarah found a new psychiatrist who specializes in anxiety. He suggested a different antidepressant—and a much lower dose—and got her into psychotherapy. Three years later, Sarah has gone from daily panic attacks to an average of one every six months. And she hasn't missed a day of work because of her anxiety in two years.

Why did it take Sarah so long to change doctors? Why *wouldn't* it? It takes a tremendous amount of courage to admit that what you've been doing hasn't worked and to seek help from a professional. When you do, it's natural to place your trust in your treater; after all, he or she is the "expert."

However, blind faith in a person just because he or she has a doctoral degree isn't always warranted.

 ANXIETY ATTACK

Research has shown that anxiety patients whose spouses or parents express hostility toward them were almost six times more likely to stop treatment than those whose families were not hostile. On the flip side, families who are too involved, or "hovering," can impede progress. Having a therapist willing to involve family members in treatment—as needed—can increase the effectiveness of treatment.

Evidenced-Based Treatments

Anxiety disorders can compromise your quality of life, to be sure. That's the bad news. The good news is that they are highly treatable: a substantial majority of anxiety sufferers get better with medication, therapy, or a combination of both. But what kind of therapy? What kind of medication, how much, and for how long?

One strategy that is increasingly being adopted by anxiety experts—and by savvy consumers—is to examine the evidence. The philosophy behind *evidence-based treatment* is simply that clinical decisions should be based on sound research and controlled observation; by looking at studies comparing treatment outcomes with different strategies, you can tease out how to get the most effective treatment. It's like going to the horse track and betting on the horse with the best odds; it doesn't mean another horse won't win, but the favored horse is the one with the proven track record.

Because the anxiety disorders share certain features, it's not surprising that the same family of medications and psychotherapy frameworks tends to work well with all of them. For instance, cognitive behavioral therapy (CBT) is the psychotherapy of choice for panic disorder, social anxiety, generalized anxiety disorder, and simple (specific) phobia. Variations of these treatments are also effective for obsessive-compulsive disorder, posttraumatic stress disorder, and major depression. CBT is a combination or a "pulling together" of various strategies, tools, and techniques to help you change the way you think and what you do in response to your fear.

ANXIETY ATTACK

Because many people have more than one anxiety disorder or may also suffer from depression or substance abuse, each person needs a treatment plan tailored specifically to his or her condition. Your clinician will recommend one—or a combination of several—for you.

Cognitive Therapy

The *cognitive* part of CBT targets the way you think. The idea is that your thoughts exert a strong influence on how you feel and what you do. A major focus of therapy, then, is helping the patient learn how to recognize and dispute maladaptive thoughts and beliefs—and replace them with more adaptive ones.

The therapist might use various techniques and strategies to meet this goal. For example, the therapist might encourage the client to pay attention to the negative thoughts that pop up automatically during the day, or that pop up in response to anxiety symptoms. Perhaps the focus will be on identifying the possible triggers (thoughts, situations, or physical sensations) that lead to a panic attack and learning to attach less importance to them. Another common cognitive strategy is playing out the "what if?" worry to give it less power. What if I panic in the store? What if I feel faint? Cognitive therapy allows you to appreciate the ways in which your automatic thoughts are often distorted. If you take the "what if" to logical extremes, you often discover that the worst-case scenario isn't as devastating as you thought.

As you can see, no matter what anxiety problem the person suffers from, the philosophy behind cognitive therapy is the same: to harness the power of your mind to positively influence your feelings and actions. The specific techniques and methods used to achieve this goal should be tailored to the particular problem at hand. One thing you can expect, though, is homework; the "assignment" part of cognitive therapy takes place in the therapist's office, but much of the real work happens during the rest of the week.

Behavioral Therapy

The *B* in CBT stands for *behavioral*. If you're really going to conquer your anxiety, you've got to face what you're afraid of (that is, do exposure therapy or other exercises involving direct action and observation).

This is where a good therapist can be critical, helping you move forward in a gradual, step-by-step process. She can convince you that the therapy will work by demonstrating how behavioral therapy works in-session, then assigning you real-world homework that is challenging but not completely overwhelming. She can help you mentally prepare for these experiences, encourage you to recognize that you can cope with uncomfortable physical sensations, and guide you through any setbacks.

ANXIETY ATTACK

One aspect of cognitive behavioral therapy focuses on learning effective relaxation techniques, such as deep breathing and guided imagery, because this helps most people move more easily through uncomfortable anxiety symptoms. Unlike with systematic desensitization, though, relaxation is generally not paired with exposures. That is, although systematic desensitization is effective, relaxation appears to slow down the process of learning that a given situation is okay.

Cognitive Behavioral Therapy (CBT)

A combination of cognitive and behavioral strategies seems to be the most effective treatment for anxiety disorders. The important elements of CBT include cognitive restructuring (changing negative and self-defeating thoughts) and exposure (gradually facing your fears). These strategies are often used side by side.

 STRESS RELIEF

Use your natural strengths to jump-start your treatment. If you're a "thinker," focus initially on restructuring your thoughts and then observe how your feelings change. If you're a "feeler," start with relaxation techniques and calming music. And if you're a "doer," focus on small behavioral goals that will get you to where you want to be.

Your cognitive behavioral therapy journey will take different twists and turns depending on your diagnosis and your personal goals/challenges. Here's a chart to give you a rough idea of how CBT might tackle different anxiety disorders.

Problem	Maladaptive Belief	Restructuring	Problem Behavior	Gradual Exposure
Panic disorder	I'll be trapped if I have a panic attack in the grocery store.	I can leave the store at any time. I'll check and see where the exits are.	No grocery shopping	Visualize going into the store, walk up to it, walk in and leave, buy one item, etc.
Phobia	The plane will crash.	The odds of a plane crashing on any given day are infinitesimally small.	Refusal to fly	Visualization, gradual exposure to airport, virtual reality to simulate flight, take real flight.
OCD	The house is going to burn down while I'm away.	I have made the house as safe as I can.	Repeated checking of stove, doors, etc.	Go through prepared safety list, stop after complete.
Social anxiety	No one will talk to me at the party. I'll look like an idiot.	There will be other quiet people at the party, too. I can help someone else feel more comfortable.	Turn down social invitations	Role-play social situations, plan conversation starters, accept invitation.

Medication

Medication is often part of the clinical treatment of anxiety disorders. The way medications are used often varies with the treatment philosophy of the practitioner or the personal philosophy of the patient. For instance, some medications can be used "as needed" for extremely stressful events, other medications can be a complement to psychotherapy, or a medication can be used on its own. Medication can be viewed as a critical part of treatment or as a stop-gap measure until the person's anxiety symptoms are manageable enough for him or her to participate in psychotherapy.

In short-term studies, combinations of antidepressants with some form of CBT have often proven more effective than antidepressants used alone.

SSRIs and SNRIs

Many medications that were originally developed and approved for the treatment of depression are also effective in treating anxiety disorders. One category of newer antidepressants are drugs called *selective serotonin reuptake inhibitors* (SSRIs). Brand/generic names include Celexa/citalopram, Lexapro/escitalopram, Luvox/fluvoxamine, Paxil/paroxetine, Prozac/fluoxetine, and Zoloft/sertraline.

Another group of newer antidepressants is the serotonin and norepinephrine reuptake inhibitors (SNRIs). Brand/generic names include Effexor/venlafaxine (including the extended release version that is dosed daily) and Cymbalta/duloxetine. An SSRI or SNRI is usually the first choice for physicians because these classes generally have fewer side effects than earlier generations of drugs. If these fail, a physician may fall back on older antidepressants such as the tricyclics (for example, Anafranil/clomipramine or Pamelor/nortriptyline) or monoamine oxidase inhibitors (for example, Nardil/phenelzine or Parnate/tranylcypromine). All of these medications take several weeks to start working, and they should typically be started at low doses to minimize the chances of a temporary worsening of anxiety.

 ON THE CUTTING EDGE

Tricyclic antidepressants (TCAs) have been widely studied in treating anxiety disorders. Tricyclics are as effective as SSRIs and are often cheaper, but they tend to have additional side effects, including dizziness, drowsiness, and dry mouth.

Benzodiazepines

Your doctor may also prescribe anti-anxiety medications instead of, or in addition to, an antidepressant. A category of drugs known as benzodiazepines eases symptoms quickly and has few side effects, other than drowsiness. You can develop a tolerance to their sedative effects, which would call for increased dosages if used for sleep, so they are often only prescribed for short periods of time. They appear less effective in reducing worry than the antidepressants, although they work very quickly to reduce physical symptoms of anxiety. Unlike most antidepressants, benzodiazepines are typically taken more than once daily.

In some cases, people suffering from panic disorder may be prescribed benzodiazepines to give an antidepressant time to work. If you have problems with drugs or alcohol, you probably will not be a good candidate for these drugs because you may become dependent on them. Some people do experience withdrawal symptoms when they stop taking benzos, although gradually reducing the dosage will usually minimize that.

Azipirones

Buspirone (brand name BuSpar) belongs to a class of drugs called *azipirones* and is also used to treat general anxiety disorder. Dizziness, headaches, and nausea are possible side effects, and like antidepressants, buspirone must be taken on a regular basis for at least two weeks before it reduces symptoms of anxiety. In addition, like benzodiazepines, buspirone should be taken more than once a day.

Before taking any medication, ask your doctor about the desired outcome of taking the drug and also the side effects. Tell your doctor about any alternative therapies, vitamins, herbal supplements, or over-the-counter medications you are using. Ask your doctor when and how the medication will be stopped and whether there are any dangers in stopping the medication abruptly. It is extremely important for some medications that they be decreased only very gradually and under a doctor's close supervision.

ANXIETY ATTACK

If you're seeing a new mental-health professional, be specific about what you've tried: medication, dosage, side effects, and length of treatment. If you have had psychotherapy, tell what kind, how often, and for how long. People often believe they have "failed" at treatment, or that the treatment failed them, when in fact it was never given an adequate trial.

Condition	Drug	Typical Dose
Panic Disorder	**Benzodiazepines**	
	Klonopin (clonazepam)	.5 mg 2–3x/day
	Xanax (alprazolam)	.5 mg 3–4x/day
	SNRIs	60–120 mg/day
	Cymbalta (duloxetine)	150–225 mg/day
	Effexor XR (venlafaxine ER)	20–40 mg/day
	SSRIs	10–20 mg/day
	Celexa (citalopram)	100–200 mg/night
	Lexapro (escitalopram)	20–40 mg/day
	Luvox (fluvoxamine)	20–40 mg/day
	Paxil (paroxetine)	50–200 mg/day
	Prozac (fluoxetine)	
	Zoloft (sertraline)	50–150 mg/night
	TCAs	100–200 mg/day
	Anafranil (clomipramine)	50–150 mg/night
	Norpramin (desipramine)	100–300 mg/night
	Pamelor (nortriptyline)	
	Tofranil (imipramine)	
Generalized anxiety disorder	**Benzodiazepines**	
	Klonopin	.5 mg 2–3x/day
	Xanax	.5 mg 3–4x/day
	SNRIs	60–120 mg/day
	Cymbalta (duloxetine)	75–225 mg/day
	Effexor XR (venlafaxine ER)	20–40 mg/day
	SSRIs	10–20 mg/day
	Celexa (citalopram)	100–200 mg/night
	Lexapro (escitalopram)	20–40 mg/day
	Luvox (fluvoxamine)	20–40 mg/day
	Paxil (paroxetine)	50–200 mg/day
	Prozac (fluoxetine)	7.5–15 mg 2x/day
	Zoloft (sertraline)	
	Azapirones	
	BuSpar	

Condition	Drug	Typical Dose
Social anxiety disorder	**Benzodiazepines**	
	Klonopin	.5 mg 2–3x/day
	Xanax	.5 mg 3–4x/day
	SSRIs	20–40 mg/day
	Paxil	50–200 mg/day
	Zoloft	10—40 mg/usually 20–60 minutes before event
	Beta Blockers	
	Inderal	75–225 mg/day
	SNRIs	
	Effexor XR (venlafaxine ER)	

The preceding list is not comprehensive; new medications are being added all the time, as are new ways to use existing ones. In fact, because the FDA approval process is expensive and time-consuming, some of the above medications are prescribed off-label; in other words, they haven't been formally approved by the FDA, although some preliminary evidence may support their effectiveness for some situations.

ANXIETY ATTACK

Support groups are often an invaluable part of treatment. These groups provide a forum for mutual acceptance, understanding, and self-discovery.

Virtual Reality

Treatment options for anxiety disorders continue to expand. One exciting development is the use of virtual reality as an adjunct to CBT. Virtual reality makes therapeutic exposure to some situations more feasible than is usually the case (other than in one's imagination). For example, it's impossible to *gradually* fly in an airplane; you're either in your seat or you're not. And most of us can't afford to take short "practice" flights in perfect weather as preparation for taking longer flights in unpredictable weather when we need to get somewhere quickly.

This is where virtual reality comes in. Virtual reality uses computer technology to simulate the real experience in the safety of the doctor's office. Dozens of studies have demonstrated that virtual reality is effective in helping people overcome their fears of spiders, heights, storms, flying, and even public speaking. More and better-controlled research is still needed to evaluate effectiveness for other anxiety-related concerns. With marked advances in technology (including availability of mobile phone apps), virtual reality is becoming more affordable and accessible to us. However, some virtual reality simulations are more realistic than others. Research has shown that if an artificial environment isn't realistic enough, it may not elicit enough anxiety in the individual for the exposure treatment to be meaningful.

Alternative Therapies

Since 1958, the American Medical Association has recognized hypnosis as a legitimate treatment. Research suggests that it can be a good relaxation tool for those of us who can use it.

How about laughter therapy? Humor visualization is another alternative therapy that can complement traditional treatment. Clinicians who incorporate humor into their work with patients suffering from generalized anxiety disorder may offer laughter to help their patients get some distance from their worries.

Eye movement desensitization and reprocessing (EMDR) therapy combines cognitive and imaginal exposure techniques with eye movements or other forms of rhythmical stimulation, such as hand taps or sounds. The theory behind EMDR is that strong emotions at the time of a traumatic event interfere with your ability to process it. EMDR is thought to integrate the intellectual and emotional aspects of the trauma. It has been most successfully used to treat trauma-induced anxiety, such as post-traumatic stress disorder (PTSD). However, controversy exists regarding what the therapeutic "ingredients" are.

 STRESS RELIEF

> Imaginal exposure is a technique often employed in exposure therapy for PTSD. It can help a person directly confront feared thoughts and memories. Imaginal exposure may also be used when it is not possible or safe for a person to directly confront a feared situation.

Energy therapies, such as thought field therapy (TFT) and emotional freedom techniques (EFT) allegedly utilize "energy healing." The theory behind thought field therapy, for instance, is that each thought you have triggers a chemical change in your body, which can produce changes in behavior and bodily sensations, including racing heart, sweaty palms, dizziness, and shortness of breath. A trained professional teaches the client how to "tap" acupressure points, theoretically disrupting the "chi" or energy associated with the unpleasant anxiety symptom. While there is anecdotal evidence of successful treatment using these techniques, the American Psychological Association has adopted the position that there is little scientific evidence to support the use of energy therapies for treatment of anxiety disorders.

ON THE CUTTING EDGE

A two-year study reviewed the usefulness of 34 complementary therapies to treat anxiety. The most effective were physical exercise, relaxation, and self-help books. Acupuncture, meditation, and listening to music also showed some degree of helpfulness.

Finding a Clinician

A good patient-clinician relationship is important, but not all patients and clinicians are good matches. And degrees and qualifications don't necessarily determine whether a clinician will be helpful; effective anxiety treatment can be administered by a psychologist, psychiatrist, social worker, or another kind of clinician. The best anxiety professional for you may be a person with experience and expertise treating your specific disorder *plus* a personality and communication style that you can relate to.

Here are a few questions you may want to ask a prospective clinician, either on the phone or in person, before signing up for therapy:

1. (If you are from a different cultural or ethnic background) How much experience do you have treating clients who are _____?

2. What is your treatment approach? What kinds of concerns do you usually help people with?

3. Are you able to prescribe medication, or can you refer me to someone who can if we agree that it would be helpful?

4. How long do you think I might need to see you?

5. How do you measure progress?

6. How often would I come, and how long does each session last?

7. Would you want to see members of my family as well?

8. Do you provide in-home treatment if necessary?

9. How much do you charge, and do you have a sliding scale if I can't afford your regular fees?

10. Do you participate with health insurance companies, and if so, which ones?

Think of the initial interview just as you would if you were interviewing job candidates. There are a lot of good "applicants" out there. If you are uncomfortable with any of the therapist's answers (or if he or she refuses to answer your questions), consider seeing someone else.

When to Say Enough Is Enough

The objective of therapy is to make the therapist expendable—at least for you. But how long does that take?

Because cognitive behavioral therapy has specific goals, it is, by its nature, time-limited. Treatment goals are generally established during the first session, as is a preliminary, agreed-upon number of sessions (perhaps 10 to 20). This range takes into account the very personal nature of every mental-health challenge (no matter how "standard" the diagnosis) as well as any setbacks/additional issues that may arise. The end of therapy is mutually agreed upon.

MYTH BUSTER

"If I start a medication, I'll have to stay on it forever." It is not clear why many people believe this. Though long-term medication may be helpful for some patients, starting a medication is not a "life sentence." In fact, the prescribing instructions for many anxiety-related drugs specify that they are intended for short-term use.

Occasionally, though, a patient gets frustrated or wants to quit therapy before the therapist thinks the patient is "ready." If this is you, before you cancel your next appointment, do a little soul searching. Why? Are you not making progress? Are you going too fast? Has your therapist said or done something you don't like? Consider discussing your concerns with your therapist, but trust your own instincts, too.

If you think you still need additional help, but you're no longer comfortable with your therapist or feel that that a particular therapy isn't working for you, tell your therapist what's bothering you. The two of you may be able to work it out, but if not, you've taken a mature, sensible step.

ANXIETY ATTACK

If you've seen a therapist 10 to 15 times and you feel that you are making no progress, it may be time to consider "firing" your therapist. At the very least, it's time to tell him that you're dissatisfied and ask whether there are different approaches you can try.

In this chapter, we've looked at the state-of-the-art in terms of anxiety disorder treatment. We've seen how cognitive behavior therapy and medication, used together or separately, work effectively for the majority of clients who use them.

In the next chapter, we take a look at anxiety and pregnancy; how you can handle your fears while your body is growing a baby and how postpartum adjustment doesn't have to mean anxiety.

ANXIETY ATTACK

Leaving therapy can be uncomfortable. If you've been seeing your therapist once a week, consider cutting down the frequency of visits gradually (for example, to every other week, once a month, etc.).

The Least You Need to Know

- Anxiety disorders are highly treatable, and a good body of research shows what treatments work best.
- Evidence-based anxiety treatment usually includes cognitive behavioral therapy, medication, or a combination of the two.
- Cognitive behavioral therapy works by eliminating negative or self-defeating thoughts and helping the patient gradually face his or her fears.
- Medication can be used by itself but may work best in combination with psychotherapy.
- The treatment relationship should be a partnership. If it's not working, discuss it with your professional.
- Don't be afraid to investigate alternative therapies such as hypnosis or acupuncture, but let all your health-care providers know what you are doing.

Keeping Anxiety from the Next Generation

An anxiety disorder does not have to be passed down from one generation to the next. In this part, we explore how new mothers—with or without a preexisting anxiety disorder—can get off to the right start with their newborns by taking active steps to manage their anxiety during pregnancy and after birth. We then turn to the relationship between parenting and anxiety and examine how your interactions with your children can either promote resilience or magnify vulnerability. Finally, we highlight the positive influence parents can have in helping their children work through normal fears and by gathering the best professional guidance when they need more than we can give.

Anxiety During and After Pregnancy

"I had a few panic attacks back when I was in college, but I could still function. I got some therapy at the university counseling center, still hung out with my friends, and made it to my classes. In fact, I graduated with honors and got a great job in the Bay area.

"Nothing prepared me for the panic attacks that hit me six years later, after my daughter was born. I got them more often. They lasted longer. I had a hard time breathing; my heart pounded so I hard I thought it would burst. It was even worse when I nursed. I got tingling sensations and numbness in my hands. I'd pound my hands together or on my leg, but it was kind of out of control, like I couldn't help it. It got to the point where I didn't want to go out by myself. Even at home, I felt uncomfortable by myself. My husband tried to help, but he didn't know what to do; I'd gone from this independent spirit to this terrified, clingy person, and he'd wind up getting impatient with me.

"Lucky for me, though, my mom was supportive because she's suffered from panic attacks her whole life. She helped me get back in therapy and gave me some 'time out' from our new baby. It's been two years now, and I feel like I'm pretty much back to normal. But I'll never forget it. We want to add more children to our family, and it scares me. At least I now know what might happen, so I can prepare for it. My doctor says there are a lot of things we can do to keep it from being so bad."

In This Chapter

- Finding out what's normal worry during pregnancy and what's not
- Shedding light on the predictors of postpartum anxiety
- Developing a plan to minimize anxiety during and after pregnancy
- Exploring the pros and cons of medication during pregnancy

By publicly sharing their painful experiences with postpartum depression, celebrities such as Brooke Shields and Marie Osmond have helped the 12 percent of new mothers who suffer through it feel less alone and ashamed. Physicians, too, are making strides in telling the difference between "the baby blues" and clinical depression.

However, it is also important to shed light on postpartum anxiety, a condition that touches 4 to 6 percent of new mothers. How does an already-established anxiety disorder impact pregnancy? What do you do about medication? What can you expect after the baby's born? We answer these questions in this chapter as we explore how to create a plan to minimize anxiety during and after pregnancy.

Anxiety During Pregnancy

Talk to any expectant mother and the conversation will likely include some concern, fear, or worry about her pregnancy. What about the drinks you had before you found out you were pregnant? How much morning sickness is normal, and what if you don't have *any?* What if you decide on natural childbirth and then can't stand the pain? How in the world are you going to juggle motherhood with your career—as stressful as your job already is? With natural concerns such as these buzzing around in your head, what mom-to-be *doesn't* worry these days?

Even the information age has been both a blessing and a curse to pregnant women. On the plus side, you can make informed decisions about your medical care. You can carefully weigh the pros and cons of amniocentesis or an at-home delivery rather than automatically take your healthcare provider's recommendation. From conception, you can "parent" your embryo, making sure your developing baby boy or girl is getting the best in-utero environment possible by taking care of your physical and mental health during pregnancy.

On the dark side, not all information is created equally. Pregnancy magazines, literature, and websites are rife with cautionary tales, sensational warnings, and information about seemingly innocent dangers that could lead to a negative pregnancy outcome. We hear terms such as *ectopic pregnancy, blighted ovum,* and *gestational diabetes,* often without understanding the true risks or likelihood. We read warnings about everything from changing kitty litter boxes to eating canned tuna to pumping gas to taking aspirin. Well-meaning friends and family members offer unsolicited advice on everything from traveling while pregnant to avoiding miscarriage.

STRESS RELIEF

Two of the most common pregnancy anxieties—miscarriage and irreversible weight gain—are largely unfounded. When a woman hears the fetal heartbeat, her chances of miscarrying drop to 2 percent. And the majority of women, without killing themselves with exercise or crash dieting, are back to their pre-pregnancy weight by their children's first birthdays. (Breastfeeding is a great help with this.)

The result? Obstetricians report a dramatic increase in anxiety-related phone calls from expecting mothers. In fact, some physicians spend up to half their patient-contact time addressing unrealistic concerns and reassuring their patients. And an anxiety-riddled pregnancy can set the stage for a difficult postpartum experience, particularly among women who are already at risk.

Postpartum Anxiety

"I was driving to the grocery store with the baby for the first time. Six blocks from home, my heart started pounding. I was sweating. I thought I was going to faint. I went back home. I didn't tell anyone because I didn't want to worry them and I felt so ashamed; why couldn't I do something as simple as go to the grocery store?

"I thought maybe I was still tired from the delivery or was anemic. But it kept happening when I drove, so I made up excuses not to drive. I refused to go out of the house for four months. Finally, my husband got impatient with me and made an appointment for me to go see a counselor. I found out I was having panic attacks. I never knew other people had the same thing; I mean, I've heard of postpartum depression, but panic attacks?"

As Angela's story illustrates, new mothers often don't recognize that symptoms such as the racing heart and sweating of panic; obsessions about cleanliness, safety, or germs; or an inability to get past the birth experience are surprisingly common postpartum emotional complications.

One reason is that postpartum depression is often used as an umbrella term for different conditions—simple baby blues, serious postpartum depression, postpartum anxiety, postpartum obsessive-compulsive symptoms, postpartum traumatic stress from childbirth, and postpartum psychosis. As a result, new moms expect postpartum depression to look just like any other clinical depression—pervasive sadness, frequent crying, lack of energy, and so on. When a new mom feels so anxious she can't sleep or finds herself haunted by irrational fears of hurting her child, she is more likely to blame herself than to look for help.

Even if she does confide in her physician, she might not get much help. Most new mothers are somewhat anxious; it's tough to be in a new role and responsible for another person. The sleep deprivation alone is enough to make new parents jumpy and irritable. Pediatricians, obstetricians, and nurses are *used to* worries, concerns, and fears and can easily chalk up clinical symptoms to normal new-mother worries. In addition, physicians are no different from regular folks in associating postpartum emotional problems with depression.

However, although it's normal for new mothers to worry about their babies, women affected by a postpartum anxiety disorder experience excessive worries and fears regarding their child as well as their own actions. A new mother suffering from a postpartum anxiety disorder finds her daily life disrupted by her symptoms and her thoughts; she is as much consumed by fear as she would be if an anxiety disorder surfaced at any point during her life.

A postpartum anxiety disorder is triggered by and occurs during a time already rife with physical and psychological stress. The dramatic hormonal shifts that occur after birth can make postpartum anxiety symptoms especially intense and unpredictable. In addition, the typical stressors of new parenting—the disrupted sleep, social isolation, and ongoing role negotiations between spouses—can be so overwhelming that you can't get enough distance to realize that your anxiety has gone way beyond worry.

Women who have experienced an anxiety disorder in the past may have an edge when it comes to recognizing their symptoms but can fall prey to another postpartum trap: the bad mother complex. Few roles carry as much psychological significance as that of "mother." As a result, new moms can feel overwhelming guilt and shame if they find themselves feeling irritable and angry when their newborn cries, are afraid to be alone with their baby, or have obsessive thoughts about harm coming to their child. *"Maybe I can't handle being a mom"* is the fear that surfaces with every anxiety symptom. Fortunately, it's often this fear—coupled with the fierce protectiveness of motherhood—that can help you get the help you need.

Beyond Worry

Postpartum anxiety typically arises within a few days of delivery. Postpartum anxiety disorders can range in severity from *adjustment disorder* to panic disorder. (From a symptom perspective, panic disorder that develops after birth looks the same as panic disorder that develops during any other stressful period in a person's life.)

Postpartum anxiety symptoms may include the following:

- Trouble concentrating and remembering things

- Difficulties finishing everyday tasks

- Trouble making decisions

- Irritability and difficulty relaxing

- Insomnia

- Exhaustion

- Feelings of extreme uneasiness for prolonged periods of time

- Loss of appetite

- Anxiety or panic attacks

- Intrusive memories of trauma from the birth experience

- Obsessive thoughts or concerns about one's child's health or about hurting one's child

Once again, you can see how the boundary between normal new motherhood and clinical anxiety can easily be blurred. What new mother isn't exhausted? Sleep deprivation can also reduce your ability to concentrate or make decisions.

When are worries about your baby's health obsessive? Instead of focusing on "how much" or "how often," perhaps the question to ask in terms of when to get help is "how painful." In other words:

- Are you so anxious that you cannot adequately care for your baby?

- Are you afraid of hurting yourself or the baby to the extent you are not sure you can stop yourself?

- Are you so anxious you cannot eat or sleep?

- Is your anxiety wearing you down to the point that you're starting to get depressed?

Answering yes to one or more of these questions suggests that you are putting too much of the burden on yourself. In particular, when talking your feelings out with friends and family doesn't help, when your life is becoming increasingly restricted, or when your symptoms last longer than a few weeks, you've probably crossed the line from normal postpartum adjustment to postpartum anxiety. No matter what side of the line a new parent finds herself on, it's not her fault. In fact, as you're about to see, whether or not a new mother experiences postpartum anxiety is a complex puzzle with some pieces still missing.

Why Me?

Like postpartum depression, postpartum anxiety problems are real mental conditions that impact thousands of new mothers every year. What is not as clear, though, is what causes them.

One theory is that pregnancy stimulates activity in certain neurotransmitters. Another popular theory is that some women have a built-in sensitivity to hormonal changes that increases their vulnerability to psychological, environmental, and physiological stressors during their reproductive years. Others argue that the genetic vulnerability is simply a biological predisposition to anxiety and that the stress of the postpartum period is no different from the stress of any other major life transition; because full-blown anxiety is often predated by a period of life stress, a certain number of biologically prone new mothers will develop anxiety during their postpartum days. This is consistent with the diathesis-stress model we discussed in Chapter 3.

 ANXIETY ATTACK

Women who become pregnant after suffering a miscarriage often find themselves in a constant state of worry and tension over the possibility of another loss. BellaOnline's miscarriage section can be a great source of emotional support (bellaonline.com/subjects/6461.asp).

Research has identified a number of risk factors that contribute to postpartum anxiety. It's likely that women who develop postpartum anxiety do have some degree of biological vulnerability, which is then exacerbated by pregnancy and after-birth stressors. The more risk factors you have, the more likely it is that you will develop postpartum anxiety. Here are the most commonly identified risk factors for postpartum anxiety.

Risk Factors for Postpartum Anxiety

Before Pregnancy	During Pregnancy	After Birth
History of an anxiety disorder	Anxiety or depression during pregnancy	Neonatal complications
Hormonal vulnerability (PMS or previous postpartum problem)	Significant loss during pregnancy (death of loved one, job loss)	Childcare stress
Family history of anxiety disorder	Pregnancy complications	Social isolation from family, friends, or spouse
Family history of postpartum depression or anxiety	Severe sleep loss during last three months of pregnancy	Difficult infant temperament
Certain personality traits (perfectionism, high need for control)	Difficult or negative labor and delivery experiences	Marital conflict
Fears/concerns about motherhood	Abrupt discontinuation of anxiety medication	Unplanned pregnancy
		Severe sleep disruption
		Being a single parent

For example, Joni's family has a history of health anxiety and postpartum panic attacks. As the oldest of three children, she did quite a bit of caretaking as a child and had some ambivalence about what the role of motherhood had in store. On the other hand, she did not have a preexisting anxiety disorder and had never had much trouble with PMS.

During pregnancy, she had a number of pregnancy-related scares and a difficult labor followed by an unscheduled C-section. Before delivery, she also experienced mild anxiety symptoms, primarily when flying and when she was in confined spaces. Post-delivery, she was lucky to have a supportive spouse and a healthy baby. On the downside, her oldest child was colicky and didn't sleep through the night until he was 9 months old.

Social support, or the lack of it, can play a major role in postpartum adjustment. Single mothers who never get a break, or whose family of origin is unsupportive and/or judgmental, can have a particularly tough time adjusting to the overwhelming demands of new motherhood. In fact, combine a lack of social support with a biological vulnerability, and a postpartum distress-free experience is likely to be the exception rather than the norm.

As you can see from Joni's story, risk factors often have a cumulative effect. There are some risk factors, though, that seem to weigh more heavily in determining the odds of postpartum emotional problems. And one of the heaviest is your emotional state during pregnancy.

ANXIETY ATTACK

Thyroid problems and anemia in pregnant and postpartum women can cause psychiatric symptoms. Ask your doctor what specific tests have been given to rule out underlying physical causes for your emotional symptoms.

The Pregnancy Protection Myth

The joy of pregnancy. Few phrases get thrown around as much as that one. Granted, there's a lot to be both thankful for and happy about during pregnancy. However, over the past few years, there has been increasing recognition that for some women, pregnancy can be plagued by mood problems. The common wisdom that pregnancy hormones inevitably create a sense of elation and calm is slowly going by the wayside. Many of the postpartum emotional complications women suffer, including anxiety, may start during pregnancy.

In fact, in many cases, a woman's emotional state during pregnancy may be the best single predictor of what is to follow. Community studies consistently show that less than half of the 8 to 10 percent of new mothers experiencing either postpartum anxiety or depression were *newly* depressed or anxious; most of them had some symptoms prior to their child's birth. Twenty percent of pregnant women suffer from some type of psychiatric disorder during pregnancy, and study after study shows that health-care providers are often unaware.

ON THE CUTTING EDGE

There may be a link between calcium and postpartum emotional symptoms. In one study, women given 2,000 mg of calcium carbonate for prevention of preeclampsia (hypertension) had significantly lower incidences of depressive symptoms 12 weeks after delivery. However, research on this topic is scant, and the jury is still out.

If pregnancy can precipitate the onset of an anxiety disorder, what effect does it have on those of us who *already* have one? It depends. Women with a history of panic disorder, for example, often report a lessening of symptoms during their pregnancy. This may be due to the hormone progesterone, which increases during pregnancy. When it drops again during the postpartum period, the woman's symptoms may return.

On the other hand, about 25 percent of women with OCD will get worse during pregnancy, with some women even seeking treatment for OCD for the first time. In addition, symptoms may ebb and flow with various pregnancy stages; many women report the greatest number of symptoms during the first and third trimesters, sandwiched around a three-month period of relative calm.

For the anxiety sufferer anticipating pregnancy, this news can be quite disturbing. However, knowledge is power. An anxiety sufferer doesn't have to choose between motherhood and mental health. By working with your physician and mental-health professional, you can create a pregnancy plan that takes into account your personal vulnerabilities and reduces your risks.

 MYTH BUSTER

> *Mothers with obsessive thoughts involving hurting their babies are likely to act on them.* Reality: it is extremely rare for a woman to hurt her infant. By definition, obsessions are intrusive, unwanted thoughts, images, or urges. Mothers who have obsessions *do not* want to hurt their babies.

Pregnancy Planning

At first glance, it might seem depressing to consider taking "pregnancy precautions" because of your struggle with anxiety. If so, let's propose an alternative viewpoint. Many of the steps in a good pregnancy plan will not only reduce postpartum risk factors, they will help *any* transition to motherhood go more smoothly.

First of all, take ownership of your pregnancy. The greater the sense of control you have over your pregnancy-related choices and options, the less often uncertainty and anxiety will plague you. Select a medical team you trust; make sure you can ask questions of your medical practitioner and get them answered satisfactorily. Have a list of questions prepared before each OB visit. Get an early ultrasound and, subsequently, whatever testing will make you feel calmer. Research birth options and agree on the birth plan long before delivery.

ANXIETY ATTACK

Your pregnancy plan should take into account how much your anxiety is presently under control. If you are currently in treatment, strengthen your therapeutic relationship. If it's been a while since you've had symptoms, consider boosting your relaxation and stress-management skills.

Because stress aggravates anxiety, one goal of a mentally healthy pregnancy should be to make it as low-stress as possible. Too many of us consider pregnancy a time to complete all of our household projects. We worry about getting the baby's room finished when all we really need when we leave the hospital is diapers, a few outfits, and a car seat. By the time we head into the delivery room, we're already exhausted. It's normal to want everything to be just right for a new baby, but you may be able to reduce your stress by making a conscious decision to let go of the less crucial details.

Instead, consider pregnancy a time to mentally and physically prepare for motherhood. Mother yourself. Accept help from others. Rest whenever you can. Take into account the physical demands of growing a baby and adjust your expectations of yourself. If you can't sleep for long periods at night, take naps during the day. Even sitting in a chair with your eyes closed can provide some respite from fatigue. Eat healthfully but don't obsess about it. The average woman's diet, although not nutritionally perfect, provides enough nutrients for a healthy baby, especially if you're taking a prenatal vitamin. Eat a variety of foods, but don't be too restrictive or obsessive about what you eat. Similarly, although you should generally stay away from caffeine, don't worry too much if you have an occasional caffeinated soda or cup of coffee. If you're having frequent morning sickness, it can be especially hard to eat a healthy diet. Do what you can and talk with your doctor about ensuring that you're getting adequate nutrition.

ON THE CUTTING EDGE

Persistent fatigue immediately following birth may be a signal that a woman will develop postpartum mood complications. Women who said they still felt extremely fatigued two weeks after having a baby were more likely to suffer from postpartum depression.

Actively promote inner resilience and calm. Keep a daily journal to help you keep track of your emotions. Practice some form of relaxation, meditation, or yoga; not only do they make a measurable difference in anxiety and tension, the breath control they promote can be a powerful aid in the delivery room. In addition, while you're developing your inner calm, don't create external chaos. Avoid major life changes; it's often too much to find a new job, move across the country, and find a house within a month before the baby is born.

Finally, surround yourself with allies. Develop a peer support system of new and seasoned parents; the former can provide the "we're in this boat together" kind of camaraderie; the latter can help you know what to expect during your first year as a mother. If you're in therapy, consider increasing the frequency of your sessions, especially during the third trimester. If you're not, getting support from a professional before pregnancy—or prior to birth—is not a bad idea. A trusted mental-health team can help you minimize risk factors by developing a plan for how to handle breakthrough symptoms during and after pregnancy and by developing a post-hospital plan that will cut down on sleep deprivation.

But what should that plan *be?* Do you go off your psychotropic medication when you first realize you're pregnant and white-knuckle it through an anxiety-riddled nine months, or stay on your meds and hope for the best? Pregnant women whose anxiety worsens during pregnancy often feel trapped; on the one hand, terrified their medication could harm the fetus; on the other, worried they won't survive without it.

ANXIETY ATTACK

Never discontinue medication "cold turkey" without talking with your doctor. Studies show that women who stopped their antidepressant during pregnancy were five times more likely to have a return of symptoms than those who decided to continue them during pregnancy.

Medications During Pregnancy

Doctors used to be very hesitant to prescribe psychiatric medications to pregnant women. In fact, most pregnant women were discouraged from taking any type of medication during pregnancy. However, not only can untreated anxiety during pregnancy put the mother in jeopardy, increasing research has shown that the mood of the mother during pregnancy can have long-lasting effects on her child's development. As a result, the decision to take psychotropic medication requires a careful weighing of the costs and benefits to both mother and child.

Potential Risks of Taking Medication

Let's first look at the potential risks of taking meds. As discussed in the preceding chapter, many of the medications used to treat anxiety fall into the category of selective serotonin reuptake inhibitors (SSRIs). Preliminary studies suggest that some of these antidepressants may carry a greater risk than others during pregnancy.

For example, preliminary results from two 2005 studies found that women who took Paxil during the first three months of pregnancy were 1.5 to 2 times more likely to have a baby with a heart defect as women who took other antidepressants or women who took no medication. Another study found that 30 percent of newborns whose mothers took antidepressants during the last trimester showed symptoms of withdrawal (sleep disturbances, high-pitched cry, tremor, gastro-intestinal problems) after birth. None required medical treatment, and symptoms subsided within 48 hours.

In general, all medications commonly used to treat anxiety should be regarded with caution during both pregnancy and lactation, and you should talk with your doctor about this. Guidelines from the American College of Obstetricians and Gynecologists (ACOG) convey clear risks for benzodiazapines in general, and the kind of benzodiazapines prescribed for sleep are contra-indicated outright during pregnancy. ACOG also notes that "risk cannot be ruled out" for other common meds used to treat anxiety. For many of them, good long-term safety information is simply not available. See focus.psychiatryonline.org/data/Journals/FOCUS/1839/foc00309000385.pdf.

Potential Risks of Not Taking Medication

To an unborn child, the risks of a mother's untreated anxiety during pregnancy can be worse. The idea that a woman's emotional state during pregnancy affects her unborn child has existed for centuries. Called the *fetal programming hypothesis,* it theorizes that certain disturbing factors occurring during certain sensitive periods of development in utero can "program" a variety of biological systems in the unborn child. This, then, affects the ability of those biological systems to change later in life, predisposing a child to certain diseases and disorders.

In recent years, this theory has been supported by science. Stress or anxiety during pregnancy are risk factors for premature birth and growth restriction within the womb, both of which are risk factors for behavioral problems in the child. In addition, a 2010 neural imaging study of 6- to 9-year-old kids showed lower gray matter density in several brain structures when their moms had been more anxious during pregnancy. Interestingly, timing of moms' anxiety mattered, as this effect was seen for anxiety at 19 weeks' gestation but not for anxiety at 25 or 31 weeks' gestation.

ON THE CUTTING EDGE

A longitudinal study followed a group of women and children from pregnancy until the children were 7. The children of mothers who rated in the top 15 percent for anxiety at 32 weeks into pregnancy (but not at 18 weeks) had double the risk for behavioral problems at ages 4 and 7. This was true for both boys and girls.

Making the Decision

Obviously, whether or not to take antidepressant medication during pregnancy is an important decision. Educating yourself is an important aspect of feeling comfortable with whatever decision you make. Weighing the possible impact of using medication against the impact of living with anxiety through pregnancy is important to assess.

Many physicians are promoting a happy medium. Because of the risk of symptom rebound, most women who become pregnant while taking antidepressants may do well to either discontinue them gradually or continue taking them. It may be prudent to reduce multiple medications down to a single agent and use the lowest effective dose possible.

Unfortunately, just as an optimal diet and exercise routine can't guarantee that you'll never get sick, no amount of prediction or preparation is 100 percent foolproof against postpartum anxiety. Should your anxiety symptoms resurface during or after pregnancy, you will hopefully take the attitude you would if you were to suddenly develop asthma or diabetes. Rather than view your symptoms as evidence that your pregnancy plan failed, you see the work you did as giving you a head start in your recovery, again, much the same as a healthful lifestyle makes recovery from physical illness easier. And rather than search for causes or assign blame, you can focus on getting the best treatment available.

ON THE CUTTING EDGE

Doctors look for three things when testing a psychiatric medication's effects on pregnancy: the occurrence of birth defects, unusual symptoms at birth, and later behavioral problems.

Treatment for Postpartum Anxiety

Not surprisingly, the most effective therapy for postpartum anxiety is often a combination of the cognitive behavioral techniques we've discussed throughout this book in combination with specific strategies to tackle the tough transition to parenthood (or having another child).

Cognitive behavioral psychotherapy for postpartum anxiety focuses on identifying and correcting inaccurate thoughts associated with anxious feelings, particularly those that center on one's sense of (in)competence as a mother and her concerns over the health and well-being of her infant. In addition, depending on her diagnosis, treatment strategies might center on halting compulsive behaviors, coping with panic attacks, or gradually approaching avoided situations.

In addition, although postpartum anxiety is not *caused* by relationship problems, it *affects* relationships. *Interpersonal therapy* is a form of therapy that focuses on interpersonal issues that can either aggravate or arise from depression or anxiety. It can help the new mother deal with her changing role and other stressors by learning how to communicate more effectively with others. Relationship issues that often surface during the postpartum period include interpersonal disputes/conflicts over the parenting role as well as grief/anger over the sudden lack of intimacy as emotional energy is consumed by the new baby. Left unaddressed, these issues can complicate a new mother's recovery from postpartum anxiety; successfully resolved, the couple's bond strengthens and serves as a vital source of emotional support.

 ANXIETY ATTACK

Check out Postpartum Support International (postpartum.net) for a wealth of information on postpartum mood disorders and a national list of postpartum support groups.

For the woman who is breastfeeding, concerns about the impact of medication on the baby can resurface. If untreated anxiety is impacting the parent-child bond, talk to your physician about possibly resuming your medication.

What About Fathers?

Throughout this book, we've discussed how helpful supportive family and friends can be in encouraging and supporting your progress. This is especially true when anxiety intrudes during the postpartum period. Husbands and partners are often the first to recognize that a new mother is exhibiting signs of postpartum anxiety and can be a lifeline to treatment and support.

A partner's leadership in providing reassurance and emotional support, not to mention picking up the slack, can make the difference between a woman's quick recovery and months filled with unnecessary shame, self-blame, and turmoil.

Of course, the postpartum period can be tough on dads, too. More than half of new fathers feel depressed sometime during the first four months following the birth of their baby. Many factors can contribute to these feelings: worries over new responsibilities and potential loss of freedom, financial concerns, and uncertainties of being a good dad. Active involvement in a spouse's postpartum anxiety treatment can not only assure new fathers that their partners are being cared for, it can also provide a safe forum to sort through their own feelings and concerns.

As you've seen, postpartum anxiety can add to an already stressful time. Identifying and minimizing risk factors during pregnancy can reduce the odds of postpartum emotional problems, but it doesn't completely remove them. As such, for women with a history of anxiety, the best defense may be a good offense: making sure pregnancy is as low-stress as possible and lining up a team of professionals ready to treat postpartum symptoms.

On the bright side, postpartum anxiety is as treatable as anxiety during any other period of a woman's life. Early symptom recognition and good professional help can minimize the impact of postpartum anxiety on the mother, the child, and the couple. In fact, some couples say that dealing with postpartum anxiety forced them to deal sooner, and more effectively, with interpersonal issues that surface among most new parents.

ANXIETY ATTACK

New fathers can find information and support about postpartum emotional complications (and lots of other stuff) at Brand New Dad (brandnewdad.com/askarmin/postpartumblues.asp). We also suggest checking out *The Complete Idiot's Guide to Being a New Dad*.

This chapter has been about the relationship between pregnancy and anxiety and how new mothers can get off to the right start with their babies whether or not they experience anxiety symptoms during or after pregnancy. In the next chapter, we take a look at what you can do to continue this "right start" throughout the parenting years—how you can raise resilient children and prevent anxiety from being passed from this generation onto the next.

The Least You Need to Know

- Feelings of anxiety and worry are common among expectant mothers, but panic attacks, obsessive thoughts, and an inability to complete daily tasks can be symptoms of an anxiety disorder.

- Postpartum anxiety is often missed by both patients and physicians. Physicians either dismiss the anxiety as part of normal new-mother worries or think postpartum mood problems are limited to depression.

- All of the clinical anxiety disorders can show up during pregnancy or after birth. The distressing symptoms are often magnified by dramatic hormonal shifts and the stress of changing roles.

- Understanding and minimizing risk factors during pregnancy can reduce the likelihood of postpartum anxiety. In particular, managing anxiety symptoms during pregnancy can benefit both mother and fetus.

- The pros and cons of antidepressant medication during pregnancy must be carefully weighed; there are infant risks associated with untreated anxiety as well as certain antidepressant medications.

CHAPTER 19

Raising Resilient Children

"Too many parents make life hard for their children by trying, too zealously, to make it easy for them." —Benjamin Franklin

"It is not what you do for your children, but what you have taught them to do for themselves, that will make them successful human beings." —Ann Landers

1. Normal children have problems.

2. *"Parents can help them."* —Dr. Stanley Turecki

3. *"… Even when we struggle with anxiety."* —Dr. Joni Johnston

In Chapter 10, we talked about how babies come into the world with built-in temperaments that influence how easily and how intensely they respond to the world around them. We also looked at parenting styles and how certain biological predispositions may either thrive or suffer in response to how primary caretakers respond to them. The baby who is unusually distressed by changes in her environment, or the toddler who is stressed by situations most others would find unthreatening, isn't *destined* to become a fearful child or anxious teenager. And anxious parents don't have to raise anxious children.

As a parent, you can help your children work with their natural temperaments. You can help your children manage stress and deal with normal childhood fears. Through modeling and hands-on parenting, you can also help your children develop resilience, the strengths that allow you to prevent, minimize, or overcome the effects of adversity; the ability to connect with others; an emotional vocabulary that promotes self-awareness and empathy; and the ability to control your behavior.

Highly Sensitive Children

From birth, Jane seemed extremely sensitive; she cried incessantly whenever her mother took her to a certain department store with fluorescent lights, and the slightest noise woke her from her nap. As a toddler, she insisted the tags be cut out of all her clothes. She had a hard time adjusting to preschool and threw a fit when her mom accidentally brought home a different cereal. Her mom quickly learned to avoid too many activities at once, because Jane became overly stimulated and was prone to temper tantrums.

Highly sensitive children can be a challenge for parents. Their senses are often stronger, sharper, and more overwhelming. A loud noise can be irritating. When they cry, they may fall to the floor sobbing. When they're angry, they may shriek and pound the walls.

Of course, highly sensitive parents often give birth to highly sensitive children. This can make parenting quite a challenge; a child's shriek or the sensory assault of toys, shoes, and clothes all over the floor can make your own negative emotions rise suddenly. You may tell yourself you should be able to comfort your child and keep your cool no matter how bombarded or irritated you feel by the noises around you. As a result, you can be tempted to ignore or deny your feelings until they overwhelm you.

And if your child is sensitive like you, with the best of intentions, you can try to protect her from anxiety-producing situations or try to "make" her be less sensitive. In fact, one of the best gifts a sensitive parent can give a sensitive child is a model for how their natural temperament can work in her favor. This means regulating your own behavior, letting your sensitivity serve you in terms of being emotionally "in tune" with your child, but also knowing how to deal with your weaknesses. Just as too much activity can send a sensitive child into a tailspin, high stimulation levels can make it very difficult for a sensitive or anxious parent to focus on a child. Know when to take a break; leave a family gathering, shopping center, or amusement park *before* you're at your limit.

As Jane grew older, her mother taught her to pay attention to stress signals. She helped Jane see the link between her thoughts and feelings and encouraged her to pace herself so as not to get overwhelmed. As a teenager, Jane has age-appropriate freedom, but a high degree of self-awareness. However, in response to her offspring's sensitive nature, Jane's mom could have easily taken on a different role—that of the protector.

ON THE CUTTING EDGE

Unmanaged stress doesn't just make your life harder; it impacts how you parent. Research has found that when evaluating the same behaviors in their infants, highly stressed mothers viewed the babies as significantly more difficult than did those mothers whose stress was under control.

Beware of Overprotectiveness

Anxious adults often had difficulties as sensitive children. Some of us may have been asked to handle situations that were not age-appropriate, without the support or warmth we needed. Or perhaps our emotional sensitivity led a troubled parent to use us as a "therapist," sharing problems with us that were too big for us to handle. Children with this experience often engage in "reverse parenting," feeling responsible for their parents' feelings and working hard to emotionally take care of them.

Couple these memories with a parent's natural distress at seeing his or her child suffer, and you can easily see how you might be overprotective. "My child will never go through that. I'm going to be there for her no matter what." You may be tempted to help your children avoid the normal trials and tribulations of childhood.

But beware: *overprotectiveness can harm your children.* Although you should respond to your child's nature with understanding, you should not let their nature become an excuse for them to avoid challenges or new situations. Being overly solicitous can unintentionally reinforce a child's belief that he *should* be afraid, that he really *can't* handle it. What you really want him to know is that his feelings are normal, that they will pass, *and* that they don't have to control him—or you.

This brings us to another potential consequence of focusing too much on your child's sensitivity or shyness. A child who clings to his father is likely genuinely afraid of separation. However, being overprotective reinforces the clingy behavior in two ways. First, the child can experience the pleasure of special attention—often highly reinforcing. Second, the child learns that clingy behavior takes away his anxiety—also highly reinforcing.

Of course, as a child gets older, the plusses of having the parent's attention are often supplanted by a desire for independence and control. Parents who continue to hover may find their child becoming secretive and aloof. This distance can make you worry even more, which can result in a vicious cycle of over-involvement resulting in rebellion, which, of course, confirms your need to control and protect.

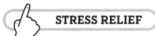

> **STRESS RELIEF**
>
> Build your child's competence by involving him in activities that contribute to a greater good, such as volunteer work or helping a kid in another class.

So what's *good enough* parenting for a naturally sensitive child? You accept his or her nature. You respond with empathy when she has a tough time. Whenever possible, you divide transitions into smaller steps; perhaps you stay a few minutes longer at a birthday party or walk with her to initiate play with a particular group. You help her prepare for new situations or events, investigating with her what to expect and exploring ways to deal with problems.

At the same time, you are cheerful, confident, and unafraid in how you take these extra steps. You're always on the lookout for signs that your child is ready to take a step toward self-reliance. This attitude—*"You can adjust to any situation and tolerate some discomfort without collapsing"*—is the most powerful factor in helping your child find her wings.

Perfectionistic Parenting

In Chapter 10, we talked about the link between perfectionism and anxiety. You saw how painful it can be to live under the constant pressure to be mistake-free and ever more successful. It makes sense that perfectionists might take the same achievement orientation to the parenting role. If you're not careful, you can expect too much from your kids and yourself.

For example, some of us may think that being a "good parent" means never getting angry with your child. If you have that belief, you may feel guilty whenever you get angry, even when anger is justified. You may then try to compensate for these very natural feelings, going overboard by giving in to your child or allowing her to talk to you in a way that is disrespectful or inappropriate.

Children benefit from a parent who can accept, and appropriately respond to, all feelings. That doesn't mean you should always scream when you are angry. It means you acknowledge when your actions and decisions are influenced by anger and correct anything that needs to be corrected. It also means helping your child accept his or her own angry feelings. "You still have to follow the rules, but it's okay to be mad at me. I know you still love me, just like I still love you, even when I'm mad."

Without meaning to, you can also project unrealistically high expectations onto your children. You can want so much for your children that you push too much, overscheduling chores, school work, and extracurricular activities. Or your worries about your child can lead you to over-focus on the imperfect; when your fifth grader comes home with a few B's, you can start ruminating about how difficult it is to get into a competitive college and inappropriately phone the teacher for a "what's wrong" conference.

Concern and advice can feel like criticism or second-guessing. You may sit down with a child, for example, with the sincere desire to hear about her day. Before you know it, you may find yourself criticizing how she's handling a teacher or a friend, then arguing, then wondering how you got there. If you do this often enough, she may start doubting herself and her ability to make good decisions—or avoiding these chats.

ANXIETY ATTACK

Play the one-minute game to teach give-and-take. Before taking action, saying something, or joining in a conversation or activity, the child can *stop* (for one minute), during which he is to *look* (at what others are doing), *listen* (to what others are talking about), and then decide to join, take action, or say or do nothing.

No matter how much your children defend themselves, they often take your criticisms to heart. Of course, a child's thinking isn't always clear, and there are times when you need to offer some advice, but it's possible to offer the benefit of your experience and maturity without undermining your child. For example, you can say, "I'm sure I would think and feel the same way if I were you. But have you thought about it this way?" Because it's true: if you were your child, you *would* think, feel, and even act the same way. When you say so, you convey understanding and respect, even as you offer another alternative.

The bottom line is that you don't need to protect your children by being perfect parents or creating a perfect world for them. Parents who allow their kids to find a way to deal with life's day-to-day stresses by themselves are helping them to develop resilience and effective coping strategies. As children grow, you need to give them room. One way to maintain peace of mind as you make this transition is to know that your children have developed the ability to bounce back from tough times. Let's look at the secrets resilient children share—and every parent should know.

ON THE CUTTING EDGE

People who doubt their own judgment are prone to mood swings, lower self-esteem, depression, and anxiety. Even if you don't agree with them, it pays to give your children a sense that their opinions are heard.

Resilience

Resilience can be defined as those skills, attributes, and abilities that enable you to adapt to hardships, challenges, and difficulties. Importantly, children *are* often resilient. In fact, most children reared in homes with mental illness, alcoholism, abuse—even war-torn communities—grow up to have successful, well-adjusted lives. In fact, difficulties can make you stronger.

The International Resilience Project has identified three potential sources of resilience—strong and supportive external resources; a clearly defined, positive self-concept; and effective strategies for interacting with the world. These are often referred to as the "I have's," the "I am's," and the "I can's." Younger children, of course, tend to be more dependent on the "I have's": *I have a person who loves me unconditionally, who encourages me to do things on my own, who helps me when I need it, who is predictable and sets limits, and who shows me the right way to do things and behave.* From a resilience standpoint, it is not as important who that person is, only that the person is accessible to them.

MYTH BUSTER

A positive attitude in the face of adversity is a state of denial. No, it isn't. Resilient people see challenge as a normal part of life and view themselves as survivors.

The same is true for the "I am's." Resilient children are taught that they are lovable, important, responsible, and able. They also know what they are not responsible for. Understandably, parents are often reluctant to discuss emotional issues with their children, and there are plenty of times when they shouldn't.

However, when a parent's symptoms are obvious to a child, or when they lead the parent to avoid important events in the child's life, it is better for them to have age-appropriate information than to be left to draw their own conclusions. On the other hand, a parent who helps her child understand that she has a problem, that she is working hard to get better, and that it's not the child's fault frees up a worried child to focus on typical kid problems.

As children get older, they rely more and more on their internal resources. The "I can" involves the child's ability to respond effectively to the world around him or her. It's here that parents can encourage a child's emotional awareness, by building his or her social skills and by teaching the art of self-control.

 ON THE CUTTING EDGE

Stress symptoms are different in children than in adults. Children commonly experience stress through headaches and stomach pains. They can also begin wetting the bed or pick up new (or regress to old) habits such as sucking their thumb.

Friendships

Protective factors such as a good support system and a lovable, capable self-concept help a child be adaptable, better able to hit the curveballs life throws at them. They buffer children from the emotional impact of unpredictable, distressing, or new situations. In particular, the ability to connect with others—to build and maintain friendships—is perhaps the most powerful protector of all.

From the very beginning, friendships are models for future relationships and how to negotiate with others. Your child doesn't have to be the most popular to benefit from the stress buffer that friendship provides. It doesn't matter whether a child has a long-term best friend or short-term regular friends. All that's needed is the ability to initiate and maintain satisfying relationships. And as a parent, you can help your child build social and emotional intelligence by doing the following:

- **Nurturing their emotional awareness.** From birth you can help your child develop an emotional vocabulary and gradually help him or her start connecting the dots between thoughts, feelings, and behavior. *"I can see that you're mad because I wouldn't buy that toy. It's scary to go to bed without your special blanket. It's frustrating when your brother keeps beating you at soccer."* Not only can you teach your child to label feelings, you can give the child permission to appropriately express both negative and positive feelings.

- **Promoting the development of empathy and the ability to take different perspectives.** Point out how your child's actions affect other people's feelings. If she grabs a toy and another child starts crying, ask her, "Why is your friend crying? Let's see whether it helps to give her toy back."

- **Teaching your child how to join in.** Show children there are many ways to make friends. A child can ask outright if he can play, he can offer to help with an ongoing activity, or he can invite others to join him in a new activity. This gives him a chance to practice different strategies and learn not to take it personally if one strategy doesn't work.

- **Teach your child to resolve peer conflicts.** Rather than swoop in to "solve" a problem, or leave young children floundering to "work it out themselves," act as a neutral facilitator. Let each child take a turn to tell her story. Ask questions that encourage them to brainstorm solutions such as "What do you think would solve the problem?"

 ON THE CUTTING EDGE

Encourage your child's sense of humor. The kinds of jokes kids enjoy tell you a lot about their worries. For instance, children going through potty training usually love bathroom humor.

Coping with Anger

Children who develop the capacity to identify, label, and verbalize their feelings have a leg up. Not only do they communicate better, but they can recognize and identify the intensity of their feelings, which actually helps them to regulate them. However, just like with adults, anger is an emotion that can give a child lots of problems.

In Chapter 14, you learned to rate the intensity of a panic attack from 1 to 10. This thinking activity actually helps you feel less out of control. This strategy can also help an emotionally intense child. Just as you learn to "observe" terrifying panic symptoms, you can teach your child to observe his or her anger and evaluate how intense the feelings are. If a child can learn to describe anger in words that capture the various levels of intensity—irritated, annoyed, furious, enraged—then she is developing an ability to step back and manage it.

Similarly, it can help the child to imagine a stop sign and think about a situation before responding. Just as you learn to pay attention to stress signals, you can help your child identify his or her early warning signs of anger (rising voice, clenched fist, gritted teeth), so that she or he has a chance to *choose* a response.

Finally, just as relaxation is a key strategy in anxiety management, many children find that self-calming activities are a first step in getting anger under control. Teach your child to take a "time out" to allow the physical symptoms to subside: he can walk away, count to 10, take deep breaths, or use coping statements like, "I can handle this." When the child has calmed down, he or she can decide how to handle his or her frustration—to talk it out, get help, or slow down and persevere.

If your child goes from calm to furious in the blink of an eye, you can make him an "anger thermometer" and assign different levels of anger to the various colors or numbers. This can help him regularly identify what thoughts, feelings, and sensations signal low-level anger and what it feels like as his anger intensifies.

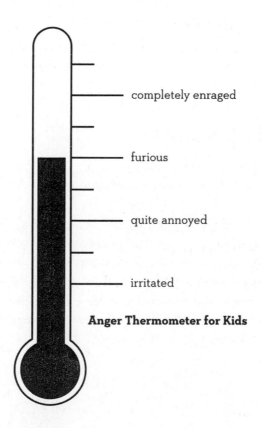

completely enraged

furious

quite annoyed

irritated

Anger Thermometer for Kids

Handling Stress

Helping children become more emotionally sophisticated and interpersonally savvy is one way you can help boost their resilience. These are skills that come in handy during good times and bad. Another is to strengthen your child's ability to handle stress. Stress is a natural part of a child's life; you can't prevent it, but you can teach them how to cope with it.

Importantly, one way children learn to deal with stress is from observing what their parents do. Parents who fly off the handle or become paralyzed with fear model these responses for their children.

On the other hand, children can handle even the most stressful situation if they understand it. A child who doesn't understand a situation may imagine the worst.

From birth, you can talk to your children about the thoughts you have about your feelings—and vice versa. As your children get older, you can teach them to observe the connection between how they think and how they feel. *"When you dropped that fly ball, what did you say to yourself? If your good friend Sarah dropped that ball, would you say that to her?"*

This is a novel concept for most children (and, as you saw in Chapters 8 and 9, for adults). However, when a child begins to be more self-aware, he or she will notice the self-talk. Even better, he or she will begin to see that it's not the circumstances that determine how you feel; it's what you say to yourself about those circumstances. And that's something a child can control.

 STRESS RELIEF

Help your child learn to recognize and identify habits of thought by playing online games. Visit selfesteemgames.mcgill.ca/games/index.htm.

Finally, the ability to take a mental break—by relaxing or distracting oneself from everyday worries and concerns—can prevent a child from becoming overwhelmed by a stressful event. As any teenager will show you, a set of headphones and an MP3 player can provide a break from the seriousness of growing up. Similarly, minimizing or denying the personal impact of teasing or rejection ("I don't care; I'm a good kid") can be useful in helping a child "defuse" his or her feelings and create a safe place in which to plan an appropriate response.

Distraction or denial can be great in reducing emotional discomfort when faced with uncontrollable events (much as TV watching can make the flu a little more tolerable). However, if you don't follow up on solvable problems, you'll feel better only temporarily.

In this chapter, we've talked about the role parents can play in rearing resilient children. We've looked at the difference between a sensitive child and an anxious one, and how the ways you parent can foster self-reliance or create doubt and worry. You've also seen how you can actively encourage the skills and coping strategies that provide protection from the inevitable stresses and challenges your children will face.

Yes, you can and should prepare your kids, by starting where they are and working forward. Sensitive kids *do* deserve special care. They don't, however, warrant excessive worry. If you're truly going to teach your children resilience, you have to deal with your own separation anxiety. You can do this through your anxiety support groups, chats with other parents, or work with a therapist. Ultimately, you have to deal with it by doing it, so that both you and your children can see how capable they really are.

 ON THE CUTTING EDGE

New research suggests that letting a child play a video game in the operating room before anesthesia is administered can promote relaxation better than tranquilizers or holding his or her mother's hand. That's the power of distraction (or of giving a child control over something)!

You also have to be realistic in terms of what you can and can't do. Normal children have fears and problems. The best-parented child can develop an anxiety disorder. Although you can help them, you can't always give them all they need. In the next chapter, we'll take a look at what you can do to soothe normal childhood fears, and when—and how—to bring in experts.

 MYTH BUSTER

Childhood mental health problems are the result of poor parenting and lack of discipline in the home. Although certain parenting styles can increase vulnerability, mental illnesses often have a strong genetic component.

The Least You Need to Know

- Anxious parents can raise normal children.
- Parents can have a big influence over whether a biologically sensitive child develops resilience.
- Overprotectiveness can be harmful to a child's mental health.
- Although children are naturally resilient, parents can encourage the skills and strengths that help children bounce back from adversity.
- Emotional awareness, good social skills, and effective stress-management strategies help a child grow up to be happy and confident.

Helping Anxious Children Recover

Are youngsters more anxious these days? Well, consider some of the stressors many parents face: divorce, less access to extended family and friends, and a lack of social connectedness. On top of this is our increased awareness of security threats such as violent crime, terrorism, child abduction, and catastrophic diseases. This increased awareness fosters both a lack of trust and an increased sense that we must always be vigilant and on-guard. The same issues that cause adults to feel anxious can unsettle youngsters, too.

If children are more anxious these days, then how much anxiety is *too* much? When is a fear "normal," and when is additional help warranted? In this chapter, we take a look at what amount of anxiety is typical of childhood and what is not. We also talk about how you can help your children with normal fears and what you can do when the problem is too big for you. No matter how large or small your child's problem is, though, keep this in mind: help is available.

In This Chapter

- Learning which childhood fears are normal
- Discovering how you can help your kids overcome typical fears and worries
- Finding out how much childhood anxiety is too much
- Checking to see how much anxiety is impacting your child's daily life
- Identifying when and how to get professional help for your child

MYTH BUSTER

Shy kids always become shy adults. Reality: only 25 percent of children classified as inhibited at 2 years of age were still rated such at age 7. And 99 percent of the "shy" children were inhibited in some situations, but not in all of them.

Childhood Anxiety

Jessica, 6, cried and refused to get out of her mother's car with her older brother on her first day of school. She has always tended to stick close to her mother and worries whenever her mother is away from home without her. She has nightmares that her parents will die in a car accident or plane crash, and she'll go on play dates only if her mother stays with her or nearby. Once she temporarily got separated from her parents in a department store and was almost inconsolable.

Ryan, 13, is so nervous around other kids that he won't participate in any school activities. He has only one friend, a child he's known since preschool. He sits in the back of the room and refuses to speak out loud in class, even though his grades suffer because of it. On days when the teacher goes around the room and makes students take turns answering questions, he breaks into a sweat and can't concentrate.

Samantha, 9, is teasingly called "worrywart" by her friends and family. However, lately her symptoms have been getting worse, and she is tense, irritable, and sleeping more poorly than usual. Her mother is concerned and frustrated by Samantha's constant worrying and need for reassurance. Samantha frets about every school assignment and whether girls in her class like her. She gets very upset when she overhears her parents arguing, and she asks her mother if they will divorce.

Jessica, Ryan, and Samantha are all struggling with an anxiety disorder. Even though their diagnoses are different and their symptoms vary, they have one thing in common: life is hard. Apparently, more and more children are anxious today; two meta-studies reported in the *Journal of Personality and Social Psychology* compared thousands of children and college students from the 1950s through the 1990s and discovered that "normal" schoolchildren by 1981 were more anxious than child psychiatric patients in the 1950s. Subsequent research has shown anxiety levels appearing to plateau around the early 1990s. They haven't worsened since then, but they're still higher than they were a few decades ago.

Importantly, childhood fears are very common. Most children have several fears at any given age; some studies, in fact, show that 90 percent of children between the ages of 2 and 14 are afraid of at least one thing—thunder, the dark, being sucked down the bathtub drain, etc. To some extent, this is a normal part of growing up.

ANXIETY ATTACK

Sleep problems can be a cause of anxiety in children. Abnormal sleep patterns (not getting enough sleep, falling asleep at school or during other activities) may result in excessive fears, preoccupations, and anxiety.

Children's fears often grow out of experiences that they can't understand or perceive as threatening. Because so much of the world is new, fears can serve a protective purpose; they encourage a child to be cautious until she or he either understands a situation better or is able to cope with it more effectively. For example, a 1-year-old may not understand why a vacuum cleaner makes such a loud noise and, as a result, is frightened by it. Common "triggers" for normal childhood fears include the following:

- **Witnessing other people's reactions:** If you're afraid of spiders, it's possible your child will pick up on this and exhibit the same response.

- **A frightening event:** A 4-year-old who gets briefly separated from his dad at the park may develop separation fears. Even witnessing someone get bitten by an aggressive dog, or observing a serious car accident, can result in lasting fearfulness.

- **Family disruption:** All families have disagreements from time to time, but if there is a constant air of hostility in your home, your child can absorb that tension. The loss of a parent or the parents' divorce can precipitate the development of fears of separation or other unpredictable events.

ON THE CUTTING EDGE

Twenty-five percent of children involved in motor vehicle accidents may show signs of acute stress disorder, even if they weren't seriously injured; symptoms include intrusive thoughts or images and sleep difficulties.

Stage Fright

As you've seen, childhood fears are common and can serve a useful purpose; they encourage a child to be cautious and provide a manageable opportunity to overcome irrational fears. Because fear is a response to real or perceived danger, it makes sense that what is perceived as dangerous will depend on the child's developmental level and natural temperament. How children think affects what they fear; preschoolers, for instance, are often afraid of monsters under the bed, whereas an older child is likely to be afraid of real "bad guys," such as robbers or kidnappers.

Here's a look at some of the common fears kids have at different stages in their childhood—and how they typically express them.

Infants

Fears: falling, being dropped, and loud noises. From 7 to 9 months until about 18 months, they're also often afraid of strangers.

Clues: crying, stiffening, and sometimes shaking.

Toddlers

Fears: strangers, separation from parents, animals, bugs, storms, sirens, large objects, dark colors, darkness, people with masks (including clowns), Santa Claus, monsters, and "bad" people such as burglars. Youngsters at this stage are often afraid of being separated from their parents.

Clues: crying, trying to avoid the person or thing they're afraid of (which can often look like a temper tantrum but which immediately ceases when the child gets away from what is feared).

Preschoolers

Fears: separation from parents, being left alone or sleeping alone, and imaginary figures, such as ghosts, monsters, and supernatural beings.

Clues: crying, physical symptoms such as stomachaches or headaches.

School-Age Children

Fears: being home alone (younger school-age children may still fear separation from parents), poor school achievement or peer acceptance, violence, kidnapping, illness or physical injury, disasters such as floods, earthquakes, and tornados.

Clues: sleep disturbances, stomachaches or headaches, excuses about not wanting to go somewhere or do something, "jumpiness," and tearfulness.

Adolescents

Fears: social rejection, poor achievement in school, unpopularity, and sexuality, including dating and sexually transmitted diseases.

Clues: withdrawal from parents, irritability, forgetfulness/distractibility, overreaction to minor changes in family routine.

Just like adults, children of all ages can become anxious about changes, such as moving to a new house or school, divorce, and so on. And, as you've seen, some children are naturally more fearful than others. However, if your child's fear isn't keeping him or her from eating and sleeping, going to school, or playing with friends, parents and children can often deal with the fears on their own.

 ANXIETY ATTACK

Children often love to hear stories about kids who have experienced similar fears. Check out ces.purdue.edu/providerparent/Child%20Growth-Development/Books_onfears_Children.htm for a list of children's books about coping with fears.

Overcoming Childhood Fears

Perhaps the biggest challenge for parents in dealing with childhood fears is understanding how differently the world can look from a child's viewpoint. It can be confusing to have a child who is enthralled with fire or fearless in the face of oncoming traffic (things you'd like them to be afraid of) become petrified by her older sister's Halloween costume or insist on a nightly search for monsters in the closet. How tempting it can be to dismiss these fears as foolish or unimportant or to try to explain to a 4-year-old that ghosts aren't real.

You can also forget that you, too, had fears that came and went and, as a result, assign too much importance to a child's age-appropriate concern. Overreacting may teach a child that when he acts afraid, he'll be sure to get attention. Alternatively, if you become anxious or worried in response to a child's fear, this may increase his anxiety level. Parents can unwittingly play a key role in reinforcing and encouraging normal childhood fears so that they continue long after their age-appropriateness has diminished. Of course, a child who is predisposed toward anxiety may tend to develop more long-lasting fears.

Finding the Middle Ground

As with many aspects of parenting, the trick in helping a child work through his or her fear is to find the middle ground between "I'll protect you from it" and "get over it." For example, helping children learn about what scares them (why fire trucks have sirens, what vacuum cleaners do) is a better strategy than arguing about whether the fear is legitimate or the situation objectively dangerous.

Talk about your own childhood fears, especially what it felt like to be afraid and how you learned to cope with your fears. Remember how much children thrive on rituals and routine and create a sense of structure and predictability in your home. Children are also less scared when they feel they have some control over a situation. Activities like field trips or fire drills can be stressful; ask your child what she or he expects and tell them what will happen. Take a child who's going into the hospital for a tour ahead of time; slowly introduce your dog-terrified child to some stuffed animals or a litter of puppies. Prepare your child for the next thunderstorm with information about lightning and thunder.

Don't forget to use your child's wisdom. Ask your child what would help him or her feel less afraid and encourage them to come up with ways to manage their feelings. Express pride when you notice their moments of personal courage, such as climbing the jungle gym or reaching out to a new classmate. As children grow older, you can use their intellectual maturity as well; for example, an older child can understand the difference between "probability" and "possibility," which can help them more realistically evaluate situations that provoke their anxiety.

 ON THE CUTTING EDGE

Here's another reason for parents to conquer their own anxiety. Research on children undergoing surgery found that the presence of a calm parent during the administration of anesthesia helped an anxious child; if the parent was anxious, however, calm children became more anxious, and an anxious child derived no benefit at all from the parent's presence.

Additional Strategies for Coping with Fears

Here are some additional strategies that can come in handy:

- Teach your child how to rate fear (just as you did with anger in the last chapter). If your child can visualize the intensity of the fear on a scale of 1 to 10, with 10 being the strongest, he or she may be able to "see" the fear as less intense than first imagined. Younger children can think about how "full of fear" they are, with being full "up to my knees" as not so scared, "up to my stomach" as more frightened, and "up to my head" as truly petrified.

Fear Scale for Kids

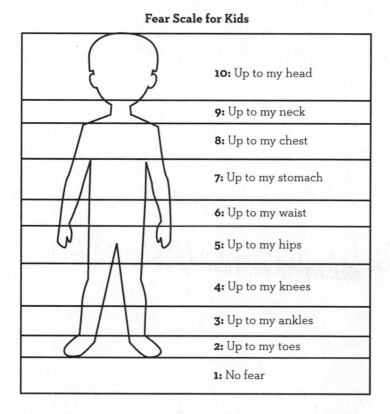

10: Up to my head

9: Up to my neck

8: Up to my chest

7: Up to my stomach

6: Up to my waist

5: Up to my hips

4: Up to my knees

3: Up to my ankles

2: Up to my toes

1: No fear

- Don't cater to fears. Avoiding vaccinations because a child is afraid of shots, or crossing the street to avoid a dog, reinforces that these are things to be feared and avoided. Instead, provide support and gentle care as you approach the feared object or situation.

- Find practical solutions. A nightlight in the hallway, for example, can ease a fear of the dark.

- Practice skills with your child. If your youngster is afraid of giving a speech in front of the class, encourage her to practice with you. If he's worried about his sports performance, spend time playing catch with him at home.

- Remind your child of other things that he was afraid of in the past but no longer fears.

- Praise small "brave" steps in the right direction.

- Give your child coping options, such as using you as "home base" to which he can return for safety. Teaching positive affirmations, such as "I can do this," and "I will be okay," can help a child feel less anxious in fearful situations. So can relaxation techniques such as deep breathing (imagining that the lungs are balloons that are inflating with each deep breath) and visualization (imagining himself floating on a cloud or lying on a beach).

- Encourage your child to exercise. This not only helps relieve stress by distracting him from what he's anxious about, but also triggers a physiological "relaxation response." Children who are anxious often feel tired (stress can be fatiguing, and it can also cause rapid, shallow breathing, which can result in feeling tired because of lack of oxygen), and so they don't feel like exercising. Exercise will improve their energy and ease their worries. If you can, join in with your kids so it will be a fun family affair, not one more chore they "have" to do.

Childhood Anxiety Disorders

Although all children are afraid some of the time, no child should be afraid all of the time. Some children *don't* outgrow their fears; instead, the fears may get worse and interfere with their daily lives. Unfortunately, childhood anxiety disorders are often overlooked or misjudged, and it's important to note that many adult diagnoses have their first manifestations in childhood.

Given that the lifetime prevalence for anxiety disorders in adults is about 25 percent, we can make an educated guess that there are a lot of children with treatable mental conditions who are suffering needlessly. In fact, a recent review of many studies showed that about 10 percent of children experience some kind of anxiety disorder.

For example, separation anxiety disorder, intense fear and worry about being apart from family members or others to whom the individual is most attached, affects approximately 4 to 5 percent of U.S. children between ages 7 and 11. Social anxiety disorder typically surfaces during adolescence, although it can be preceded by a period of shyness in childhood. In addition, children can—and do—develop specific phobias (many of which have their onset in early childhood), generalized anxiety disorder, panic disorder (more rarely), and related conditions like obsessive-compulsive disorder (OCD), post-traumatic stress disorder, and depression.

Symptoms of Separation Anxiety

Although separation anxiety is normal during a period of infancy, growing kids may develop a more intense version that can interfere with everyday life. Here are some signs that a child might be experiencing serious separation anxiety:

- Constant thoughts and intense fears about the safety of parents and caretakers

- Refusing to go to school

- Frequent stomachaches and other physical complaints

- Extreme worries about sleeping away from home

- Being overly clingy

- Panic or tantrums at times of separation from parents

- Trouble sleeping or nightmares

Symptoms of Phobia

As you saw in Chapter 15, people can develop phobias about many common objects or situations. If you think your child might have phobic anxiety, here are two hallmarks to watch for:

- Extreme fear about a specific thing or situation (for example, dogs, insects, or needles)

- The fears cause significant distress and interfere with usual activities

Symptoms of Social Anxiety

Although many kids feel a little shy in new situations, there may be more to it if you see the following in your child over time and across a range of situations:

- Fears of meeting or talking to people

- Avoidance of social situations

- Few friends outside the family

Other Symptoms of Anxious Children

Kids have many ways of expressing their fears, but here are some of the more common behaviors to watch for:

- Many worries about things before they happen

- Sleep deprivation due to worry, fear, or attempts to control these concerns

- Constant worries or concerns about family, school, friends, or activities

- Repetitive, unwanted thoughts (worries or obsessions) or actions (compulsions or avoidance of certain situations)

- Fears of embarrassment or making mistakes

- Low self-esteem and lack of self-confidence

- Family conflict over seemingly mundane issues (such as going to school or a minor change in routine)

In evaluating whether or not a child has an anxiety disorder, professionals often consider four factors:

- How intensely does the child experience the anxiety symptoms? Do they make her physically ill? Do her worries take up much of the day?

- How long have the symptoms lasted? Anxiety that lasts longer than a month may indicate a need for professional treatment.

- How age-appropriate are the child's fears? Separation anxiety at 1 year is not a matter of concern; it might be if the child is 9.

• How much do the anxiety symptoms prevent the child from engaging in, and enjoying, regular activities? Is the child missing sleepovers or not getting ready for school in the morning?

For you as a parent, though, your primary questions are often how much emotional pain your child is experiencing and how you can help lessen it.

Red Flags

Because anxious children may be quiet, compliant, and eager to please, their difficulties may be overlooked. Parents may be the first, or the best, ones to recognize when a child's problems are too much for him or her to manage. In looking at this checklist, the focus is on the perspective of the child—not on clinical diagnosis; what matters is the amount of distress and pain your child is experiencing.

❏ Has your child's anxiety lasted more than one month?

❏ Does your child worry a lot about the future?

❏ Does your child often ask unnecessary questions and repeatedly ask for reassurance?

❏ Does your child worry excessively about a number of events and activities?

❏ Does your child get frequent stomachaches and headaches at school?

❏ Does your child have nightmares about being separated from you or excessive fears about something bad happening to you?

❏ Does your child seem exceedingly anxious or uncomfortable with peers, to the point that she or he avoids them?

❏ Does your child feel extremely nervous when she has to do something (play a sport, speak up in class) while others watch her?

❏ Have you noticed your child's school work or social activities declining?

❏ Does your child seem to make a lot of excuses to avoid school whenever possible? (An example would be "illnesses" that magically improve as soon as he or she is allowed to stay home.)

❏ Does your child throw temper tantrums to avoid certain activities or objects?

❏ Does your child constantly worry about things that have already happened?

❏ Does your child have certain rituals or routines that are extremely distressing when disrupted?

❏ Does your child worry to the point that she feels physical symptoms (like throwing up, dizziness, shakiness, or sweatiness)?

❏ Does your child redo tasks because he's never satisfied with his performance?

❏ Does your child constantly worry about how well she is doing at school or in competitive activities?

❏ Is your child consistently afraid to meet or talk to new people?

The more items you recognize in your child, the better the odds you can benefit from the advice of a professional.

Differences in Expression of Anxiety Symptoms in Children

When it comes to anxiety in children, an educated parent is the best advocate for his or her child. Having a clear understanding of what anxiety disorders look and feel like can be a great aid in understanding when a fear is just a "stage" and when it's a warning signal. Parents who have struggled with anxiety themselves can be quick to pick up on the current of fear running through a child; used wisely, your sensitivity can enable you to help your child work quickly through normal fears and get early treatment when the child's fears are excessive or limiting.

However, although anxiety symptoms are often similar in adults and children, they are sometimes expressed differently. Unlike adults, child anxiety sufferers often can't manipulate their environment to avoid a frightening situation. For example, socially anxious children *must* attend school and *will* be asked to read out loud, take part in a class project, or go on a field trip. As a result, in an attempt to better manipulate their environment, children with anxiety disorders may be angrier and more defiant in comparison to their grownup counterparts. Anxiety or fear can result in temper tantrums.

ANXIETY ATTACK

Pay attention to what turns a temper tantrum on and off. If your child's "fit" immediately and consistently stops when you allow him or her to avoid a certain situation or event (go to school, attend a birthday party), that's a clue that the temper tantrum was about that activity.

Similarly, anxiety symptoms in children often reflect their level of intellectual development. For instance, all children engage in magical thinking, an immature thought process that confuses correlation with causation. *I was mad at my dad and then he died; therefore, I caused his death.* In this worldview, effects and their causes are not objectively determined, but mediated by the child's own desires; *it is raining because I am sad.*

STRESS RELIEF

It can be challenging to balance promoting self-confidence in new situations and teaching your child to be cautious in potentially dangerous ones. The best defenses against the real dangers of the world are age-appropriate supervision, knowledge (safety rules, emergency procedures), and preparation (code words, how to say "no").

Helping Your Children Recover

Not only are we recognizing that many adult anxiety disorders begin in childhood, we are more and more aware that the sooner an anxiety sufferer gets help, the better off she or he will be. In recognizing that a fear has gone on too long or is taking its toll on your child's social or academic life, you can get your child the help she or he needs and prevent additional problems such as lack of friends, school difficulties, and low self-esteem. You can also prevent your child's anxiety disorder from causing family problems or robbing you of the joy of parenting a happy and well-adjusted child.

So what can you expect when you take that leap of faith and schedule that first appointment? You can expect your child to get better; the vast majority of children treated for an anxiety disorder show significant improvement in three to four months. You can expect your child to gradually face his or her fears. The most common (and research-validated) psychotherapy approach is gradual exposure to scary situations and objects, similar to that discussed in Chapter 17. Depending upon the severity of your child's symptoms and your personal values/beliefs, you should be prepared to discuss medication.

ANXIETY ATTACK

When seeking a mental-health professional for your child, consider talking over your concerns with your child's pediatrician, teacher, or guidance counselor. Not only do they know you and your child well, but they should also be involved in any assessment of the problem.

You can also expect to take an active role in your child's recovery. You can do your homework and make sure the therapist you choose has specific experience working with children who have anxiety disorders. You can work with the therapist to make sure the messages you give your child at home are in sync with your child's treatment. You can discuss ways you can encourage your child to practice their newfound skills. You can explore ways you can simultaneously support your child, set limits on inappropriate behavior, and keep your family on an even keel. In the process, you can remind yourself of the big picture; no matter what genetic cards your child is dealt or what comes up, you as a parent are a powerful coach in helping your children develop the coping skills to succeed.

 MYTH BUSTER

If my child needs help, I must be a bad parent. No one would think less of you if your child had diabetes or cancer. A mental illness is no different. The greatest harm comes from leaving a mental illness untreated. But just like with physical problems, the prognosis is better when a mental health problem is treated early.

The Least You Need to Know

- Worries and fears are a normal part of growing up.
- Parents can help their children overcome age-related fears by finding a balance between "get over it" and "I'll protect you."
- When childhood fears last too long and disrupt a child's daily activities, she or he may have an anxiety disorder.
- Children can be diagnosed with the same anxiety disorders adults have. However, the expression of their symptoms can be different.
- Parents can play an active role in their child's recovery by getting the right professional help and working with the therapist to reinforce new skills at home.

Glossary

adjustment disorder   A maladaptive reaction to an identifiable stressful life event, such as divorce, loss of job, physical illness, or natural disaster. This diagnosis assumes that the condition will go into remission when the stress stops or when the patient adapts to the situation.

agoraphobia   Abnormal anxiety regarding public places or situations from which the person may have difficulty escaping or in which he or she would be helpless in the event of incapacitation.

amygdala   The part of the brain's limbic system responsible for regulating emotions and triggering responses to danger.

anxiety   Apprehension without apparent cause. It usually occurs when there's no immediate threat to a person's safety or well-being, but the threat feels real.

anxiety disorder   An illness that manifests as an intense, often unrealistic and excessive state of apprehension and fear. This may or may not occur during, or in anticipation of, a specific situation and may be accompanied by a rise in blood pressure, increased heart rate, rapid breathing, nausea, and other signs of anxiety.

assertiveness   Generally, assertiveness is characterized by behavior that enables people to act in their own best interests, to stand up for themselves without undue anxiety, and to express their personal feelings comfortably. Assertive behavior differs from aggressive behavior in that people exercise their right of self-expression without denying the rights of others.

autonomic nervous system   The part of the peripheral nervous system that controls the internal organs.

behavior therapy   A type of therapy with emphasis on changing specific, countable, observable behaviors. Based on well-supported learning theory, clients learn tools to observe and manipulate aspects of their environment to make their own desired behaviors more rewarding or to make undesired behaviors less rewarding. Classical and operant conditioning are key mechanisms in this approach. A behavior therapist's tag line might be, "If you can learn something, you can unlearn it."

belief   Any cognitive content held as true.

classical conditioning   When an animal (or person) learns to associate a stimulus with a reinforcement or aversion. For example, bullying or teasing experienced early in life may reflexively elicit feelings of anxiety that become conditioned, creating patterns of emotional responses that carry over into adult life.

cognition   The formal word for "thinking."

cognitive distortion   Triggered by inappropriate or irrational thinking patterns, called automatic thoughts. Instead of reacting to the reality of a situation, an individual automatically reacts to his or her own distorted view of the situation. Cognitive therapy strives to change these thought patterns (cognitive distortions) by examining the rationality and validity of the assumptions behind them. This process is termed cognitive restructuring.

cognitive therapy   Similar to cognitive-behavioral therapy but with primary emphasis on the cognitive aspect: clients learn to identify, evaluate, and change their thinking to help them reach their goals. They also learn specific problem-solving skills. Many cognitive therapists incorporate behavioral techniques as well, even if they don't call themselves cognitive-behavioral therapists.

cognitive-behavioral therapy   A highly structured psychotherapeutic method used to alter distorted attitudes and problem behavior by identifying and replacing negative inaccurate thoughts and changing the rewards for and reactions to behaviors.

compulsion   An irresistible impulse to act, regardless of the rationality of the motivation.

defensive pessimism   A strategy of imagining the worst-case scenarios for every situation, used by anxious people to help them manage their anxiety so they can work productively. Defensive pessimists lower their expectations to help prepare themselves for the worst. Then they mentally play through all the bad things that might happen. Though this might be depressing, defensive pessimism can actually help anxious people remove the focus from their emotions so that they can plan and act effectively.

diagnosis   The process of identifying an illness by its signs and symptoms and results of various diagnostic procedures. The conclusion reached through that process is also called a diagnosis.

diathesis-stress model   Involves understanding mental illness as being caused by a combination of "nature" (genes, heredity) and "nurture" (family upbringing, life events, social environment). Individuals may inherit a predisposition to mental illness and then experience a stressor that results in the emergence of an illness.

distraction   A condition or state of mind in which attention is diverted from an original focus or interest.

emotional hijacking   According to Daniel Goleman, this occurs when the planning rational mind is hijacked by emotional response. A hijacking occurs in an instant, triggering this reaction crucial moments before the thinking brain has had a chance to fully glimpse what is happening, much less evaluate what is going on.

emotional intelligence   The ability to successfully understand and use emotions. It involves a group of skills, including the ability to motivate ourselves, regulate our moods, control our impulses, and empathize with others.

exposure with response prevention   A form of behavior therapy in which patients intentionally approach situations (places, specific animals or insects, body sensations, thoughts) that make them feel fearful (the "exposure") without leaving the situation or engaging in any avoidance behaviors. The approach may be done gradually ("graduated exposure") or suddenly ("flooding"). The exposures are repeated until the person no longer feels fearful in the situation.

fear   An intense aversion to or apprehension of a person, place, activity, event, or object that causes emotional distress and often avoidance behavior.

fetal programming hypothesis   A theory that certain disturbing factors occurring during certain sensitive periods of development in utero can "program" set points in a variety of biological systems in the unborn child.

fight-or-flight response   The theory states that animals react to threats with a general discharge of the sympathetic nervous system, resulting in immediate physical reactions by triggering increases in heart rate and breathing, constricting blood vessels in many parts of the body. In layman's terms, an animal has two options when faced with danger: either face the threat ("fight") or avoid the threat ("flight").

generalized anxiety disorder   A mental illness characterized by chronic, excessive worry, and fear that seems out of proportion to the situation. Persons with generalized anxiety disorder often worry a lot about things such as future events, past behaviors, social acceptance, family matters, their personal abilities, and/or school or work performance.

habituation   The process whereby a person becomes so accustomed to a stimulus that he or she ignores it.

highly sensitive person   A term Dr. Elaine Aron uses to describe a biological sensitivity that causes the individual to process sensory information (noise, lights, emotions) more intensely than 80 to 90 percent of the people around her.

interpersonal therapy   A form of psychotherapy that targets helping a person deal with changing roles and other stressors by gaining insight into his or her unique relationship patterns that maintain problems and learning to use clear communication to change those patterns.

magical thinking   The thought process whereby a person mistakes correlation for causation. For example, someone may believe a shirt is lucky if he has won a bowling competition in it. He will continue to wear the shirt to bowling competitions, and though he continues to win some and lose some, he may chalk up every win to his lucky shirt.

modeling   Learning through observation, the process by which we learn new behaviors by watching others perform them.

obsession   A persistent, repetitive, and unwanted thought, image, or urge that the person cannot eliminate by logic or reasoning.

obsessive-compulsive disorder (OCD)   A problem characterized by *obsessions,* recurring unwanted thoughts that are difficult to stop, and/or *compulsions,* rituals or repetitive actions often carried out in an attempt to relieve the thoughts.

operant conditioning   A process by which the results of the person's behavior determine whether the behavior is more or less likely to occur in the future.

optimism   A life view in which one looks upon the world positively.

overprotectiveness   A parenting style by which parents attempt to protect their child from emotional/physical harm to the extent that the child is not permitted to engage in the kinds of trial-and-error learning involved in developing a sense of independence and mastery.

panic attack   An extremely intense and sudden feeling of fear and anxiety. It is associated with many physical symptoms, such as rapid heartbeat, trembling, rapid shallow breathing, pins and needles in the arms and hands, and feeling faint.

panic disorder   An anxiety disorder during which the person experiences recurrent out-of-the-blue episodes of extremely intense anxiety and physical arousal lasting up to 10 minutes.

parasympathetic nervous system   The part of the involuntary nervous system that allows a person to relax.

perfectionism   A learned internal motivation to strive for perfection based on the belief that self-worth should be judged by optimal performance.

personality   The unique bundle of all the psychological qualities that consistently influence an individual's usual thoughts, feelings, and behaviors across situations and time.

personality disorder   An enduring pattern of inner experience and behavior that differs markedly from the expectations of the individual's culture, is pervasive and inflexible, has an onset in adolescence or early adulthood, is stable over time, and leads to distress or impairment.

phobia   A fear that is extreme, persistent, often leads to avoidance, and interferes with a person's functioning or well-being.

post-traumatic stress disorder (PSTD)   A debilitating condition that can follow a terrifying event, causing the person who survived or witnessed the event to have persistent, frightening thoughts and memories, or flashbacks, of the ordeal. Persons with PTSD avoid reminders of the event, have changes in mood and thinking about the world, and are hyperaroused. Once referred to as "shell shock" or "battle fatigue."

postpartum depression   A complex mix of physical, emotional, and behavioral changes that occur in a mother after giving birth. It is a serious condition, affecting 10 percent of new mothers. Symptoms range from mild to severe depression and typically appear within days of delivery. Symptoms may last from a few weeks to a year.

procrastination   Putting off or delaying an action until a later time.

rapid eye movement (REM) sleep   Sleep that is characterized by rapid eye movement, brain activity close to that of wakefulness, and a complete absence of muscle tone. Most dreaming takes place during REM sleep.

resilience   The process of, capacity for, or outcome of successful adaptation despite challenging or threatening circumstances.

risk factors   Characteristics that increase the likelihood that one will develop a particular condition.

rituals   A set of actions performed mainly for their symbolic value. In obsessive-compulsive disorder, rituals take the form of particular mental or physical tasks that serve to temporarily alleviate anxiety.

selective serotonin reuptake inhibitors (SSRIs)   A class of antidepressants that block the reabsorption of serotonin in the spaces between nerve cells in the brain. SSRIs include citalopram (Celexa), escitalopram (Lexapro), fluoxetine (Prozac), fluvoxamine (Luvox), paroxetine (Paxil), and sertraline (Zoloft).

separation anxiety   A developmental stage during which a child experiences anxiety when separated from their primary caregiver (usually the mother). It is normally seen between 8 and 14 months of age.

separation anxiety disorder   Excessive, prolonged, developmentally inappropriate anxiety and apprehension in a child concerning removal from parents, home, or familiar surroundings.

serotonin and norepinephrine reuptake inhibitors (SNRIs)   A class of antidepressants that block the reabsorption of serotonin and norepinephrine in the spaces between nerve cells in the brain. SNRIs include desvenlafaxine (Pristiq), duloxetine (Cymbalta), and venlafaxine (Effexor).

social anxiety   Excessive fear of embarrassment in social situations that can have debilitating effects on personal and professional relationships. Also called social phobia.

stress   A state of mental or emotional strain during which the perceived demands of the environment exceed the perceived ability/resources to cope.

sympathetic nervous system   The part of the involuntary nervous system that activates the internal organs in response to real or perceived threats.

systematic desensitization   A process whereby people gradually expose themselves to the things/situations/events they fear the most, using relaxation to make exposure more tolerable.

temperament   The way a child responds to and interacts with people, materials, and situations in his or her world. Temperament is a baby's personal style of relating to the world that is wired in before family and cultural factors have a chance to influence it.

thought-stopping   A process by which one can cease dwelling on a bothersome thought. Effective thought-stopping techniques include replacing, substituting, and distracting oneself.

trait   A stable characteristic of a person.

values   Personal beliefs in which we have a strong emotional investment.

worry   To feel concerned or uneasy about something to the extent that it disturbs one's peace of mind.

Resources

Websites

The internet is a wonderful resource for anxiety sufferers as long as we're informed consumers and consider the source. We've focused on those that provide fairly independent information. Note that many of the organizations listed here also have very helpful websites, with search engines to find anxiety disorders experts.

Anxiety

anxieties.com
anxieties.com
An excellent self-help guide.

algy.com/anxiety/about.php
algy.com/anxiety/about.php
A self-help network dedicated to the overcoming and cure of debilitating anxiety. Includes definitions, treatments, support, and links.

anxietypanic.com/index.html
anxietypanic.com/index.html
Search engine and more.

healingwell.com/anxiety
healingwell.com/anxiety
Health articles, medical news, doctor-produced video webcasts, community message boards and chat rooms, professional health-care resources, email, newsletters, books and reviews, and resource link directories.

socialphobia.org

socialphobia.org

Social Anxiety Association, a nonprofit organization, seeks to educate the public about the most common anxiety disorder—social anxiety.

webmd.com

webmd.com

A vast array of information about both physical and mental health issues, including information about psychological treatments, drug therapy, and prevention.

womensmentalhealth.org

womensmentalhealth.org

Information on anxiety and depressive disorders during and after pregnancy.

selfesteemgames.mcgill.ca/index.htm

selfesteemgames.mcgill.ca/index.htm

Online games for children that promote self-esteem.

Stress and Stress Management

cmha.ca/mental-health/your-mental-health/stress/

cmha.ca/mental-health/your-mental-health/stress/

Sponsored by the Canadian Mental Health Association.

stress.about.com/od/?once=true&

stress.about.com/od/?once=true&

A group of articles about stress and stress-reducing techniques.

helpguide.org/mental/stress_management_relief_coping.htm

helpguide.org/mental/stress_management_relief_coping.htm

Expert, noncommercial information about coping with stress.

stressbusting.co.uk

stressbusting.co.uk

Self-help strategies for reducing stress and anxiety.

mindtools.com

mindtools.com

A comprehensive list of tools that can help you master stress.

Organizations

Agoraphobics In Motion (AIM)
PO Box 725363
Berkley, MI 48072
248-547-0400
email: anny@ameritech.net
http://aimforrecovery.com

American Psychiatric Association
1000 Wilson Boulevard, Suite 1825
Arlington, VA 22209
800-357-7924
psychiatry.org/mental-health

American Psychological Association
750 First Street, NE
Washington, DC 20002-4242
800-374-2721
apa.org/helpcenter

Anxiety and Depression Association of America
8701 Georgia Avenue, #412
Silver Spring, MD 20910
240-485-1001
adaa.org

Association for Behavioral and Cognitive Therapies
305 7th Avenue, 16th Floor
New York, NY 10001
212-647-1890
http://abct.org/home

Beyond OCD
2300 Lincoln Park West, Suite 206B
Chicago, IL 60614
773-661-9530
email: info@beyondocd.org
http://beyondocd.org

Freedom from Fear
308 Seaview Avenue
Staten Island, NY 10305
718-351-1717, extension 19
freedomfromfear.org

International OCD Foundation
PO Box 961029
Boston, MA 02196
617-973-5801
email: info@iocdf.org
ocfoundation.org

National Alliance on Mental Illness
3803 N. Fairfax Drive, Suite 100
Arlington, VA 22203
703-524-7600
nami.org

National Institute of Mental Health
http://nimh.nih.gov/health/topics/anxiety-disorders/index.shtml

Self-Help Books

There are hundreds of anxiety-related self-help books; the key is to pick the one that "speaks" to you.

Anxiety Disorders in Adults

Antony, Martin, and Richard Swinson. *The Shyness and Social Anxiety Workbook: Proven Techniques for Overcoming Your Fears.* Oakland, California: New Harbinger Publications, 2000.

Baer, Lee. *The Imp of the Mind: Exploring the Silent Epidemic of Bad Thoughts, Reissue Edition.* New York: Plume, 2002.

Beckfield, Denise. *Master Your Panic and Take Back Your Life.* Atascadero, California: Impact
  Publishers, 2000.

Bourne, Edmond. *The Anxiety and Phobia Workbook.* Oakland, California: New Harbinger
  Publications, 2010.

Buell, Linda Manassee. *Panic and Anxiety Disorder: 121 Tips, Real-Life Advice, Resources and More,
  Second Edition.* Poway, California: Simplify Life, 2003.

Carmin, Cheryl, Alec Pollard, Teresa Flynn, and Barbara Markway. *Dying of Embarrassment: Help
  for Social Anxiety and Phobia.* Oakland, California: New Harbinger Publications, 1992.

Crawford, Mark. *The Obsessive Compulsive Trap.* Ventura, California: Regal Books, 2004.

Gardner, James, and Arthur H. Bell. *Overcoming Anxiety, Panic and Depression: New Ways to Regain
  Your Confidence.* Franklin Lakes, New Jersey: Career Press, 2000.

Dayhoff, Signe A. *Diagonally Parked in a Parallel Universe: Working Through Social Anxiety.* Placitas,
  New Mexico: Effectiveness-Plus Publications, 2000.

Hilliard, Ericka B. *Living Full with Shyness and Social Anxiety: A Comprehensive Guide to Gaining Social
  Confidence.* Emeryville, California: Marlowe and Company, 2005.

Hyman, Bruce M., and Cherry Pedrick. *The OCD Workbook: Your Guide to Breaking Free from
  Obsessive-Compulsive Disorder, Second Edition.* Oakland, California: New Harbinger
  Publications, 2005.

Jordan, Jeanne, and Julie Peterson. *The Panic Diaries: The Frightful, Sometimes Hilarious Truth about
  Panic Attacks.* Berkeley, California: Ulysses Press, 2004.

Orsillo, Susan, and Lizabeth Roemer. *The Mindful Way through Anxiety.* New York, New York:
  Guilford Press, 2011.

Ross, Jerrilyn. *Triumph Over Fear: A Book of Help and Hope for People With Anxiety, Panic Attacks, and
  Phobias.* New York, New York: Bantam, 1995.

Shipko, Stuart. *Surviving Panic Disorder: What You Need to Know.* Bloomington, Indiana:
  Authorhouse, 2003.

For Children

Pando, Nancy. *I Don't Want to Go to School: Helping Children Cope with Separation Anxiety.* Far Hills, New Jersey: New Horizon Press, 2005.

Crary, Elizabeth. *Mommy Don't Go.* Seattle, Washington: Parenting Press, 1996.

Huebner, Dawn, and Bonnie Mathews. *What to Do When You Worry Too Much: A Kid's Guide to Overcoming Anxiety.* Washington, DC: Magination Press, 2005.

Lite, Lori. *A Boy and a Bear: The Children's Relaxation Book.* Plantation, Florida: Specialty Press, 1996.

———. *The Goodnight Caterpillar: Muscular Relaxation and Meditation Bedtime Story for Children,* Marietta, GA: Litebooks.net, 2004.

Penn, Audrey. *The Kissing Hand.* Washington, DC: Child and Family Press, 1993.

Romain, Trevor, and Elizabeth Verdick. *Stress Can Really Get On Your Nerves!* Minneapolis, Minnesota: Free Spirit Publishing, 2000.

Childhood Anxiety

Chansky, Tamar E. *Freeing Your Child from Anxiety: Powerful, Practical Solutions to Overcome Your Child's Worries and Phobias.* New York, New York: Three Rivers Press, 2004.

———. *Freeing Your Child from Obsessive-Compulsive Disorder: A Powerful, Practical Program for Parents of Children and Adolescents.* New York, New York: Three Rivers Press (Crown Publishing Group), 2001.

Spence, Sue, Vanessa Cobham, Ann Wignall, and Ronald M. Rapee, eds. *Helping Your Anxious Child: A Step-by-Step Guide for Parents.* Oakland, California: New Harbinger Publications, 2000.

Spencer, Elizabeth Dupont. *The Anxiety Cure for Kids: A Guide for Parents.* Indianapolis: Wiley, 2003.

Postpartum Anxiety and Depression

Bennett, Shoshana S., and Pec Indman. *Beyond the Blues: Prenatal and Postpartum Depression.* San Jose, California: Mood Swings Press, 2002.

Kleiman, Karen, and Valerie Raskin. *This Isn't What I Expected: Overcoming Postpartum Depression.* New York, New York: Bantam, 1994.

Misri, Shaila. *Shouldn't I Be Happy? Emotional Problems of Pregnant and Postpartum Women.* New York, New York: Free Press, 2002.

Sabastian, Linda. *Overcoming Postpartum Depression and Anxiety.* Omaha, Nebraska: Addicus Books: 1998.

Index

W-X-Y-Z

CHECK OUT THESE BEST-SELLERS

More than 450 titles available at booksellers and online retailers everywhere

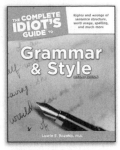

THE COMPLETE IDIOT'S GUIDE TO

Rights and wrongs of sentence structure, word usage, spelling, and much more

Grammar & Style

Laurie E. Rozakis, Ph.D.

978-1-59257-115-4

THE COMPLETE IDIOT'S GUIDE TO

301 twisters and teasers for a stimulating mental workout

Word Search Puzzles

Matt Gaffney

978-1-59257-900-6

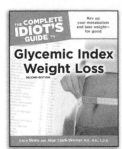

THE COMPLETE IDIOT'S GUIDE TO

Rev up your metabolism and lose weight—for good

Glycemic Index Weight Loss
SECOND EDITION

Lucy Beale and Joan Clark-Warner, M.S., R.D., C.D.E.

978-1-59257-855-9

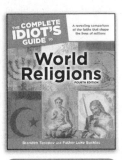

THE COMPLETE IDIOT'S GUIDE TO

A revealing comparison of the faiths that shape the lives of millions

World Religions
FOURTH EDITION

Brandon Toropov and Father Luke Buckles

978-1-61564-069-0

THE COMPLETE IDIOT'S GUIDE TO

Give your resume a professional makeover and stand out from the pack

The Perfect Resume
FIFTH EDITION

Susan Ireland

978-1-59257-957-

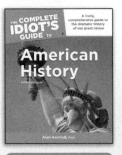

THE COMPLETE IDIOT'S GUIDE TO

A lively, comprehensive guide to the dramatic history of our great nation

American History
FIFTH EDITION

Alan Axelrod, Ph.D.

978-1-59257-869-6

THE COMPLETE IDIOT'S GUIDE TO

Calculus
SECOND EDITION

Sail through class with foolproof explanations and dozens of practice problems

W. Michael Kelley

978-1-59257-471-1

THE COMPLETE IDIOT'S GUIDE TO

Easy, effective, and enjoyable methods for you and your dog

Positive Dog Training
THIRD EDITION

Pamela Dennison

978-1-61564-066-9

THE COMPLETE IDIOT'S GUIDE TO

Money-management tips and investment strategies to put your money in your pocket

Personal Finance in Your 20s & 30s
FOURTH EDITION

Sarah Young Fisher and Susan Shelly

978-1-59257-883-2

THE COMPLETE IDIOT'S GUIDE TO

Tips and tricks to organize your house in a jiffy—one room at a time

Organizing Your Life
FIFTH EDITION

Georgene Lockwood

978-1-59257-966

CD INCLUDED!

THE COMPLETE IDIOT'S GUIDE TO

Audio exercises let you listen, learn, and practice.

Learning Spanish
FIFTH EDITION

Step-by-step lessons help you speak Spanish like a native

Gail Stein

978-1-59257-908-2

THE COMPLETE IDIOT'S GUIDE TO

Refine your taste for the finest in vino

Wine Basics
SECOND EDITION

Tara Q. Thomas

978-1-59257-786-6

THE COMPLETE IDIOT'S GUIDE TO

Make friends with the social network

Facebook®
SECOND EDITION

Mikal E. Belicove and Joe Kraynak

978-1-61564-118-5

CD INCLUDED!

THE COMPLETE IDIOT'S GUIDE TO

Audio CD: The Complete Idiot's Studio for Training Course

Music Theory
SECOND EDITION

Michael Miller

978-1-59257-437-7

THE COMPLETE IDIOT'S GUIDE TO

Walt Disney World

Doug Ingersoll

978-1-61564-112-

ALPHA

idiotsguides.com